Bringing Peace To Our World, One Chocolate Story At A Time

20 Reflections & 20 Routines From 2020

Keep
The
Faith!

Erin Kanno Uehara
Business owner of Choʻo leʻa
& @yourchocolatefriend

Bringing Peace To Our World,
One Chocolate Story At A Time
20 Reflections & 20 Routines
From 2020

ISBN: 978-1-946106-59-9

Glorified Publishing
PO Box 8004
The Woodlands TX 77387
www.GlorifiedPublishing.com
Printed in The United States of America

DEDICATION

For Chris, Aubrey, & Conner.
My first book is dedicated to my family.
There's no one else I would have wanted to share
this stay-at-home quarantine life with!

ENDORSEMENTS

"Erin's chocolate stories are raw, real-time and always heartfelt. During a time of uncertainty, fear, and change, her stories and reflections brought hope, peace and always shed light on a path leading back to God. Her routines inspired me and my family to LIVE and thrive during a pandemic and even when this pandemic is done, we will continue to reflect, live and thrive everyday." -Shandis Ching

"Little did I know when I offered to help Erin with 'whatever she needed' a couple of years ago, that it would lead to playing a small part in realizing her dream to write a book! She is that person, friend, sister in Christ, who always, always, brings truth into my life, whether through spoken or written words. Reading through this collection of her reflections and routines feels just like having a conversation with her, with lots of laughs, occasional tears, and ultimately, hope." -Tabitha Chiu

vi

CONTENTS

CONTENTS

CONTENTS

CONTENTS

ACKNOWLEDGMENTS

First and foremost glory be to God for putting the dream in my heart over 10 years ago to write a book. It was a struggle to get here, but taking one faithful step at a time, He has led me to this book you now hold in your hands. My deepest gratitude to my parents Reagan and Rene Kanno, my sister Evie Joy Chan and family, grandma Jane Hiranaga, in-laws Russell and Carolyn Uehara, sister-in-laws, Nicole Higa, Summer McDonald, Laurie Uehara and families, my chocolate parents Colins and Joan Kawai, and my entire family including those that have already gone to be with the Lord, for their endless support, help with childcare, volunteering with the business, everything imaginable in between!

Thank you to my Chocolate Family past and present, Tori Tajiri, Ally Kuranishi, Christine Guiyab, Casey Hara, Rena Jumawan, Teri Castillo, and Carol Tominaga...you're the dream team! A huge mahalo to my contributing editors, Shandis Ching and Tabitha Chiu who walked with me through my writing in the pandemic week after week. And thank you to the rest of my extended chocolate family Cherise Kang, Tamura Team, Sanford Morioka, Elise Ono, CFC Kazoku, Murakami Family, and so many others. (We have a big chocolate family!)

Thank you to my community of supporters and friends who have encouraged me to put out this book over and over again! To name a few, Traci Gushiken, Noe Takayesu, Alyssa Kapoano, Trisha Shibuya, Cat Toth Fox, Tanna Dang, Kim Ta, Pam Higa, my entire small group of ladies, my girls, my many Hawai`i small business friends- you know who you are, the list goes on and on. Thank you for being my cheerleaders! My mentors here in Hawai`i Keith Ogata, Mark Ibara, Joseph Burns, Pastor Norman Nakanishi, Pastor Billy Lile, and Pastor Tim Ma, thank you for your guidance. And to my mentors I've never met, Dr. John C Maxwell, Rachel Hollis, Emily Ley, Trent Shelton, Pastor Greg Groeschel, Pastor Wayne Cordeiro, Pastor Mike Kai, Camille Styles, and many other authors, thank you for paving the way to help me believe in myself and what's possible!

Special thanks to my invaluable partners in this process Bryan & Cathy Yamashita and Kurt and JoAnn

Kagawa, couldn't do this without you guys! To my editor Edie Bayer, you are my match made in heaven and to my publishers at Glorified Publishing, thank you for believing in this and His calling. Thank you to my printers and long-time loyal partners, Edward Enterprises. As always, thanks to my design partner, Stacey Nomura, photography by my talented sister in Christ, Karen De Borja of Karen DB Photography, hair and makeup by Cathy Yamashita and outfit by my faves at Allison Izu. You guys helped bring it all together and made it happen! A big shout out to everyone mentioned or featured in this book for being a part of the stories to bring peace and hope to others! To all of our chocolate friends, my supporters who have encouraged me to stay sweet and to keep creating whether it was with more chocolates or more encouraging emails, thank you, thank you, thank you from the bottom of my heart!

Last but not least, thank you to my daily loves and inspiration, Aubrey, Conner and my husband, best friend, and #1 supporter, Chris. I love you all.

— INTRODUCTION —

This book was carefully crafted like our artisan chocolates, but unlike our chocolates, it has no shelf life or expiration date. However, our lives here on Earth does, and so may these stories lead you to live a sweeter and fuller life starting now. You are about to indulge in the 40 stories of lessons learned in my 40 weeks in the pandemic of COVID-19 and how I found peace in it all. A peace that you can have too.

Aloha! My name is Erin Kanno Uehara and I am the owner of Choco le`a, a gourmet chocolate company in Manoa Valley, Honolulu, Hawai`i. I am honored that you picked this up and am so excited for you as your friend, that you're about to experience a taste of what life was like here in Hawai`i as a full time small business owner, wife, mom, and human being just like you, trying to process a suddenly very different world. I know that the lessons I learned can be applied to your own life wherever you are now.

I love my work and still feel like a little girl in a chocolate shop just doing what I can do to fulfill our mission of "Bringing peace to our world, one chocolate at a time." We have been fulfilling this through starting sweet connections and building relationships through the universal love language of chocolates. Through our retail shop, corporate accounts, wholesale accounts with the tourism industry, export sales to Japan, pop-up events and catering, in-class hands-on chocolate making workshops, and an in-house dining cafe, we were living out our mission through multiple channels and growing rapidly in our first five years of business.

Then in March 2020, I had to suddenly temporarily shut down my business. During this time, I experienced a 100% loss of sales, was forced to abide by a stay at home order, while taking full-time care of my three and five year old children and transition them to distance learning at home while I worked at home. To help process what felt like an out-of-control new life, I began journaling my weekly reflections of daily struggles, simple things to celebrate, and my experiences during the pandemic. COVID-19 imposed so many new challenges on my family and my business. Little did I know that writing was helping me to reflect and find meaning through the mess. Despite the challenges and with God's grace, I found a way to continue living out our mission, "Bringing peace to our world, one chocolate **story** at a time" and began sharing these personal journal entries with all of my chocolate friends.

My circle of chocolate friends began with a list of several thousands of people who were on our business email list. This included customers, corporate clients, business partners, suppliers, employees past and present, family, basically anyone who visited our chocolate shop at least once. At this point with pretty much nothing to sell and no opportunity to do so, I felt like they all simply became, friends. People I appreciated and cared for. It was thanks to them and their years of support and love, our business grew to what it was and over time, they had become what I referred to as "chocolate friends," or people I met through chocolates.

I didn't communicate regularly through email with our chocolate friends except maybe once a month just to announce new seasonal specials. But as I began to worry with all of the sudden unexpected changes in COVID-19 and searched for peace in what was becoming the "new normal," I began to wonder if they were searching for a little peace too? Something to lift them up, bring a little joy, and a little sweetness to their life? I was used to doing this through chocolates, but now I had nothing, but my thoughts, my reflections, and an email list to connect with them. So, I sent out our first weekly email recapping the first four weeks immediately when the pandemic hit Hawai`i in an email titled "Finding the Good on Good Friday." On this Good Friday, I wanted to share some of the GOOD, despite all that had happened in weeks #1-4.

It was my greatest hope that with no chocolates, these emails could continue to live out our company mission. And so it began, a chocolate chronicle of emails, a blog of stories, "Bringing peace to our world, one **chocolate story** at a time."

As a former teacher, I believe there is a lesson to be learned in EVERY moment. As a current business owner & mom, I see an opportunity in EVERYthing. As an aspiring author and speaker, I wanted to start giving hope to EVERYone.

So my heart-felt stories begin with 20 reflections followed by 20 routines implemented to live in the pandemic of 2020. In each of the 40 weeks of stories, I share with you the lesson learned, the opportunity now, and the hope for our future. I pray that these stories and scriptures help you to become the best version of yourself and who God created you to be, to live out your sweetest life to the full.

With love always,
Your chocolate friend, Erin

— MARCH 16—
Week No. 1
Reflection 1: Loss

"Changes to shop hours due to coronavirus."
"Curbside pick-up only due to coronavirus."
"Shop temporarily closing due to coronavirus."
"Shop temporarily closed due to coronavirus."

That seemed to be the thing I was writing on every email, social media site, app platform, vacation message...and it kept changing! It was such a weird thing since in our 6 years in business, we've never closed for an extended period of time, not even for vacation. It was so surreal.

The feeling that summed up week #1 of COVID-19 hitting us in Hawai`i, was "**loss.**"

It all happened extremely fast. This week was a

complete blur and felt like my world was changing every few hours. Major decisions needed to be made as I watched our company experience loss after loss:

Loss of our wholesale channel to hotels and travel companies; our corporate sales to large companies who were supposed to fly in for events or who were canceling on the mainland; our event sales for pop ups and collaborative opportunities; our custom and catering sales to brides and grooms and others with large gatherings banned; our party favors sales for bridal and baby showers for the smaller gatherings banned.

Our export sales to Japan halted and we had to decline invitations to shows overseas. Our own in-house hands-on chocolate making workshops were shut down as health concerns grew. Our omiyage made in Hawai`i gift sales slowed to zero as less and less people traveled to Hawai`i and less of Hawai`i traveled away to share our chocolates. Thankfully, there were a few loyal chocolate loving locals left (thanks chocolate friends).

There was no manual for this and I had no prior

professional development training to help me prepare. What I ended up doing was listening to the news and reading tons of information. I found myself calling more experienced business owners and mentors and asking what they suggested. I can still see myself in a nice pink dress, pumps, hair and makeup done, with my team bustling inside, while I was outside in the garage. I was in what I called my "private office": a rusted patio furniture hand-me-down table and fold-out chair, sitting in my dusty corner of the garage near the back of our shop. I was on the phone, quietly and nervously whispering to a more senior entrepreneur, "What are we going to do?"

Then, at some point, I got totally overwhelmed and just went with my gut. What could I live without?

Loss of all revenue for the business? I guess so.

Loss of personal income? Ok.

Loss of perfectly good product? Yes.

Loss of life of a team member, a customer or their families getting the virus? No.

Loss of sense of self, values and the mission? No.

I made the quick decision of two last days of curbside pick-up only (though I had no freaking clue what curbside was, as that wasn't even really in our vocabulary yet. I didn't think of how that would logistically work with over 200 cars coming to our little curb at random times in a short time period.)

I then shut down production and service completely until it was safe to reopen. It was the craziest week of Choco le`a life that I had ever experienced. It really tested me as a leader of this company. The worst was saying "goodbye" to the faces I respected and cared for so much, not knowing when we might ever be together again. My chocolate family. I was absolutely heartbroken.

I felt like I was in a nightmare, not really even sure this was really happening, but trying to stay focused and think and move forward. It was like you're supposed to do in those old carnival fun houses where the walls around you spin in blurry circles, but actually the floor beneath you is still. If you just keep your focus ahead, feel the floor beneath you, and keep moving without letting the overwhelmingness around you throw you off balance, you'll make it out of the tunnel okay.

We actually started 2020 prepared for a year of exponential growth with new hires, new accounts and had invested for the first time in major equipment. We had the whole year planned out in advance with specials for every holiday and a calendar with deadlines and systems falling into place.

Then suddenly...nothing. Everything was unplugged; no smell of chocolate; no tapping of moulds to get the air bubbles out; no laughter in the office and no talking story in the shop.

I cried...really hard, all alone in the dark deserted shop as I had done many times before when something really junk happened. But this was so different. How did THIS all just happen? My business, my job, my dreams, my team, my years of sweat and sacrifice seemed to suddenly all be lost in a matter of days.

Lesson Learned: Everything can be lost. Everything is temporary. And no one is immortal.

Opportunity Now: Stay alive. Keep everyone safe and figure out what's next, but not even one week or day at a time...just one decision, only one minute at a time.

Hope For Our Future: If our business survives, we

can try again. But even if we don't, we can rise up from this and try again. It's only the end if we make it the end. Stay alive.

My prayer for you, my chocolate friend, is if you are experiencing immense loss, you choose to do whatever you can to stay alive and keep those around you safe. We will figure this out…somehow. The end of a business, a job, a whatever may just be a temporary end and ultimately, everything will come to an end one day. We will lose our life here on Earth, but there is the hope of eternal life and the hope in God that can never be lost.

With love always,
Your chocolate friend, Erin

"For God so loved the world that he gave his one and only son, that whoever believes in him shall not perish but have eternal life." -John 3:16

— MARCH 23 —
Week No. 2
Reflection 2: Strength

After the tears came the strength.

It must have been sheer adrenaline that just pushed me to get done what needed to get done as the leader and owner of this business. The disciplined decision to do what needed to be done to "shut down" the right way and not simply "run away."

I took over multiple positions in addition to the several different hats I already wore. I took over four more email inboxes and wrapped up conversations in multiple social media inboxes. I tied up the incomplete jobs, paid the outstanding bills, asked for extensions on the incoming bills (oh my gosh the non-stop incoming bills)!!!

I had a clipboard I looked at every single day full of bills...so many that my gold clip didn't even "clip" anymore and the papers would sometimes fall out from being too thick. Old school style, I wrote out every single bill I had so it was engraved on my heart. This way I knew what the goal was that I had to pay off. I knew what I needed to do to get our company out of all debt and be free and clear of all of our responsibilities.

I applied for the loan opportunities, the new grant opportunities, and then tried to keep up with the changing opportunities. I honestly wanted to make a big bonfire and just burn everything, but instead, I logged every receipt left, answered every message from "Can I cancel my wedding favors?" to "Can I still buy stuff from you?" I was also trying to write words of encouragement to every single person we have ever worked with, "Please take care and don't worry. We will get through this together." I tried to be strong for everyone.

And when I heard that partners I had worked with for years were suddenly "gone" and their email message popped up as, "I've been let go. Thanks for everything." I sent messages back immediately of "Thank YOU for everything and please stay in touch. I wish you well. I hope we can have an opportunity to work together again." Just in case they read it one more time before leaving their job forever! I powered through hard conversations with other small business owners, hotel general managers who sat in completely empty hotels, suppliers, distributors, friends on the island, on the mainland, and in other countries. We were all doing our best to stay strong, to put our head down and do the work we could and needed to do.

Lesson Learned: There is a strength inside of me - inside of us - that comes out when it's time for battle. When you're really fighting for something, fighting to save whatever you can, fighting to stay in this, a fire is ignited and the burn can give you what you need for the next few fights.

Opportunity Now: Use that fire for good and fight for what's right.

Hope For Our Future: If we can continue to use that spirit for the right things, who knows what we can accomplish in the midst of absolute loss, chaos, and uncertainty.

My prayer for you my chocolate friend, is that you stay strong. You fight. And remember the Lord your God is always with you.

With love always,
Your chocolate friend, Erin

"Do not despair, for the joy of the Lord is your strength." -Nehemiah 8:10

"So do not fear, for I am with you; do not be dismayed, for I am your God. I will strengthen you

and help you; I will uphold you with my righteous right hand." -Isaiah 41:10

— MARCH 30—

Week No. 3
Reflection 3: Exhaustion

Then I was tired…so very, very tired. I was ready to take an unemployed break, only to remember that I needed to now be a full time teacher with two three- and five-year old pre-schoolers to care for. I had to get the home-school schedule in place to keep their life balanced with some structure, some play, and lots of positivity as we all stayed home and adjusted.

I wanted to curl up in a ball in bed and tell them to watch the TV as much as their hearts desired, but limited it to their choice of "Frozen II" once a day. Yes, once a day. I have memorized the entire soundtrack.

Thankfully with my teaching degree and past experience I was able to whip up lessons on the fly. I know how important routines are for kids and how it sets them up for success. Which by the way, now I needed to set myself up with a new routine of work-at-home and be a full-time stay-at-home mom! My 4:30 A.M. morning routine was, at this point, non-existent. My three year old was now sitting up next to me in bed at 6:00 A.M., telling me to, *"Wake up, Mommy."*

Sigh.

In my journal this week I wrote, *"I have a headache and a slight scratchy throat! Is this from the pile of finances I've been working on? I started crying...I cannot be separated from my kids if I have COVID-19! What is this thing? I have to be with my family!"*

Next day I wrote, *"Be content with what you have. I have no income. Maybe I could be a poor pastor?"*

Next day I wrote, *"This week we gave over $5,000 in chocolates away. I applied for a grant. I went through a huge pile of unfinished finances and made a "F-it" pile. (Please excuse my French). Then I got a headache, a really sore throat, and came home defeated. I want to forget it all and quit."*

The very next day I wrote, *"Today is a new day and I put my trust in God again. Want me to be a pastor? A stay at home mom? What do you want me to do? Not do?"*

The next day I wrote, *"Why can't I hear God clearly during this time? I'm losing my motivation and energy."*

Lesson Learned: This is exhausting. Do I have to learn anything in this? (insert delirious laugh) Perhaps what I learned is being a full time mom is a full time job and having a full time job to save your business is another full time job = exhaustion and this cannot last forever. I cannot live like this forever.

Opportunity Now: Rest. Then do what I can.

Hope For Our Future: This is a season. It will pass. Suck it up and I will look back at this one day and be grateful God told my body and mind to rest and let Him work a bit on my behalf. He can do so much more than we ever can and sometimes, we need to learn to rely more on Him. It's not until we're at a point when we feel like we have nothing left, but very little, and that very little is all we need to give to God.

My prayer for you, my chocolate friend, is that when you are exhausted, you rest and let God help carry you. Just take the very next step in obedience. Even if it's just bathing your child, tucking him in, then putting yourself to bed. He renews us every morning and will renew you, too.

With love always,
Your chocolate friend, Erin

"Come to me, all who are weary and burdened, and

I will give you rest. Take my yoke upon you and learn from me, for I am gentle and humble in heart, and you will find rest for your souls. For my yoke is easy and my burden is light." -Matthew 11:28-30

"Every new morning...Because of the Lord's great love we are not consumed, for his compassions never fail. They are new every morning; great is your faithfulness." -Lamentations 3:22-23

— APRIL 6 —

Week No. 4
Reflection 4: Focus

It was a better week. I finally started focusing on the good. I started finding myself again, spending way more time in devotion and prayer, clearing the clutter in my head and turning off social media for a week to gather thoughts and put it down on paper. I didn't want to miss the lesson, the opportunity, and the hope that could be shared with others if I just focused.

I now have a plan - a focus - and can set new goals, even if they are small and short term. For us, that means moving it all back to the original one space and start moving furniture again.

In this time, I realized that our business foundation was perhaps not as strong as it should be for the growth I had been planning and hoped for. The opportunity now was a chance to rebuild, start again, reset and change things. The hope for the future was that the death of a dream, business, or idea can come back to life...BETTER.

So here is what I gathered in the first four weeks of this pandemic when I put it all into focus!

Lesson Learned: There is so much to be grateful for if you focus on the good. I've had a really good team, a really good six years of sweet memories, and still ongoing support from loyal chocolate friends, waiting for the good times to come back. I got to personally connect with each person on my team through all of this. We had a chance to say the things we've always wanted to say, but were afraid to like the real meaning behind our company mission statement. We bonded even more as a chocolate family, as chocolate friends, as a business community, as a state, nation, and world. We all have a current common experience that is connecting us and we have something to be grateful for whether it's health, family, food, shelter, nice weather, more time to exercise, or a job.

Opportunity Now: As an entrepreneur, this is a time

22

to not wear all of the hats and worry about the day-to-day operational things that kept my head down in the business, but an opportunity to take care of "all of the other things I never had time to do." Things that were critical to strengthening the foundation of our company from reviewing statistics, analyzing data, re-evaluating, re-envisioning, making changes, and maybe even scaling back to do a few things really well, rather than many different things. At home, it's an opportunity to really spend time with family. For me, it's a precious young age to homeschool my kids, and watch their crazy little brains absorb everything, as they process this "new normal" in their own unique way.

Hope For Our Future: What we CAN do with this time, is give hope to others, because there are so many who need it. Through email, Zoom, phone calls, hand-written cards...we can still connect. We even launched a secret "final mission" where we called out each team member one more time and a few "chosen ones," to pick up the "secret stash of chocolates" and give hope to others. The "final" mission, was to live out our mission of "Bringing peace to our world, one chocolate at a time." These chocolates were delivered to heroes in healthcare, the front line first responders, service men and women, leaders in government, volunteers helping the less fortunate, and the heroes staying at home doing their part. Even if we don't have chocolate, or we can't be with people, we can still find ways to give hope.

So what will week #5 be? I'm hoping the emotion is **"hope"**.

I will be re-structuring the business and preparing for its re-opening day. I will be re-evaluating what we are really good at, and what we're not. I'll be setting up new goals to get us back to doing the parts of the business we loved the most. I'll be setting up a new schedule that will allow us to love ALL the things in life we have realized we cherish so much in addition to this business...like spending physical and intentional quality time with others.

So, Happy Easter everyone!

My prayer for you, my chocolate friend, is that as you see cute images of chocolate bunnies, shiny eggs, and baby chicks, may they serve as reminders of life, the rebirth. Just as Jesus Christ rose from the grave, we too can rise out of the ashes of this pandemic, love one another, and start again.

With love always,
Your chocolate friend, Erin

"He is not here; he has risen, just as he said."
-Matthew 28:6

"I am the resurrection and the life. The one who believes in me will live, even though they die; and whoever lives by believing in me will never die." - John 11:25-27

— APRIL 13 —

Week No. 5
Reflection 5: Hope

So I said week #5 would be one filled with the emotion of "hope." Thankfully, it did end up being that because of so many others, including you. If I can be honest, it didn't come from deep within me this week. In week #5, it came from five different groups of people, who carried me through the week.

1. Responses from YOU our chocolate friends!

Thank you for your outpouring of love to my "Finding the Good on Good Friday" email. I was overwhelmed with positive responses, well wishes, and gratitude. Of all the emails sent out in our six years of business, this one by far received the most feedback! It gave me so much hope to hear that you can't wait for us to come back and that you would be here, at our shop, as soon as we open again. Thanks to you, we are hoping for the best and you've given us purpose to continue planning for our return. We've started by rearranging some things in the shop for smoother service!

2. A Birthday Surprise from the Team

The fact that my crew, aka my chocolate family, put together a secret birthday surprise while separated from each other in quarantine, and yet were still able to pull together the birthday shout out on me...that gave me hope!

It was not the fact that they worked together (I knew they could), but really the fact that this camera shy crew took selfies! I found out they coordinated this remotely in a few hours and got photos from the team, which is always a struggle for me. This is why you always see ME in photos and videos! They posted it to our Instagram MyStory @chocoleahawaii.

This just reminded me of the culture of love and teamwork that all of them have built together. They brought hope on my quarantine birthday! It has always been one of my favorite moments as their leader, when the team worked together to make something happen, all on their own, in their own unique way, while making sweet memories and sharing laughs doing it!

Our best specials, promos, and events, have come about as a result of this kind of team effort with the goal of the recipient in mind.

3. Business Community

My email inbox began filling with different kinds of correspondence from other local business owners and entrepreneurs who helped me feel connected to the business community. They started sharing how they're dealing with everything: their tips, the silver lining in the extra time they have, how they've applied for this and that, and the best one this week was hearing that some of my business friends were approved for the PPP loan! Hooray!

Hearing the hope again in their voices made me smile. One in particular, who has been sharing a lot of what he is doing (as he always does), is a business friend that I love talking with, Jimmy Chan (owner of Hawaiian Chip Company). In fact, right before COVID-19 hit Hawai`i, we had just spent a couple of hours at his factory, talking story about the future and our goals and dreams (and eating his ono chips of course)! Just a few weeks later, here we were talking about pivoting and how we were going to keep fighting for our businesses.

We've got to keep ALL of these amazing local businesses going! Hearing the leaders share their persistence and passion gives us all hope!

4. A Three & Five Year Old

I've been spending a lot more time with my three year old son and five year old daughter daily in home-school. They love "preschool with Ms. Mommy" and they give me hope that even though I am making up lessons on the fly, and I'm tired, they can't wait to learn what the day will bring.

Their little brains absorb everything! I mean they even got super excited learning how to grind coffee beans and measure ingredients to make coffee when I ran out of ideas for a hands-on math lesson…plus I needed more caffeine anyway. No need to send me more ideas. I didn't really run out of ideas, I just ran out of energy!

Kids remind us of the little things that matter. Their zest for learning, their energy to play, their childlike faith they have in us as parents to teach and prepare them for life. It's astounding! Their hope in the situation of shelter-in-place is that they get more time playing and learning together as a family!

5. The Working World

Finally, seeing the working world of friends still on the job reminds me that there still is life and activity bustling out there. For those of us hunkered down at home, THIS is our world. We forget that some people are still getting dressed, still going out of their houses, still having income to go shopping online, and still busily working.

Whether you're in accounting or healthcare, making deliveries or prepping food, re-stocking the market or farming, serving in the government or providing mental and emotional support via telehealth … your commitment to and consistency in your expertise to serve others is giving hope that the rest of us will be able to jump back in and contribute our part to society as well.

Of course, as we started this past week with Easter Sunday, I was also reminded of the constant hope we have in our constant God. Right now, He's telling me to just write. So for week #6, I'll share more of the lessons learned, the current opportunity, and the hope for the future. I'm hoping the feeling I have will be "energized!"

Lesson Learned: Sometimes, we rely on others to give us hope and so we must not isolate ourselves. It's hard for us to feel hopeful all of the time. But when we stay connected and see it in others, it reminds us that we can have hope too.

Opportunity Now: Pass it on to people around us, who still need to be reached, may feel forgotten, or are on the verge of having hope again. Just send them a quick message asking, "How are you?" You never know peoples' stories and what they're going through until you ask.

Hope For Our Future: YOU, yes YOU, simply by reading this, have given me hope and purpose to continue sharing my story, with vulnerability and transparency, in the hope that it "Brings peace to our world, one chocolate story at a time." Thank you for being a hope giver!

My prayer for you my chocolate friend is that you never lose hope.

With love always,
Your chocolate friend, Erin

"And the God of all grace, who called you to his eternal glory in Christ, after you have suffered a little while, will himself restore you and make you strong, firm and steadfast."
-1 Peter 5:10

"We remember before our God and Father your world produced by faith, your labor prompted by love, and your endurance inspired by hope in our Lord Jesus Christ."
-1 Thessalonians 1:3

"Let us hold unswervingly to the hope we profess, for he who promised is faithful." -Hebrew 10:23

— APRIL 20 —

Week No. 6
Reflection 6: Forgot

Yup...I forgot to write about week #6 on my reflections of COVID-19. I also forgot already what happened.
#mommybrain #andallthemomssaidamen

That's all I wrote in my email blog. I looked back at that week and my journal and tried to remember what happened. A lot of crying, nightmares, interrupted sleep, and frustration. No wonder I forgot what happened. I think I was trying to forget it all.

Lesson Learned: It happens. We're human. Give yourself some grace.

Opportunity Now: Oh well. Move on.

Hope For Our Future: We all forget sometimes. No big deal.

My prayer for you, my chocolate friend, is if you forget, give yourself a break and carry on! The good news is God never forgets.

With love always,
Your chocolate friend, Erin

"...for the Lord your God goes with you; he will

never leave you nor forsake you.". -Deuteronomy 31:6

— APRIL 27 —

Week No. 7
Reflection 7: Perspective

COVID-19 from the Point of View of My Two Kids

Children's Day & Mother's Day is just around the corner, and I am reminded day after day just how challenging and rewarding the job of a mom is! With my five year old daughter and three year old son and a shelter-in-place, I've been home with my preschoolers. And if you're a mom or know one, then you'll want to read to the end of this email for a change in perspective!

Week #7 was a lot of letting go of the work and the business for a while, and shifting my focus to my kids. I'll sum it up as the week of perspective. Because of them, I've been learning to adapt my point of view to theirs.

Children really have put this whole COVID-19 experience in perspective. Honestly, if it wasn't for them, I'd be in way worse shape. On the days I felt like really just not doing anything, I looked at them and was quickly reminded that they needed me. They were counting on me. This wasn't their fault. I needed to get my "sorry for myself" butt out of bed and make breakfast, teach school, get to work, model for them chores, a good behavior, and a good attitude, etc., etc., etc.

"Mommy I love this lock down. I get to be with you every day." Yup, that's just what my daughter said from her car seat behind me after a drive home from the chocolate shop, and just like that, my negative mindset was reset. To me, every day feels "about the same." It feels boring…feels uncertain, and feels limiting. But to these little kids, the world is BIG. The unknown is thrilling. The possibilities are endless. There are so many adventures to behold.

I've watched them "hunt for treasure" below my clothes in the closet with a flashlight. They've gone on "fishing explorations in the great ocean" in the laundry basket in the living room, with a belt hanging over one side and the other end gripped tightly in their hands. They've "built their own carnival" with chairs, pillows and cardboard boxes as they hopped from "ride to ride" and "there were no lines and it was free!" They've "scared away monsters" yelling at geckos on the sidewalk and "made beautiful bouquets" from the weeds and fallen flowers gathered along our same old, same old walks.

One Coin

On one particular day, I stared at the computer screen intensely and when my daughter, Aubrey, asked what I was doing, without thinking, I rambled, *"I am trying to figure out how to pay all of these bills that I keep getting with no income and no money."* I heard her run off to their room and rustle around in things for a few minutes. Then she came running back to my desk, and super proudly, placed a very shiny bright penny on it with the hugest, most accomplished smile on her face.

"There!" She exclaimed. *"Now you have one coin. And no matter what, you will always have at least one coin."* I had to let out a tear and a laugh at the same time. I know she had just taken this from one of

the Easter eggs I had hidden for them in our home, and that she had then happily put in her wallet for her savings. Here she was giving what little she had to me, without a second thought. Then she skipped off, as if she just solved my really hard problem, and we could all move on and play now.

God's Night Sky

My son, Conner, always enjoys peeking out the window to take a look at the night sky and find the moon to tell it "Good night" before going to bed. Now with a little more time at night, we stare out a little longer and sometimes even stand outside under the night sky. He always admires the stars and the planes that fly and says, *"Wooooooooooow,"* in the quietest stretched out whisper, as if it was the very first time he was seeing these things.

I was feeling particularly lonely one night, missing others in my family, my friends and people in general, because I love being with people. I texted my mom and told her to look at the moon right at this minute because we were too. I knew that even though we weren't together, I found some comfort that we were looking at the same moon, under the same sky, created by the same God, and He was in control.

When Conner saw me tear up, He asked, *"Mommy are you crying because you're happy or sad?"* This time, it was a little of both: sad to not be with all the people I love like we once were able to, but happy that I could hold him in my arms, at this very moment, the way my mom would hold and take care of me. *"Don't cry mommy,"* he responded as he shoved his little face into mine.

Lesson Learned (from my kids): Though the days run together and sometimes look and feel exactly the same, it's our perspectives that CAN change. It's our way of looking at things that can see a day full of new lessons to learn and adventures to go on, or the same old, same old. We can see a solution to a problem, or still not enough; a beautiful creation for all of us to stare at in amazement from God, or just another routine thing to look at, at the end of the day.

Opportunity Now: Write down more of what kids teach us, and apply it to our lives to help change our perspective. Let's look at everything through their little eyes, with their little hearts and minds full of innocence, full of faith and full of wonder.

Hope For Our Future: These little people around us ARE our future. They will come out of COVID-19 and live a life like no one else. They may remember this as a time that we were altogether a lot, that they learned a lot, that they explored everything around them in creative new ways again and again. It was a time when they grew up literally before our eyes, and it forced them (and us) to adapt to a different and new way of learning, communicating, connecting, and solving the problems in our world for a stronger and better future.

To all of the "moms" out there: THANK YOU. Thank you for pouring into our future during this time. And to all of the children out there, thank you for leading us at times, for giving us the strength to change our perspectives, and push onward.

My prayer for you, my chocolate friend, is that if you are a "mom," (dad, grandparent, guardian…) THANK YOU. Thank you for pouring into our future during this time. To all of the children out there, thank you for leading us at times, and for giving us the strength to change our perspectives and push onward.

With love always,
Your chocolate friend, Erin

"So we fix our eyes not on what is seen, but on what is unseen, since what is seen is temporary, but what is unseen is eternal." -2 Corinthians 4:18

"'For my thoughts are not your thoughts, neither are your ways my ways,' declares the Lord. 'As the heavens are higher than the earth, so are my ways higher than your ways and my thoughts than your thoughts." -Isaiah 55:8-9

— MAY 4 —
Week No. 8
Reflection 8: Gratitude

Happy Teacher Appreciation Week! Happy Nurse Appreciation Week! Happy Mother's Day! We have all been influenced in some way or another by these people. This past week, I spent a lot of time in reflection and **gratitude** for them as we come to the close of a school year, saying "goodbye" and "thank you" to teachers, congratulating graduates, continuing to celebrate our healthcare workers, and recognizing moms everywhere. In this vein, I am sharing gratitude with three personal (and slightly embarrassing) little stories of three people who cared.

1. Teachers

My teachers from preschool through graduate school, really shaped who I am today. In fact, a few of them actually come to visit me at the chocolate shop and check in (Hi Mrs. Sproles, Ms. Yorioka and Mrs. Matsuura)! Even now, some teachers (who were never MY teachers then, but are now), are taking the time to care and write back to my emails. They offer criticism and compliments on my writing, which are really encouraging me to continue to practice.

Teachers Who Care, Let You "Fail"

Ms. Higa showed me care and love in a way I didn't understand in high school and didn't really appreciate until after I graduated. I signed up for honors physics because, quite honestly, it would look great on my class schedule. I'd be with the brightest in the bunch. Feeling proud, I went into class and quickly learned I was feeling pretty stupid. This was way too hard for me. What was I thinking? But too full of pride to withdraw, I figured I'd fake my way through and memorize what I needed to take the tests.

But Ms. Higa's class was not about tests; instead, it was a lot of hands-on demonstration of our understanding. Unfortunately, I had no clue what I should be understanding.

I remember during round robin reading as a little kid,

I used to count ahead which paragraph would be mine to read, and rehearsed it in my head so that I would sound perfect when it was my turn to read aloud. I'd sound great, but totally missed everything prior because I was too busy practicing my part, rather than listening through the whole thing for understanding. I cared more about appearing smart, rather than actually getting smart!

Well, Ms. Higa would not let me get away with something like that. She would not just give me an A. In fact, she gave me a C! I had to go in after school for extended time to finish my work. I had to try things over and over until I could show her I got it. I had to sit with her one-on-one during free periods for extra tutoring so she could slow things down for me and try to explain it a different way. But she was there for me, again and again, so that I would get it, and so that I would really understand what she was trying to teach me. I would have to work for it and earn it. She was the "toughest" teacher I had, but now looking back, she was actually one of the most caring teachers.

Ms. Higa, if you are reading this, I want you to know how much I respect and appreciate you for not giving up on someone like me and believing I could do better. Thank you for always being available when I decided I was ready to really learn. I'm sorry that I was so bitter with you sometimes because you woudn't simply give me what I wanted. Instead, you let me "fail" until I realized that I could really learn if I cared to apply myself.

2. Nurses
Nurses Who Care Bring You Orange Jello

I've had shingles on my wedding day, lost my sense of smell twice, gave birth twice… and have had different rotations of nurses in different hospitals, for different reasons. Some were super sweet. Some were funny and gave me a laugh I needed. And some just did their jobs really quickly and efficiently and gave me confidence that I could rest and they would take care of everything.

When you're in a state of such vulnerability, pain, or discomfort, nurses are the angels by your bedside. And when it's your own kid, or loved one, who needs the medical care, and you're freaking out and need to be by their side, those nurses are holding your trembling body, hugging you when you cry, and gripping your hand and making you look at them in the eyes and repeat back the words, "It's going to be okay."

I remember one nurse in particular, though I don't remember her name, brought me the orange jello I really wanted...twice. That little thing really meant a lot. When you can finally have something besides water and ice chips and all you want is the jello (IF it's available), and usually they only have red (and you don't like red), but sometimes, sometimes, there's orange flavor (and you really want that one)! Well, this nurse reassured me she would find me my orange jello and that she would check all the different refrigerators on the different floors at different times on the days when they restock.

I don't remember much except that she dropped it off with a sly smile, and threw me a silent fist bump across the bed, like we had just accomplished some secret mission together. She did this for me twice...even if I wasn't on her watch! I've seen so many nurses, I forgot a lot of their names. But I never forget how they made me feel...cared for. Even if just for a jello run that made me feel "worth it!"

3. Moms
Moms Who Care Will Be Your Blanky

I could write a novel about my mom - how she's the most generous, compassionate, organized, smart, humble, and respectful person I know; but, I'll sum it up with one small story

It was my first experience of losing a loved one. I couldn't understand how I could go on without her.

My mom searched everywhere with me again and again. She listened to me as I tried to talk through remembering when I last had her. She held me as I sobbed buckets of tears. She offered suggestions on what we could try and do. Mostly, she just made sure to be with me through it all. My mom took care of me when I felt like I couldn't take care of myself.

It sounds like a small and silly story now, but as a little kid, it was like losing your best friend. There my mom was to fill the gap. SHE was my constant comfort, before, during and after. Through the loss and heartache of so many things experienced in life, mom was there as my "blanky."

Now, as a mom myself, my heart hurts the most for anyone who had no mom or mom figure who could care for them. My heart aches for those who weren't told they are worthy, that there is hope, that they are loved, there is a God and that they were "fearfully and wonderfully made."

If that person just so happens to be you reading this, I hope you find comfort in knowing that I care. I can be a "teacher" that will share life lessons. A "nurse" that can help ease the pain with comforting chocolates and prayer, and a "mom" who will be a caring voice, constantly sharing the abundance of things to be grateful for. In fact, we can all be that for someone.

Lesson Learned: There are many people around us to be grateful for. Teachers, nurses and moms are just some of them who cared for us along the way.

Opportunity Now: It is never too late to thank them...no holiday or appreciation week needed. Find a way to share your gratitude today.

Hope For Our Future: We can also show our gratefulness by paying it forward and acting as "teachers," "nurses," and "moms" in the lives of others. We can make an impact on the next generation that will one day take care of us.

My prayer for you, my chocolate friend, is that you know just how grateful I am for all of YOU as I tested out a Mother's Day curbside sale. I learned a lot from this last one about how to make it better. Even criticism is something to be grateful for...because it is often like the best teachers, nurses, and moms, who tell us what we might not want to hear, but need to.

With love always,
Your chocolate friend, Erin

"...She works with eager hands...She gets up while it is still night; she provides food for her family...She sets about her work vigorously; her arms are strong for her tasks...She is clothed with strength and dignity; she can laugh at the days to come....She speaks with wisdom, and faithful instruction is on her tongue...She watches over the affairs of her household...Her children arise and call her blessed; her husband also, and he praises her: "Many women do noble things, but you surpass them all." Charm is deceptive, and beauty is fleeting; but a woman who fears the Lord is to be praised. Honor her for all that her hands have done, and let her works bring her praise at the city gate." -Proverbs 31

"And we know that in all things God works for the good of those who love him, who have been called according to his purpose." -Romans 8:28

— MAY I I —

Week No. 9
Reflection 9: Seasons

Happy Graduation Season! I want to take this time to honor our graduates. Whether you are graduating from high school, college, preschool or any school or program, whatever route you chose, you stuck with it, you worked at it, and you have accomplished a lot to get to where you are. And even though things are different and you may be having drive-through graduations, or are standing on the side of the road as cars honk "congratulations" to you, we hope you feel celebrated during this time!

This IS an exciting time! It is the start of the next chapter. I believe that we go through different seasons in life, as the book of Ecclesiastes in the bible says:

There is a time for everything, and a season for every activity under the heavens:
A time to be born and a time to die
A time to plant and a time to uproot
A time to tear down and a time to build
A time to weep and a time to laugh
A time to mourn and a time to dance
A time to embrace and a time to refrain from embracing (can't wait to embrace again)
A time to keep and a time to throw away
A time to be silent and a time to speak
A time for war and a time for peace.

I was in the middle of reading this particular book in the bible, when COVID-19 began. It was as if God was saying to enjoy the season we were in.

Enjoy? I understand "enjoy" was not the word I would have chosen, but maybe at least I could start with recognizing the season we're in, and realizing it will only last, good or bad, for so long.

During this graduation season, I've found myself reflecting back on my own time in school and hope that these little stories, will give you some encouragement and guidance.

NO 4.0

From my early elementary days, I decided I was going to graduate high school with a 4.0 Grade Point Average. It was one of my top three goals growing up because I wanted to "be smart." That goal was what I stayed focused on.

Well, I graduated with a 3.98. I remember crying so hard to my friends outside of the school's office courtyard, after hearing the news and getting told "no" after asking if they would just round those decimals up. I realized I came so close to my long time goal, only to fall short by 0.02. I remember not being invited to the special lunch with the principal to receive the Koa wood bowl with embossed gold plaque and other accolades.

It sounds silly, but when that was such a big aspiration of mine and I didn't accomplish it, I felt like a failure. I remember having to process through it and accept that I gave my everything and I should be proud, even if at commencement, I was not sitting in the front row where I always imagined I would be. Also, that I would not be selected to make the inspiring speech at the massive Aloha Stadium, in front of our friends and family, to celebrate that very special moment.

I had to decide not to let myself be defined by a number, a score. Not anymore. I had already thrown that graduation cap up into the air, as if releasing it all up to the heavens and saying, "Okay, what's next? Let the sky be the limit!

Back to School
From there, I went on to college, received a Bachelor's Degree in Education and became an Elementary School Teacher. I remember driving to work at 6:30 in the morning and leaving the campus at 6:00 at night. I remember crying in the school courtyard with Liane, a very close teacher friend, who was also my roommate at the time. We cried because no matter how many hours we put in, we still felt like we didn't know how we could help some of our students keep up.

After burning out and quitting teaching in 2008, I found myself at the downturn of the economy and unable to find a full time job. When I did get back into full time work, my then bosses, Scott and Beryl, encouraged me to get my Master's Degree in Business. It sounded like a good idea because a lot of the job positions I had applied for would have accepted me if I held a degree in business instead.

MBA = Making Brilliant Acquaintances

I studied and got accepted into the part-time Masters in Business Administration (MBA) program at the Shidler College of Business at the University of Hawai`i as I continued to work a full time and part time job. During the first orientation weekend, the professor said to all of us in the lecture hall, *"Say goodbye to your personal life. Many of you will break up with your boyfriends or girlfriends and you'll have no time to go out with your friends."*

I don't remember the entire "welcome" speech, exactly, but I remember thinking, *"Oh no! Maybe this is going to be harder than I thought!"* But then they said, *"Let's review calculus."* Calculus! I can't do a review, when I never even took that class before. I only needed to take Math 100 in my undergrad.

I remember crying, again, but in a different school

61

courtyard. I called my teacher friend, Shauna, and said, *"I can't do this."* She told me, *"Yes you can. You will figure out how."* I remember hanging up quickly during our short break, wiping away my tears, and making my way back into the lecture hall.

I looked around to plan who I could be in a group with since this coursework required a lot of group work. What I discovered is that I could get through the program because I teamed up with people who had the knowledge, experience, and expertise in the areas that I did not have. (Thank you Kanani, Daren, Kai, and Dayna!)

We met together all of the time, but took turns taking the lead in the areas of study that we each excelled in. We studied hard, but we also decided to have fun while doing it, because as the professor had prophesied, "that was the only life we had."

I remember it was in college that I began to learn my strengths, my weaknesses, my frustrations, and my areas of joy. Friends made throughout my school years helped me to understand myself better, and supported me in my personal and professional growth, even if I wasn't exactly sure what I would do next with an MBA.

Building a Team

Fortunately, I did take what I learned about being stronger and better together into Choco le`a to build my next team. Completing the MBA program involved me **M**aking **B**rilliant **Ac**quaintances. To create and build this business was the same. Choco le`a is what it is because of the people! I was very fortunate to find the right people the company needed, at the right times, and it always aligned with where they were in their personal lives as well as our professional aspirations. Each and every person along the chocolate journey left their mark, and contributed in some way for the season they were with us.

As for YOU, our chocolate friends, your support, feedback, and encouragement has also shaped and formed Choco le`a as we shifted with changing times and the needs and wants that you shared. Altogether, as a chocolate family and chocolate friends, we have cried together through the hard times, when things were out of our control, and when we made mistakes.

But we also cried together tears of joy in seasons of

accomplishments. When we saw you get married. When you said you were having a baby. When you came in with a stroller barely surviving and our shop was your break to get out. When you told us you were finally retiring. When you came in with your grandkids and took your time getting them (and yourselves) whatever you wanted; when you got exactly what you needed to celebrate and thank someone else very special in your life. Even when you had to celebrate the life of a loved one gone, who loved our chocolates and would have wanted our chocolates at their final goodbye. In every season, we've been honored to celebrate with you.

Today's Graduations

Just the other day when driving home from the chocolate shop, I was reminded of this season of graduation as I passed Roosevelt High School and saw their drive through graduation. About 10 cars were lined up at a time with graduates walking up the hill and two hugging at the bottom of the stairs before taking a picture together, diploma in hand.

I saw congratulation signs with your names on them along street poles down the road. I saw red and yellow balloons swaying in the wind. I don't know what came over me, except that I started crying and silently saying from my car, "Congrats you guys!" It was there, outside in their school courtyard, that they held their celebration in real-time.

I cried tears of sadness that this is what their celebration looked like compared to my own from Mililani, but also tears of happiness for you, that YOU DID IT! Regardless of what it looked like, not comparing it to anyone else's, this was YOUR graduation. In this season, this is how we will celebrate all of YOU!

There were two similar themes throughout my school journeys. One was tears; tears of struggle; sadness and disappointment. But also tears of joy, relief, contentment and happiness. Tears falling because of all the feelings and it's okay to feel it all. The other was really great friends. We need each other. We need some really great friends and family to help us get through THIS season and the next.

Lesson Learned: You are not defined by a number, a score, or 2 or 3 letters behind your name. Though you may earn it, you still need to decide what you will do and who you will be with it. You are also not defined by a job or lack of a job. You are still somebody. Figuring out who that is and bettering that person is a never-ending season of growth.

Opportunity Now: Celebrate what you have accomplished and as you continue to move into the next season, don't forget the friends who helped you in this past one while you make some great new friends in the next one. Celebrate the graduates around you with the drive-by's, the homemade card and lei, the social media posts, a quick text or call, or simply share with them this message!

You may be wondering how you can make friends in quarantine? Start by showing the world who you are, your dreams and what you want to contribute to this world. You will attract the kind of people who will nurture and support you and what you set out to accomplish, who will join alongside you on the journey.

Hope For Our Future: This season will end and the next one will start. So try to enjoy the one you are in now.

My prayer for you, my chocolate friend, is that you celebrate! Congratulations class of 2020 and to all "graduates" who feel like celebrating (in safe ways) that we got through this particular COVID-19 season together!

With love always,
Your chocolate friend, Erin

"The Lord has done it this very day; let us rejoice today and be glad." -Psalm 118:24

67

"Rejoice in the Lord always. I will say it again: Rejoice!" -Philippians 4:4

— MAY 18 —
Week No. 10
Reflection 10: Faith

Hawai`i and retail continued to open slowly on week #10. In addition to beaches and parks, places of worship, and soon to come, dine-in restaurants. Everyone is getting ready to welcome people as the government and public's faith in the safety of re-opening our economy grows.

For us, we did not open because our time is not right now. Although we're sorry this is disappointing to many of you who are loyal chocolate friends wanting to support us (thank you, thank you, thank you), we ask that you have faith along with us that we will be able to return in the near future.

In our company's journey of grow, grow, grow and a personal lifestyle of go, go, go, this shut down has been very different and has forced me to rely on my faith in a very uncertain time. Though it was very hard to slow down and accept it at first, it did force me to read, pray, journal, and just listen to others more. The past two months have further stretched my faith in God to refocus on the basics: His purpose, the why, the what and for who. We have clarified those points, but we're not open yet, because we still need to iron out the how.

The neat thing I realized while rereading our original strategic plans for 2020, is even though almost all of our goals for the second half of the year will not be met, the greater vision can still be accomplished! Although I've made so many different plans, timelines, and the details having changed again and again, I am confident in the things that will NOT change, as we re-commence this business in faith:

1. We will stick to our same values and mission of "Bringing peace to our world, one chocolate at a time."

2. We will do it again, but focus on getting better...not bigger.

3. We will be creative and flexible as we adapt with changing times and needs.

4. We will build an even stronger foundation, on which we can further use this platform, to sweeten the lives of those around us.

Following in Faith leads to Major Milestones of Growth

Throughout our six-plus years, there have been many moments of preparation for growth as we took steps of faith. Those moments actually felt similar to times like now. The future was so uncertain, and all I had was a prompting in my heart from God and the word to guide us to do the next thing.

2013: It all began by building out a commercial kitchen in the back of Linda Sugihara's dress shop in Manoa, because of a vision from God of a building with a white picket fence. (Long story, but basically I jumped in my car and drove around Oahu until I found a commercial property with a white picket fence - what you now know as our Choco le`a shop!)

2014: The front space (dress shop previously known as LMS Boutique) suddenly became available when Linda decided to retire, and we were forced to decide if we wanted to quit, move operations, or acquire the front to open our own shop to try the retail business and expand. Again because of God's plan (not mine), I returned from a mission trip in Japan, and went with the last option.

2015: We started a family with our first little one and me going into labor, literally in our shop, during a meeting.

2016: Why can't I remember this year? I know I had a 1 year old, just built and moved homes, and was pregnant with our second so maybe that's why this whole year was a blur!

2017: Our family grew with a second baby and our business grew with a second space. When our neighbor in the building moved out, we acquired the space and invested again to build out a second commercial kitchen, just before the end of the year and our holiday rush.

2018: Aloha Japan! We began exporting and selling our products in the country of people who always came to find us in Manoa! This was a year of exponential growth.

2019: Aloha outer-island and outer-state friends! We took a leap of faith and offered shipping to the neighbor islands and mainland during the holidays! We also expanded our shop into a mini-cafe with freshly brewed coffee and homemade ice cream, and began offering hands-on workshops in our kitchen.

2020: At the start of this year, we invested in a lot more to expand again and were on the verge of announcing our next big plans...when COVID-19 hit.

Now: Though a lot has certainly changed, one thing hasn't changed: My faith. Whatever comes next, God, at the top of our organizational chart, has always made the final decision.

Lesson Learned: Taking a pause, can really help actually prepare you for a different kind of growth. We may not be getting bigger as a company, but we can get better as a group of people. Professionally, we will get better at our craft. We will grow together working as a tight team. We will get to know our chocolate friends on a deeper level. We will be able to serve this world with our platform of chocolates in an even more meaningful way. Personally, we will get our priorities in order. We will have more gratitude in our hearts and serve more with our hands. We will take more pauses to reflect and fuel our faith.

Opportunity Now: The plans are in the works behind closed shop doors, but the emails (like this one) and posts on our Instagram (@chocoleahawaii and @yourchocolatefriend) are going out into the world now to share this faith. We want to start by connecting on a deeper level with each of you, share our why and who we truly are, who we've always been, and what we've always believed, but with a new found faith that there is a purpose to His plan. If you own a business, are currently working or trying to get back into work, don't worry about getting bigger. Work on getting better.

Hope For Our Future: We hope you will love Choco le`a version 20.0! In the year 2020, we were striving for version 3.0, but after COVID-19 and change after change, we will be re-emerging with version 20.0. It will be smaller and simpler, but still as sweet and satisfying.

My prayer for you, my chocolate friend, is to keep the faith. We can't wait to welcome you back into the shop, but until then...

Order online from wherever you are.
Pick up curbside from the comfort of your car.

Enjoy at home, your own chocolate dessert bar!

With love always,
Your chocolate friend, Erin

"Now faith is confidence in what we hope for and assurance about what we do not see." Hebrews 11:1

— MAY 25 —
Week No. 11
Reflection 11: Movement

There was a lot of movement going on in week #11. The definitions for the word "movement" include:

1. An act of changing physical location or position
2. A change or development

This week, we did both. We moved everything we could from our second commercial kitchen that we built and occupied for two and a half years, back to our original little commercial kitchen behind our shop that we built seven years ago.

We gave up the space we had grown into. For us, this move was kind of a big deal.

I walked around the kitchen and ran my hand against the remaining cold, clean, stainless steel tables, refrigerators, and racks and in the same breath whispered "thank you" and "goodbye." What I loved about this space is it that it had the "luxurious elbow room" we had always dreamed of, and allowed us to train more chocolatiers, without having to say, "Excuse me, excuse me, excuse me!" every time you had to slide by to get to another corner of the room.

For me, this space was a representation of what working together can accomplish. My production team planned it all, laid it out, and picked the equipment they wanted. I was so proud of what they built as a team. We also got our daily exercise running back and forth between this kitchen and our shop with rolling coolers of fresh chocolates.

After saying my goodbyes and sitting around reminiscing for closure, (because honestly the "temporary shut-down" happened all too fast), I started messaging and sending photos to our chocolate family. They too came and said their "goodbyes," helped with the move and reminisced about the good times.

In fact, one of our sweetest employees, Carol, once occupied this same kitchen back in 1998-1999, where she ran her own chocolate company and was known as the "chocolate lady in Manoa." Before I even hired her, Manoa residents would ask me if I knew her, and while I didn't know her, fate would have it that she applied and was hired to work at Choco le`a. I didn't realize we had this connection with her until she was with us for about one year. And here she was, in her old space with us, saying "goodbye" once again.

We also had to move out everything else that couldn't fit into our original kitchen (which was A LOT) into the homes of chocolate family and chocolate friends, neighboring businesses and to The Salvation Army.

I had to call in the "boys" to help, AKA all of my and my husband's friends and their friends' friends! To give you a visual, in just one day alone, we had our air conditioning friends, property manager friends, security friend, electrician friend, new plumber friend, chocolate friend, and two little friends (my kids), in and around the building, doing their thing to get the space back to its original condition...well there were actually upgrades made so better than original condition! But the most heartwarming thing of all was when they came in to do "their job," they ended up doing one or two more tasks. I watched as they, without being asked, helped each other carry the weight (literally) of our move.

Saying "goodbye" to this space was truly sad. But honestly, watching the perfectly good things in it go to people we truly loved, and seeing how happy it made them, helped make this a merrier move. I thought I would shed more tears as the thousands and thousands of dollars we invested went out the door too soon. But instead, the people who took them provided laughs and laughs and "thanks" and "thanks."

These material investments were now being invested into these friendships as the pieces found new homes where they would help friends to better organize or even start dreams of their own. Plus they even fed us manapua, pork hash, pastries, and desserts on these days. It almost felt like a party and a celebration in some ways.

When my kids saw that everything had gone, my son innocently said, "Hey mom, there's no chocolate in here!" When I explained to him the reason why, he then proceeded to say, "Well, let's play hide and seek." I looked inside and was like, "Seriously?" He was serious. He ran to hide behind one of the only pieces of furniture left.

As my parents helped me pack up the last of the small items to donate, my small kids thought it looked fun and jumped in to help and thus played a small part in this whole, very long process. I had to stop and take photos of everything throughout because I didn't want to forget these super sweet moments of how family and friends turned what could have been a very sad move, into a movement towards our future.

There is one thing that we could not take out of this space, and that was the life and spirit that was poured into it along with the many other small businesses before us (like our old friends Tom's Terrific and Line & Dot). Each business gave it their all and left it a little better for the next group coming in, to live out their dreams and contribute to this community and our world.

To whoever the lucky new tenants of this space will be,

I pray you create your own sweet memories here. I pray your team can make it feel like home and fill it with aloha. And we look forward to meeting you since after all, we will be neighbors in this building along with small local businesses that we love (shout out to Ku Day Spa, Hawai`i Doggie Bakery, Three Dogs & A Girl, Unity Chiropractor, and M's Massage.)

For the past six plus years, we've always made our chocolates the same way, by hand, on-site, in small batches with aloha and will continue to do it the same way, but in the original space that we started in, back in 2013.

Lesson Learned: The best investments are made in people. Things come and go. You can get shiny new equipment but even the best stuff gets old and breaks down. Spaces become vacant and businesses grow out of it. But the people in your lives, even if they've moved on, those who really love you will show up with just a quick call. When I said, "Ok I can't do this on my own. I need help", so many of them came. Even if I hadn't seen a few of these friends for months, even if some of them have moved on from our crew, they will always be chocolate friends and family in my heart, who had a part in this chapter of our story.

Opportunity Now: Ask for help. We never knew back in the day that we would grow so much so soon and also never thought we'd have to let part of it go so soon either. Whether building and starting up or moving and starting again, it is not something that can be done alone.

No matter what God has in store for us next, the same holds true. The focus has always been about bringing people together, sweetening relationships and bringing peace to our world. This move, this "sale," this ask for help, brought people together. The hardship of owning a business and the lack of work during this COVID-19 pandemic, sweetened the bonds that we all shared in some way and started conversations.

The common goal of cleaning out this space brought peace as I watched everyone work together, not because they had to, but because they wanted to help. This aloha culture we have here in Hawai`i is our hope for this whole world. So if you're like me and sometimes have a hard time asking for help, you could be missing out on being a witness to the coming together, bonding, and joy it can bring others, when they have the opportunity to help and be a part of something. Just ask.

Hope for Our Future: Movement can be a change for good. Although letting go of this space was physically and emotionally difficult, it puts us in a better position for sustainability as we develop and build again. We're going back to our humble beginnings that will still allow us to keep our focus on the business we've always said we're in...the people business. (Chocolates just happen to be a sweet platform for our work.) We are ALL in the people business in some way. After all, if the work we are doing isn't helping anyone, isn't making anything better, then we need to change our position, and "move!"

My prayer for you, my chocolate friend, is that you can find our move (and perhaps your own) to smaller and simpler to still be sweet and satisfying.

With love always,
Your chocolate friend, Erin

"Two are better than one, because they have a good return for their labor:" -Ecclesiastes 4:9

"Though one may be overpowered, two can defend themselves. A chord of three strands is not quickly broken." Ecclesiastes 4:12

— JUNE I —

Week No. 12
Reflection 12: Kindness

A lot of different words came to my mind during week #12. With all that's happening in the world on top of COVID-19, from racial injustice, flaws in our systems, anger and violence, destruction of property, loss of lives, protests, overwhelming sadness, and so much more...I felt so many emotions for our hurting world.

To be honest, I was confused as to which word best described the week. So much so, that I even found myself immobilized at times, consumed by all the media I was reading and watching. But when I sat down to start my journaling to help me process what I was feeling, I did what I always try to do when I am searching for answers. I went to the Bible, and read:

"Love is patient, love is kind. It does not envy, it does

not boast, it is not proud. It does not dishonor others, it is not self-seeking, it is not easily angered, it keeps no record of wrongs. Love does not delight in evil, but rejoices with the truth. It always protects, always trusts, always hope, always perseveres. Love never fails." -1 Corinthians 13

So, as I watched events unfold between our own humankind, I chose a word to focus on that didn't come automatically at first, but more of what I hope to see more of in our world: "**kindness**."

At first, I hesitated, thinking this is too cheesy for me to send out to all of you. But through your responses to these emails, and even at our curbside pick-up on Saturday, confirmation came through just about every single one of you who said, "*I love reading these blogs and emails. It brings me hope.*"

With a mission of "Bringing peace to our world, one CHOCOLATE at a time," I realized that with the temporary closing of our shop and not as much chocolate to share, I needed to find a new way to bring this peace and so began doing it, one EMAIL at a time. These emails are simply snippets from my journals that

I've long kept to myself because it can be scary to share my heart with a world that can sometimes be very unkind.

I personally know that kindness doesn't always come easily and is a choice I need to make again and again. It is not among the top words I would choose to describe myself. But kindness is free. It doesn't cost us anything, and kindness can easily be spread.

Kindness is also what I felt like I was the recipient of this week from so many customers turned chocolate friends. If you are like me and need to hear some hope, during a time of such hurt, here are a few little stories of how others chose kindness this week.

It began with me checking our mailbox, and instead of the usual bills and scam mail, my focus shifted to a few unexpected hand-written cards in the pile. One was from a former teacher, Mrs. Sproles, in response to my email on "gratitude" and one was from a long-time customer, Sue, turned chocolate friend.

This friend was actually one of the last people to pick up her chocolates before we temporarily closed our doors. Sue was also one of my first customers who took a chance on me when I would make 20 boxes of random truffles each month, and would meet at Manoa Marketplace shopping center for a drop off.

I remember looking into her eyes that day during week #1 of "loss" and saying "goodbye" because I had no idea when I might see her again. And now, almost three months later, she made a choice to check in on me and write words of encouragement on a Cinderella card, which is also a movie with the lesson to "Have courage and be kind." She encouraged me to stay in it and reassured me that she along with many others were waiting to support us at our re-opening because "everyone deserves a happily ever after, one chocolate at a time."

I then began the busy week prepping for our second curbside pick-up. Tuesday's 12 P.M. launch opened and I was overwhelmed as I watched everything sell out in about ten minutes. Even though inventory once again went so quickly, this time, rather than emails of frustration and sad emojis, you chose to send me emails of understanding and congratulations on the demand, with hopeful optimism for the next round of pre-orders.

When all the chocolates were gone and only shirts left for sale, I watched as some of you were eager to purchase one to wear proudly as an ambassador alongside us for "world peace, one chocolate at a time." Your kind response to something you longingly waited for, and did not receive, motivated me to get back into the kitchen and start planning another curbside pick-up.

The kindness continued as a message came in on our Instagram @chocoleahawaii that I did not expect. A local whiskey loving group of friends (we will call them our whiskey chocolate friends) had a conversation reminiscing how much they loved our Yamazaki 12 truffles we once had. In their own creative challenge to support a small local business, one friend dared another to give up his Yamazaki 12 bottle to us, and his kind heart gladly stepped up to the challenge. I received a random surprise message that he was dropping off a bottle. For real?

Unbeknownst to him, I was originally scheduled to be

in Nagoya at the Takashimaya Fair right then, and would probably be trying to hunt down a bottle of this whiskey during my free time to bring back! Yet, here he was choosing to give it to us, not expecting anything in return. His act of random kindness challenged another friend to donate HIS Hakushu 12 bottle and then another Hibiki bottle. This means what we now have, my friends, are the ingredients we have been searching for to be part of our annual Father's Day special! Thank you Brett, Brent, Carli, and all the whiskey chocolate friends for this kindness challenge.

I also want to take this time to express a heartfelt "Domo arigato" to our Nagoya friends as well for the invite to the Takashimaya Fair! I wish I could have been there with you again this year. Even though last June was my first time to that city and I did not have any friends, your hospitality and kindness shown to me was unlike anything I had ever experienced, and I will never forget it.

As week #12 continued, so many of you chose to show undeserved kindness, for no reason at all. It ranged from snack deliveries, to homemade masks left on the doorknob of our shop for my kids (thanks Alisa), cute little keepsake signs (thanks Rachael), and good old phone calls checking in. So many of our customers have become friends and during this pandemic, you chose to be kind, despite everything you yourself have been going through. As one of you said, *"I have become sweeter from eating all of your chocolates!"*

Over the years we sometimes had customers yell at us when they weren't happy with our packaging, or the price, or our limited hours, but we always chose as a company to respond in kindness. It paid off. Everyone is going through something and we don't know everyone's story so we did not want to further inflame the anger. When we responded in this way, we have found time and time again that dissatisfied customers often became our loyal friends.

In the same way, YOU have all showed us kindness again and again as WE have made mistakes. Honestly, the times we've been most beaten up in this business is when we messed up and felt so horrible that we let you down. When we miscounted. When we put the wrong product in the bag. When we had to call to apologize and take accountability. Yet you showed us undeserved grace and kindness in response. Thank you, thank you, thank you.

Many of you have also showed kindness by taking the time to write back and share how our emails are bringing some peace, love, and hope to your world. You've opened your heart to share your own stories of hurt and how you had to once close your own business. How you lost a marriage over business and was left completely heartbroken. How you missed your kids growing up when you were consumed with work. And how you sometimes feel so discouraged, confused, angry, sad, and lost in this world as I do sometimes, and are searching for hope or the right word to focus on. Some of you have even been passing our emails on. One chocolate friend, Alex, said he shared our emails with his admin ladies in the office, as a way to spread hope. As a result, we are forming new friends through old friends. Through it all, we really have become chocolate **friends.**

Finally, with all that's happening, I continue to find myself taking a few minutes before bed to talk about different things in life with my kids who are three and five years old. This past week, the topics were kindness and respect. How God calls us to love all people. We talked about the values that are important to us as a family and as a chocolate family, because the values, both at home and at work, are the same. Finally, that we all have a choice, and I pray that they will always choose kindness.

Lesson Learned: Choose what you want to focus on. Sometimes, so many things in our world happen that seem out of our control, or beyond our comprehension, or are simply overwhelming. But we need to choose what we will believe in. What we stand for, and what we want to share. I am not always kind, and realize that even the good feelings and actions take an intentional effort. But it is a choice. Kindness is free. What you focus on most, you find, you live out, and you can spread.

Opportunity Now: Perform a random act of kindness. This is not something new, but it still works. It starts a chain reaction. It can create a change in heart in both the recipient and you. Here are a few ideas:

1. Take the time to listen to someone else's story. Even if that person doesn't look like you, act like you, or like

the same things as you. We can learn a lot from each other.

2. Send a "thinking of you" card in the mail to someone and write three uplifting sentences about the other person, to make them feel seen, feel valued, and feel heard. You can even leave it anonymous!

3. Give up something you love that you know someone else will love, and share it with them instead.

Hope For Our Future: Our world is more connected than ever before, giving us the chance to spread hope faster and further than ever before. Using technology and social media, information, photos, music, videos and so many other things can easily spread. Even COVID-19 showed us how quickly and easily a pandemic can spread. But good can be spread too: real information, encouraging stories, helpful tips; great laughs, compassion, empathy and kindness can all easily be shared and spread all over our connected world unlike ever before.

My prayer for you, my chocolate friend, is for you to decide what we will stop the spread of, and what we will start the spread of. Let's start by spreading **kindness**.

With love always,
Your chocolate friend, Erin

"Be kind and compassionate to one another, forgiving each other, just as in Christ God forgave you."-Ephesians 4:3

As we just moved back to our original tiny kitchen and are busy setting it up again, a major challenge will be trying to make sure the temperature, humidity, and everything in the space is JUST right again. Then we will slowly get into the groove of making chocolates in this old/new space. It is honestly frustrating at times for us to not be able to produce as much as we know we once could, and are now restricted by space, time, finances, and storage. But in these moments, we are learning to be **kind** to ourselves and be content with what we CAN do.

— JUNE 8 —

Week No. 13
Reflection 13: Fun

Wow...are we really on week #13? It has been twelve weeks (or three months) of being home with the kids + attempting to home-school + work + we still have another one and a half months to go (assuming they return in August in person, and no distance learning)! Is anyone else going a little crazy? On top of it all, we're staying home alone a lot as the days get hotter and the "fun" of summer and no school starts to wear off.

Let me preface this by saying that I am extremely grateful that I have the opportunity to care for my kids every day, but if you are a mom, dad, or any caretaker in this position right now, can I just get an "Amen?!" With a just turned three year old who sometimes still puts his pants on backwards, a five year old who misses her friends, teacher, and playground, and what seems like a never ending cycle of food prep, dishes, teaching or entertaining, cleaning, feeding, dishes....I think we all need a little more fun or FUNny moments to keep us going so we don't lose our sanity.

Yes, there was some fun this week. Like getting in the kitchen and playing with chocolates again. Hiking with a friend. Having dance battles in the living room with my kids. But a lot of it wasn't fun. I feel like the weeks and the news every day has been heavy. Our country and our world has been going through a lot. And although I don't want to ignore it, I needed to lighten my load, lighten the mood, and make my own fun to give myself a break and keep it together.

Hearing how excited you all were with the announcement of Crunch a le`a was so FUNny and it sincerely gave me some good laughs! Real quotes from YOU, chocolate friends:

-"I was wondering if you are all getting closer to making the Crunch a le`a. No pressure just checking if I could get my hands on it. :)"
-"That's the crack!" (referring to IG post of Crunch a le`a)

-"I want $100 worth. Can't wait to try it." (from a chocolate friend who hasn't even tried it before)
-"I hide my Crunch a le`a from my kids and husband in the freezer. I still have some from last Christmas, but am running out!"

Fifteen of you following on my personal Instagram (@yourchocolatefriend) commented when I posted a pic for fun and the caption, "Should I just sell these big boys in bulk?!" You responded with cries of "YES!!!! Pleeeeeeeassssse!" I thought it would be fun to just try it, put it in untraditional packaging that I will call "Choco le`a consumption wrapping," and ask if you wanted to be a test group friend to which one-hundred percent of you agreed! So one night, I made an impromptu trip to the chocolate shop to get out of my comfort zone, and have a little fun in the kitchen to make this test batch for you.

With kids pretty much always in tow, THEY DO make super simple things fun! My son thinks it's soooo much fun to play hide-and-seek in our super small shop even though he hides in the same obvious spot over and over and I have to pretend like I can't find him.

He is also very particular that his and his sister's reward for when they come with me to work at the chocolate shop, is a Birthday Cake truffle. I found that he will only eat the truffles with a blue sprinkle on it. No blue sprinkle, and it doesn't pass his "quality control check." Slightly annoying, but learning to laugh about it and packaging all of the Birthday Cake truffles with no blue sprinkles to randomly give away in this week's curbside "FREE surprise extra kindness giveaway." Also giving away the "Cruncha le`a Crumbs" I usually enjoy. Have fun eating the "scraps!"

When I think of FUNny, I think of the guy that makes me laugh the hardest...my dad. He's still got it and has those "dad jokes" that are only funny when he says it, in the moment, and even funnier because it was kind of bad! You know what I mean? And he'd make everyone laugh at work too. You could hear him always rustling through the "crew snack bin" or sitting down with our customers making friends. Or getting the biggest kid-like smile when we said that we had a new flavor or product he could try. This always made him super happy even though his favorite is still the mint chocolate chip truffle. I "pay him in chocolates" since he's my volunteer Maintenance Manager who comes in to clean the air conditioners, change the light bulbs, and do pretty much whatever maintenance is needed.

Just before this lock down, I took a kind of impromptu one-day trip with him to Maui, and we laughed so much on the long car rides from visiting our friends at the Grand Wailea, to UpCountry Maui, and finally to Lahaina. He even modeled for me when I asked him to pose for a pic I could use on IG later for Father's Day...and here it is! Love you dad!

I married a guy who is the fun one in the family. Definitely more easy going than me, less serious, and always down for an adventure. He also THINKS he's funny, which sometimes, actually makes me laugh! Fun fact: Chris is actually the one who wanted to learn how to make chocolates from my uncle, not me. I just wanted to eat it. So the very start of Choco le`a was fun because it was something we learned and figured out together.

I still remember when we purchased our first used refrigerator and stainless steel table in 2012 and put it right in the middle of the living room in the place we were renting because it was the best spot for the air flow from the air conditioner. It looked ridiculous and how I imagine all businesses start, like Apple in Steve Job's garage. There was our set up. A stainless steel table and refrigerator right next to some fishing gear and a couch in the middle of our living room. I wish I had a picture from then!

And so, a quick shout out to my dad, my husband, my father-in-law, and all of the "dad" figures out there! We raise our glass to you (or chocolates I should say) and wish you a "Happy Father's Day!" (For those of you who are the ones staying home with the kids, I really hope you get the whiskey truffles at our next pre-order.)

Times are tough for sure. Many things are not a laughing matter. But God didn't create us to just be miserable every day of our life. I know I've always loved my job and mostly had fun at work. But without the same work, I've once again had to search for fun in different ways. If I can be honest, when I sometimes began to feel guilty about having too much fun during times like this, I was reminded in the word:

"This is what I have observed to be good: that it is

appropriate for a person to eat, to drink and to find satisfaction in their toilsome labor under the sun during the few days of life God has given them - for this is their lot. Moreover, when God gives someone wealth and possessions, and the ability to enjoy them, to accept their lot and be happy in their toil - this is a gift of God." -Ecclesiastes 5:18-19

So here are some real quotes for fun, just because, and the best part is that all of these are courtesy of chocolate friends who sent them to me. I'll keep it anonymous, but really, if you recognize one of the below as yours, thank you for putting a smile on my face this past week. Know that you're making more people smile right now! Thank you for having a great sense of humor when you couldn't get an online pre-order, when your favorite product was not available, or if you're just going crazy during this shut-down not having your Choco le`a stash.

The Crazy Things You've Said In Quarantine:
"I will be ready for tomorrow's pre-orders. Alarms are set."

"We are in quarantine having been on the mainland! Can you extend this offer? We can then leave our home!"

"My young daughter has been going through Choco le`a withdrawals! Thank you for setting the quality of chocolate standard high!!"

"This grandma is too slow at ordering online."

"My mom is signed up for emails but she forgets to read them haha so I'm signing up now."

"I'm wearing your Choco le`a shirt and a lady at the dentist place knows you."

"You know what's funny? I lost weight when I started working at Choco le`a too! It was an active job at Choco le`a...that or chocolate is the unknown secret diet that we all need!"

"People are only upset because they are having Choco le`a withdrawals."

"Gave grandma a nine-piece truffle box. She's savoring it and eating 1 truffle every three days...but that's still not enough to get her through one month!

"How about Oreo cookie week? I'm kinda freaking out cause I really need one. You can charge me double I'll be okay with that!"

"I noticed you are using less commas in your email now :D (they were kinda everywhere before !)"

And to wrap it up, many of you can relate to this chocolate joke. Some of you may laugh and some of you may cringe because this actually happened to you!

"There was a box of chocolate with a note on it saying, 'Don't eat me!' Now there's an empty box with another note on it saying, 'Don't tell me what to do!'"

Lesson Learned: There are a lot of things out of our control. Sometimes all we can do is laugh and try to move on or turn it into something fun. Laughter IS great medicine! It's an old saying, but we need to stay well and take care of not only our physical and spiritual health, but our emotional health too. I'm learning to have more fun, laugh out loud until it hurts, laugh at myself, and spend time with people who can laugh at me.

Opportunity Now: Make your own fun or find the fun in whatever you are doing, and sometimes, even be okay with making fun of yourself. If you don't get what you want during our pre-order hour, laugh about being "too slow," then send me a message saying, "Put me on a wait list for Crunch a le`a," or whatever product it is you crave. Or send me a fun idea to make it work for you! Seriously, I am open to new ideas, I am willing to fail and make mistakes, and open to trying new things that are out of my comfort zone. That's how all of the videos on Instagram MyStory and the taste-testing videos you all LOVE, happened. I did it as a joke for fun when trying to figure out what Instagram Stories was, and you all asked for it again and again. Let's keep having fun with chocolates!

Hope for Our Future: Even though they drive us nuts, kids do make us laugh! If you are also counting down the days of when they will go back to school because you can't find a summer FUN program to give you a break, write down the funny things they say and the funny things they do, because one day, you'll forget and will longingly look back for a laugh. If your kids are all grown up and you're caring for your dad, grandpa, uncle, or other family member getting older, write down the funny things THEY say and the funny things they do, because one day, they won't be here and we will need to recite their final fun moments and sweet stories, for future generations to learn from.

My prayer for you, my chocolate friend, is that you find the fun, or make the fun, and let those moments lead to smiles and sweet laughs.

With love always,
Your chocolate friend, Erin

"A joyful heart is good medicine…" -Proverbs 17:22

Just For Fun

I wanted to experience the whole crazy online pre-orders from your perspective, so I watched a friend try repeatedly to purchase Asato Family sherbert (great job guys and great stuff)! The anticipation and refreshing rush as she waited for the spinning circle to let her know....that...she...got it! I watched her bite her lip, pump a fist to the ceiling, then cheer as she let out a sigh of relief because minutes later, the notice appeared that they were "all sold out!" Oh man I wish I could see your videos of what your reactions are on the other side.

Last joke for fun: "What kind of candy is never on time? ChocoLATE!"

— JUNE 15 —

Week No. 14
Reflection 14: Uncomfortable

Wearing a mask is uncomfortable. Making sure we stand six feet apart is still uncomfortable. Not being able to kiss on the cheek when we greet each other is uncomfortable. Not hugging after a long, difficult, or deep conversation is uncomfortable. Not being with people like we once used to, is for me, very uncomfortable.

If I can be honest, I am STILL trying to adjust to all of this. Yes, I know we are on week #14 already, but I am a social "people person" and what IS comfortable to me is hugging. Standing close to one another. Putting my arm around friends when we laugh and share food. This whole "distance" thing is still a struggle.

There were also a lot of uncomfortable conversations

in the past week. Conversations about the "Black Lives Matter," movement. Conversations about police officers and their service to our communities. Conversations about the systems and policies in our government and political leaders. Conversations about opening up to tourism for the economy versus staying hunkered down for health reasons. Conversations about religion and heaven versus hell.

In an interview this past week, I was asked some hard questions that I was uncomfortable answering. So much so that I literally had to say, "I'm not comfortable answering this question." The hardest was when there was no openness to any conversation.

A really great quote I heard recently is, "People fear one another because they don't KNOW one another. They don't know one another, because they don't communicate with each other." You are learning more about me as I communicate through these weekly email blogs and I have been learning about you as we have conversations, break down barriers, and begin to feel more comfortable with one another.

For some of you, shopping online is uncomfortable.

Some of you vent to me that you still struggle with not being able to come into the shop, to custom order whatever you want from our wide selection, and instead, have to "fight for it" as things sell out in minutes on our website. Some of you have left me voicemails asking me about online shopping carts and why things can disappear from your cart, since in real life at the store, people don't grab things out of your cart and once it's in, it's in and yours. But online, you have to pay in order to actually 'have it' otherwise people would just hoard everything and hold it in their carts while they think. I understand that this can be very frustrating and uncomfortable, but I am grateful that you still try.

I'll be the first to admit that I am not an online shopper. It took me years to buy anything on Amazon and I still miss the malls, touching the products, and wandering around browsing the whole store first while taking in the decor, the smells, the music, the people, and the entire experience. But, the only way to get comfortable with something new, is to try it again and again. So, I am learning to shop online and trying to find the fun in experiencing other small local businesses in the same pre-order/curbside way that we've been doing it, but from your perspective.

Through this research, I'm finding what is unclear to me and what is frustrating, and what is awesome! Sometimes, I myself am uncomfortable asking the other businesses for clarification, because then I'll look dumb if I can't find the answer myself on the website. I want you to know that I appreciate those of you who ask, share, and speak up, because what may seem crystal clear in my eyes, are the things that may still be an area to improve on. Thanks to you for sharing how uncomfortable you feel about ordering online. It has challenged me to create tutorials to help you feel less uncomfortable with this new way of shopping.

Even making bamboocha, big, bulk Crunch a le`a for this past curbside service was a bit uncomfortable for me because I was not happy with the packaging. The finished look wasn't polished. It didn't match the brand standards I had set for the business. But YOU all loved it! You all wanted it…AND you still want more. To let it leave my hands in this new bulky form was quite honestly, a little uncomfortable because I felt like I hadn't perfected it.

I have been getting more comfortable with our pre-order and curbside pick-up way of operating and look forward to seeing everyone! BUT I am uncomfortable asking, "What name is your order under?" as I look at long-time loyal chocolate friends who look unfamiliar because of your face masks, or because it's been awhile since I worked "front of the house" and saw all of you. All the while you politely chuckle and say to me, *"Hiiiiiiiiii, Erin!"* (insert that emoji of the girl slapping her forehead here)

With the COVID-19 numbers rising again here in Hawai`i and around the world, lots of people became uncomfortable going out, changed their minds about sending kids to summer school, or postponed their planned re-opening dates. I feel uncomfortable opening for many reasons ranging from finances, our dependency on markets that have so many uncertainties right now (tourism, large corporate orders, hotel wholesale orders, export sales, non-profit gala favors, and gifts for other large events), to the health risks, to questions of childcare, to just not being ready to return until I felt like we changed enough with the changing times.

By that, I mean taking care of things both as a business and personally. The things that I long knew I needed to take care of, and create new routines that I was "too busy" to take care of, and to get those priorities in order before returning.

It's totally uncomfortable for me to say this, but part of making positive change starts with facing the things that are really uncomfortable and admitting it's not what we want it to be.

One of my greatest fears of coming out of COVID-19 is remaining exactly the same person I was before, and returning to the exact same thing. No difference. If we're returning to a "new normal," wouldn't that require a "new me?" Or rather I should say, a better version of myself? A better version of the business? A better way of living this life together?

Uncomfortable as it is, we know that change, new beginnings, great ideas, stronger bonds, deeper friendships, healthier relationships, and new ones, begin outside of our comfort zone. It's when we are willing to walk into a room where we don't know people, or when we choose to sit on a table with people out of our usual "circle" of people that we look like.

It begins when we are forced to think creatively and out of the box. When our world gets flipped upside down. When death is just around the corner for a loved one. When someone says something that challenges us or shifts our thinking from what we know, to have to research, read, learn, and look outside of what we possibly grew up understanding. It begins when we sit for hours with someone, and listen to their story. When we hear what they've been through, or what they're going through now, but have masked their challenges with a smile or a perfect Instagram feed.

No one likes to be uncomfortable. Hell, I was never comfortable writing these emails and am still not. (Am I allowed to write "hell?") I had a whole other topic written out and re-read tons of times to go out on Monday, but gave up as I was just really uncomfortable with how unauthentic it felt.

Even when things messed up last week and a draft of "week #13: Kindness" and a final of the same email went out back to back due to technical difficulties, I cringed thinking about which one you all read and that a bunch of you probably read the one that wasn't supposed to go out. But that kind of discomfort should not stop us from moving forward and paralyze us from being willing to mess up again in order to make progress.

When you give me credit for being so strong and so brave with my transparency, it's really not me who deserves the credit. These emails are something I felt God put in my heart as something I should have shared and written about YEARS ago. For years - yup, before Choco le`a even began, I felt God telling me to write and share, and I have been writing. But I never shared any of it. Because...I was scared. I was uncomfortable. I was unsure of what everyone would think of me when they read it, if they read it at all, because for all I know, who cares what I might have to say.

But moving in this direction of authenticity, way out of my comfort zone, and writing and openly expressing my faith, is a prompting in my heart from my Lord and Savior that I cannot deny. The honest reason why I started writing these emails, other than a lack of a shop or chocolate and a struggle to find a way to still live out our mission of "Bringing peace to our world, one chocolate at a time," when we were on lock down with no inventory of product, was that I simply felt like if this was it, I needed to be obedient, and do what I know He has been calling me to do and share.

Just say it. Just write it and send it even if it sucked. That this could be my final chance with this sweet business platform to reach whoever I could over the years of sharing chocolates. That this ship could go down (though I don't plan for it to go that way). That tomorrow could be my last day, and all of these things are things we know, but COVID-19 made it more urgent and more real. It brought up all of the feelings locked away deep inside that were suppressed because it's more comfortable to wear a mask, smile, and go on like everything is okay. Even if it's not.

Lesson Learned: Stepping out of my comfort zone, again and again, is what God calls me to do. I am brought to my knees and rely on Him and His strength and not my own. Doing things that make me uncomfortable gives Him the glory, keeps my pride in check, and gives Him the opportunity to shine.

At the end of the day, that's really all I want to do. My heart's desire is to live out the will of my Heavenly Father. But life is sometimes so much easier to live IN our comfort zone, to live IN our comfortable homes, with familiar people, in our stable or successful jobs, doing things in our control, and what the world expects us to be.

Opportunity Now: Sometimes, the BEST lessons come during the times of greatest discomfort. But in any uncomfortable situation, it is our human nature to seek comfort. For me, I find that comfort from the words and messages in the Bible. Read the word. Every answer to every question I have can be found in the Bible. It makes me so uncomfortable to sound so preachy when I am so far from perfect. I know I am flawed and only human, but I know the Bible is the one place I can always go back to for answers. HE is the one who has never failed me.

I'm sorry if reading this makes you uncomfortable, but if this was my last message, or my last day, I would want to go knowing that I shared the gospel, the truth, the life, and the way with all of you. After all, friends share the truth, even if it makes the other person uncomfortable.

Hope For Our Future: We grow when we get out of automatic, out of the routine of day-to-day, out of the monotony of what's expected, and do the unexpected, the untraditional, the seemingly impossible, the scary, the uncomfortable. When we lean on Him, something greater than our goals, our idols, our leaders, and ourselves can be accomplished. At the end of the day, what we are all looking for is to be comfortable with who we really are. To be loved. To be comforted in the times that we feel uncomfortable. He will not fail us. He is always with us, and He LOVES us ALL.

My prayer for you, my chocolate friend, is that you step out of your comfort zone and into the comforting embrace of our Lord and Savior who is waiting with arms outstretched.

With love always,
Your chocolate friend, Erin

"Praise be to the God and Father of our Lord Jesus Christ, the Father of compassion and the God of all comfort, who comforts us in all our troubles, so that we can comfort those in any trouble with the comfort we ourselves receive from God." -2 Corinthians 1: 3

"No, in all these things we are more than conquerors through Him who loved us. For I am convinced that neither death nor life, neither angels nor demons, neither the present nor the future, nor any powers, neither height nor depth, nor anything else in all creation, will be able to separate us from the love of God that is in Christ Jesus our Lord."
-Romans 8:37-38

— JUNE 22 —

Week No. 15
Reflection 15: Perseverance

It's week #15 guys. Or day #105 of this...whatever this is. COVID-19 pandemic. Temporary "world" shut down. All I know is that it has been a long time with a long time more ahead.

Like clockwork, every day my routine loving three year old son wakes up early in the morning, and says, *"Breakfast mommy. Can I have a lot of circle cereal in my Lighting McQueen bowl with my blue spoon and milk and milk in the cup and I will pour the milk from my cup into my bowl please?"* #verbatim

On the mornings I play "dead" and try to pretend I'm still asleep, he persistently stays by my side for a very long time repeating this drawn out sentence and tapping me on my arm. As always, his perseverance wins and I reluctantly get up, make his breakfast, and turn on the news.

I am reminded every morning on the news that just as we began to open up again as a nation, we find ourselves faced with rising cases, with some places hitting new highs. We anticipated this in our "second wave," but here we are still trying to push through the "first wave." Well friends, it looks like we are going to be in this fight against COVID-19 and will need to persevere through all of this for a lot longer.

Although I've been eager to get back to business, this pandemic has put a hold on a lot of things like tourism, travel, special events, and large corporate accounts, which we once so heavily relied on. With our return to a "new normal" delayed, writing my reflections for COVID-19 on a weekly basis was something I found myself doing to reflect and sort through what I was feeling. Sharing it with all of you has been something that many of you mentioned you consistently look forward to in your inbox to read. (Thank you!)

But if I can be perfectly honest with you all, this week, I literally walked among the trees in the mountains and thought to myself, "What's the word for this past week?" The word sets the tone to write. The word describes the week and pulls all of the different things that happened, or the lack thereof, together.

I've been "late" when I wanted to send out my email blogs. I've made mistakes sending out my email blogs. I feel like I am running out of "ideas" or "words" for my email blogs. In fact, I sent a first draft of this to a friend that really just felt like, "blah, blah, blah" to me, but to my surprise my friend replied, "I love it!" "You need to keep writing these," she said. "I think that's what people need to hear right now."

She told me to keep going and I realized that though many of you may need to hear my words right now, it is actually YOUR words that keep ME persevering. Your stories and responses are inspiring me to press on!

After sharing a second draft with my 2 chocolate friends, (whom I will tell you about below), and feeling their joy and tears in their responses, I literally had an epiphany, like a whisper from God, that my emails are also an opportunity to share YOUR stories that are inspiring me!

So, as I persevere onward with a lack of content for the week, I would like to share the stories of 2 chocolate friends, who have given me permission to freely share with all of you their stories of persistence and perseverance that came at the expense of their pain.

GLORY To God For A Miracle
The first story comes from my first chocolate friend, Glory, who I "met" after posting this on my Instagram @yourchocolatefriend in February 2020:

"Exactly one year ago, I COMPLETELY lost my sense of smell and taste. Yes, you read that correctly. I'm already hearing impaired with 100% loss in one ear, feels like I'm about legally blind with a -9.25 prescription, and then this.

Thankfully, by some miracle, both senses returned after a couple of months, but it was such a heartbreaking moment as I felt like a part of me died and I would never experience life the same again. I'll never forget finally admitting to my team that I

132

couldn't taste the Valentine's Day chocolates they made and broke down and cried in front of them as we had to carry on as a company.

After visits to doctors and tests and tears and prayer, I finally made peace with how life was going to be and recorded this video so I wouldn't forget what I had to push through..."

Glory reached out to me on this post and commented: *"I'm crying right now. I was introduced to your chocolate a few weeks ago...and have been watching this page because I love the texture of the Crunch a le`a. Now I see this. I completely lost my sense of smell and taste in April. I know exactly how you feel, and I am still hoping and praying that my senses will return."*

From there, we connected and I learned more about Glory. A wonderful woman, wife, and mother of a beautiful family. She lost her sense of smell (and taste) due to a traumatic brain injury. The likelihood for her recovery is extremely low.

She continued, *"Sometimes I have panic attacks when I remember that I can't smell. I am a major foodie and love to cook. I have children and a husband I wish I could smell. I feel so disconnected and pray that it will come back. I fell in love with the Crunch a le`a that a friend introduced me to. It's the texture that I found to be so satisfying. It feels so good to speak to someone who knows exactly what I'm going through. God works his magic in so many ways and I believe this is one of them. It's so crazy!"*

Since then, Glory has been a friend on Instagram and persistently watches our page for her next opportunity to purchase Crunch a le`a. Just the other week at our last curbside pick-up, I reserved one of our bulk Crunch a le`a bars for Glory. When I finally met her in person, she had the brightest smile on her face and the most sincere gratitude in her heart. *"The crunch was so amazing!"* she reported. *"The texture really hits home for me. I'd love for you to share my story. I hope it can reach someone, the same way yours did."*

Thank you Glory. Even as you push through life without your sense of smell and taste, I admire your persistence in continuing to cook for your family, continuing to go out and enjoy the foods you love based on your memory because you can no longer taste it, and even the simple things like waiting for our chocolates so you can enjoy its texture. I pray that you will persevere in your perspective on life and prayer and never give up on our God and the miracles that only He can do. We will continue to be praying alongside of you during this challenging time.

Gina - One Chocolate Truffle Per Day
When COVID-19 first began, the posts on our Instagram @chocoleahawaii changed slightly. It was less about what we were making and what was available for sale, and more about reminiscing the sweet memories made as we stayed in shelter-in-place. The changed content on our page, created a change in the conversations we had in our Direct Message inbox. It was there that I connected with chocolate friend Gina, who had an energy that made me smile with her every response.

She wrote: *"Before this craziness I bought 2 boxes of the Signature Set Truffle Box. One for my boyfriend and one for me...then COVID happened and the highlight of our day would be to open our box and decide which truffle we would enjoy together via FaceTime."*

I learned that Gina is a nurse at a local hospital, and when this first happened, she wanted to take extra precautions and made the difficult decision to stay separated from her boyfriend for about 3 weeks and son for about two long months. Her perseverance to do her heroic work at the sacrifice of being with the ones she loved, only to be rewarded by a small morsel of a chocolate truffle per day, shows her strength in character and care for others.

Now reunited with loved ones, she used our chocolates from a recent curbside pick-up as a gift to help her to take a big step after years of working through the opposition to begin forgiving a lost loved one. She wrote, *"Your chocolates are truly spreading peace one chocolate at a time...peace, forgiveness, grace...thank you so much."*

And as Gina said, *"God never wants us to waste a hurt so instead of being bitter, let's be better."* Thank you for sharing this Gina, for your steadfast service, and for continuing to share chocolates with those you love, and are learning to "love" again, one truffle, one chocolate, one day at a time.

Throughout week #15 there was a Zoom meeting, a phone call, a visit, a voicemail, a LINE message, an email, and a discussion with several other small local businesses about what's next. How are we going to do this? Should we combine forces to survive, then thrive? What are the next steps to keep going? These conversations can easily make me feel like it would all be easier to just give up.

But one voicemail left by an elderly chocolate friend and neighbor, (who sounds like she could be my grandma's sister or long time close relative by the tone in her voice), was, *"I'm so glad that you are not closing. I'm not able to go out anymore and used to enjoy watching people come in and out of your shop from my window. It makes me happy to see you coming in and out again. You really do have GOOD chocolates."*

In hearing you root for us while seeing the hurt all around us, we find the fight within us, to persevere, and let the GOOD win and His glory, be revealed in the days to come.

We WILL persevere because our mission is "Bringing peace to our world, one chocolate at a time." But gosh, we still have a lot of work to do. With the peace that comes from God within, we can fight for peace and freedom from the opposition of COVID-19 and other "plagues" of hate, jealousy, pride, and destruction in this world.

Lesson Learned: We must persevere. Even if we don't feel like it. Even when YOU feel like you can't possibly go on or continue, there are others cheering you on, who have stories to share to inspire you, and we must continue to persevere together. God has not given up on us and we cannot give up on Him. We should also not give up on ourselves or on others and the possibility that change can happen and miracles can still prevail.

Opportunity Now: Keep fighting, whatever you are going through. As one good friend repeatedly told me this past week, *"Don't give up. Whatever you do, don't give up."* It brought me to tears because in some areas of life, it would be so much easier to just give up. But that's what the enemy wants.

We shall not surrender. We shall instead find our strength in the Word. We will set up success for ourselves with words of encouragement and quotes in our faces that we need to read and remember daily. With photos of loved ones that we will not give up on. With little treats or gifts to reward ourselves and celebrate along the way. With music that will inspire us and move our soul. With surroundings of memorabilia of past successes or a nice spot outdoors for a fresh new perspective. With a run to feel like we are going somewhere, even if only to move our body to better health. With meditation to clear our mind and prayer without ceasing. We can keep fighting and persevering with consistent reminders to each other.

Hope For Our Future: Perseverance has prevailed. We see "walking miracles" today in the difficulties others have overcome. A lost limb, post-traumatic stress disorder, a loss of sight, loss of a loved one, the close of a business, the end of a dream, all could mean "the end," but some have chosen to use the pain as gain. The choice to persevere, to keep on praying can result in answered prayers of babies born, homes rebuilt, marriages saved, and wayward children and soldiers brought back to home sweet home, and so

much more. I choose to persevere, and I hope you will, too, in whatever you are facing.

My prayer for you, my chocolate friend, is if you are reading this you are a part of this! WE are a community of chocolate friends. Just remember that if you ever need a little chocolate, you know where to find us, and you're always welcome. In any case, I pray that this week, you have an extra dose of 'perseverance' defined as "the persistence in doing something despite difficulty or opposition or delay in achieving success."

With love always,
Your chocolate friend, Erin

"Let perseverance finish its work so that you may be mature and complete, not lacking anything." -James 1:4-6

"Not only so, but we also glory in our sufferings, because we know that suffering produces perseverance; perseverance, character; and character, hope." -Romans 5:3-4

"Therefore, since we are surrounded by such a great cloud of witnesses, let us throw off everything that hinders and the sin that so easily entangles, and let us run with perseverance the race marked out for us, fixing our eyes on Jesus, the pioneer and perfecter of faith. For the joy set before him, he endured the cross scorning its shame and sat down at the right hand of the throne of God. Consider Him who endured such opposition from sinners, so that you will not grow weary and lose heart." – Hebrews 12:1-3

— JUNE 29 —

Week No. 16
Reflection 16: Excellence

This week I was given a topic to think about: "Excellence." I prepared for my first webinar as a guest speaker, thanks to an invitation from Hawaii Baptist Academy. In addition, I prepared to mentor a high school student with great potential, grit, and enthusiasm for business and entrepreneurship. For the webinar I was asked to reflect on my thoughts on 'Leadership & Excellence.'

As I collected my thoughts on this topic, I figured, why not kill two birds with one stone? That way, I could share these preparations with you, in hopes that anyone reading this might also be inspired to reflect and think of your own answers, or share them with someone else. So this week I share with you six questions and reflections on excellence.

143

Question #1: What does excellence mean to you?

The answer to this question didn't come easy. I honestly laughed sarcastically to myself when I first received the list of questions that included this one, and immediately thought, "Excellence can ONLY be accomplished with God."

After shaking it off and trying to get serious, since this seemed like such a stretch of a topic for a week like this, I came up with my own definition for 'excellence': "Living out God's purpose for your life, with the abilities He gave you, to the damn best of your ability, while valuing others, and glorifying Him."

Then I looked up the actual definition of 'excellence' and read, "the quality of being outstanding or extremely good."

I sarcastically laughed again! Yup, like I said,
"Excellence can only be accomplished with God."
I feel like excellence is at a whole other level from good, great, or even awesome.

I honestly feel like on some days I'm 'good' at best. Rarely do I ever feel outstanding or extremely good.

144

Especially now-a-days. Reflecting on excellence for the week, and being with inspiring leaders in our community, really kicked my butt in gear to clean up. I knew I needed to switch it up to the next level.

Question #2: What do you believe drives you or guides you to pursuing excellence?

Like I mentioned in question one, I believe excellence is accomplished WITH God. So what drives me to pursue excellence is the fact that it points people to Him. I want to be a light in this world. With all the "noise" and chaos in it, in order to get someone's attention, one must do something outstanding! As the definition says, this would cause people to actually stop to look and ask, "Why?" or, "How?" My response to which would be, "Because of God."

The greatest opportunities to follow in faith and please Him usually come in the face of adversity and hardship. Those are the moments that others are looking to see what you will do and how you will react. Everyone expects "excellence" when things are going well, are easy to do, and well within our comfort zone and capabilities. But when they are not and we still pursue excellence, it really gives us the opportunity to be the light.

My personal mission in life is: "To live a life of faith, leading others through His love." To lead and love requires other people; to attract people, we must do and be something "extremely good."

"In the same way, let your light shine before others, that they may see your good deeds and glorify your Father in heaven." -Matthew 5:16

"I am the light of the world. Whoever follows me will never walk in darkness, but will have the light of life." -John 8:12

Question #3: How can young leaders meaningfully and effectively serve in the community with excellence?

My answer to this is by serving from your heart, for the right reasons. Do not worry about what everyone else thinks, or who will see what you do, or how it will make you look. When you wholeheartedly serve with the intention in your heart to genuinely help others, God sees that and knows our hearts. That is when we find we are the most focused and most effective at doing the work, and also when the work becomes the most meaningful.

I also believe that when you focus on your purpose or contribution to this world and your God-given abilities, you will begin to find where you naturally excel at serving and can best contribute there. If you're not sure where to start, look for a non-profit organization whose mission and values align with your own, and who have other leaders serving that exemplify what serving with excellence looks like to you. When you take your focus off of yourself and how you might look, feel, or be treated, and focus it on others, you will find yourself serving with a cheerful heart.

"Not looking to your own interests but each of you to the interests of others." -Philippians 2:4

"Do not conform any longer to the pattern of this world, but be transformed by the renewing of your mind." -Romans 12:2

Question #4: What keeps you up at night and what are you doing to solve it?

Nothing keeps me up at night! I am exhausted by the end of the day and fall asleep when my head hits the pillow. Just kidding!

But really, if something does keep me up at night, it's usually me wishing that there were more hours in the day, or that I had more energy to accomplish more of what I wanted to do because there always seems to be more to do than there's time to do it.

There are two things in particular that I will stay up a little longer for and lose sleep over. The first is to read a little because I want to keep growing and learning from other leaders, expand my thinking, get inspired, and invest in my personal growth. The second is that I am whispering to my five year old daughter or three year old son, telling them about Jesus.

My deepest conversations with them, happen when there are absolutely no distractions, no other sounds, no lights, and all they hear is my voice and feel my breath cuddled up right next to them in bed. There in the intimate darkness, I share almost like it's a secret, how they have the power of the Holy Spirit inside of them, how Jesus loves us all; how God never leaves us; how much they are loved and what their God-given abilities and qualities are and how grateful we should be.

I feel like there's just too much that needs to be taught and said and we can never take a single day of life on earth for granted. My way of solving my anxiousness when there's too much to do, and not enough time, is to at least do these two things. One, invest a little in myself so I am fueled to invest in others. Two, invest in my family. Then, no matter what happened earlier in the day, I know I did something that will make me better tomorrow than today, and I said what really needed to be said. Then as I drift to sleep, I pray that tomorrow I get another chance to get all that other stuff done.

Question #5: What gets you up in the morning and how do you engage and excite your team?

The first thing I do every morning is read my Bible, write five things I am grateful for from the day before, and journal. I do this all with a good cup of coffee in my favorite mug on a pretty coaster, something sweet (usually chocolate), in my quiet house with just some soft spa-like background music playing, and Christmas lights twinkling, while the world is still sleeping. I feel like it's my only quiet, alone, and intimate time with God and I absolutely love it. My morning routine helps me set the perspective for the day even prior to reviewing my calendar and the day's events. Setting myself up for the day then helps set myself up to be there for my team.

I am excited every day for work because I feel that I've been blessed with a SWEET platform (pun intended). I have been given chocolates, something that just about everybody loves or can relate to in this world, as my way to share God's goodness! All kidding aside, I do feel it is my responsibility and I can't take this given opportunity lightly.

The story of how I got into this business, how the location of our shop was selected, how we grew and received such recognition are all testimonies. The people I lead both on my team (aka my chocolate family) and my customers, suppliers, partners, community members (aka chocolate friends) are all my opportunity to turn people to Him, or away from Him, by how I live day after day.

For the team I work with, not all who are believers, I excite them by reminding them of our opportunity and responsibility to bring joy to others through chocolates, sweeten relationships, and live out our mission of "Bringing peace to our world, one chocolate at a time." I consistently show up and make time for them to feel engaged with their hard work by sharing stories from our chocolate friends about how much they love everything, the photos they share on social media, and how grateful I am for them.

Valuing each person on my team includes knowing their likes, their personalities, etc. This helps me to communicate and excite them most effectively via their love language. For some, I will praise them in front of the group and post a photo of them on our social media, then give them the next creative and difficult assignment. For others, I'll give them a fist bump, not say a word, and slip them one of their favorite plate lunches. I've seen time and time again, when they know that I KNOW each of them and genuinely care, then they care to do their job well and are excited to work too.

Question #6: What do you think we, as individuals, can do to build a stronger, sustainable future and community post COVID-19?

Take care of ourselves and take care of each other.

"My command is this: Love each other as I have loved you." -John 15:12

It seems so simple but that's exactly what God calls us to do. I feel more than ever that during this time, He is looking down on us, asking us to stop our sinful living and turn to Him; to stop hurting and start showing love to one another.

It starts with us and when we are rooted in the right things, we can lift up others around us. It's almost like we should use this 'quarantine' to care for our physical, mental, emotional, and spiritual health and see Jesus as our 'vaccine'. By giving our life to Him, we can begin to live for His purpose with our God-given abilities. This way we can contribute, to the best of our ability, to the needs of our family, teams, businesses, schools, and communities, adding value to others, while glorifying Him. In other words, according to my personal definition, we should pursue to live a life of excellence now, to build a stronger and sustainable future together.

Being invited to speak at this webinar during COVID-19 was a great experience. As I went through each question, it became an exercise and preparation for me to reflect on something greater, something that I was not really thinking of, or striving for, during this temporary long shut down. It's easy to get lazy, give up hope, or just settle for survival, but that was not what we were about pre COVID-19, and it will not be what we are about post-COVID-19. So, in closing, I'd like to share with you one chocolate story that reminds me of excellence.

Dark Mac Nuts for the Moana Surfrider

A sweet sample story of excellence comes from my experience with The First Lady of Waikiki. In my opinion, one of the most beautiful historic hotels in Waikiki, has always been the Moana Surfrider Hotel.

It's a level of luxury that I never thought I would have the opportunity to work with. But when I followed the God-given assignment to leave my full time job and comfortable income for no income, no customers, and no promise of a thriving business, the very next day after taking the leap of faith and giving up my full time work, I received a call to work with the Moana Surfrider Hotel.

They wanted chocolate covered macadamia nut clusters. But not just any chocolate covered mac nuts! They wanted our high quality signature chocolates, locally hand-made in a very specific way. But we didn't know what that way was yet, or how we would accomplish it. I just knew this first opportunity with The First Lady of Waikiki needed to be a product of the utmost excellence for her. This would give Choco le`a a chance to be on the map as a sought after artisan chocolate product that was not only locally made, but beloved by people from all around the world.

Using only the best locally grown whole and half style mac nuts, we went through many, many versions to create samples of this product so that it would be exactly how a very high-powered, specific group of individuals wanted it. It was honestly rejected repeatedly. We were given harsh criticism during the process of creating it. But we were also given multiple chances to perfect it until it was exactly as it is today…with just the right size, texture, taste, ratio of salt, look, and packaging.

I wish I had kept track of how many hours were spent of trial and error creating; how many miles driven back and forth to make sample deliveries; how many parking tickets paid for meetings for discussion, and how many pounds of chocolates and macadamia nuts were logged as 'waste'. All of this before creating something 'outstanding' and 'extremely good' for the people who were giving us the opportunity for our first great stream of revenue

It was a God-given opportunity in my perspective to have this as our first account, the first day after taking a huge leap in faith. It required the God-given skill set of multiple people to help me create this again and again. It required a lot of hard work giving it our absolute best to achieve the excellence we were called to. We did it because we valued this hotel, this team, this opportunity, and the fact that it would ultimately give God the glory one day. And now you know the story.

Lesson Learned: Excellence is something we should continue to strive for! Why settle only to survive, when WITH God we CAN thrive? During this COVID-19 season, I've been hoping for just a few great days. I have been content with the good days and just relieved when I don't have another hard day, since some days are really hard. I even forgot about striving for days of excellence, days WITH Him to help me accomplish more. I mean, this is not going to magically all go back to normal in a few days and I've allowed it to lower my standard of living and expectations. In my reflections, as I prepared to inspire others, I found myself being inspired and am reminded of what I strived for pre-COVID-19.

Opportunity Now: Sharing reflections on our thoughts, our experiences, and our lessons learned is the opportunity. We can surely learn a lot from one another by asking to be mentored, or asking others to speak and share, or volunteering to be a mentee are all opportunities to keep inspiring each other. In doing so, we find ourselves lifting others up, which can force ourselves to get up and take life to the next level.

I was just feeling sorry for myself at the start of writing this after receiving more bad news; however, knowing that a very energetic high school student eagerly awaited me to inspire and share with him, made me think back to how I felt when I was sixteen. I had so much more energy and a future of what looked like endless possibilities. I'm not sixteen anymore, but I can still get energized and excited about the future!

Even if you don't think you have anyone to inspire or you're not sure what to say to inspire others, you can simply send an email to one person you know. Maybe contact a student who is not asking for a mentor, but reaching out to them may spark in them their God-given purpose and abilities that they didn't know are inside of them.

Hope For Our Future: Two generations in particular come to mind. The one after us, and the one before us. I feel that this next generation that I am mentoring is super smart, ambitious, has a heart for their community and their world, are quick to action, are creative, and searching for answers and change. They're going to move us in new directions, create new things, and set new frontiers while adapting to our changing world.

The generation before us still has a lot of life, wisdom, resilience, generosity, and adaptability in them, too. I've seen how many of you "didn't stand a chance" with our online orders the first time, tried and "miserably failed" the second time, tried and almost got it a third time, and finally figured out what could work the fourth time, and are ready to "beat the young generation" the fifth time...by working together WITH them! Haha. Yup, some of you have shared with me that you asked your grandchild to order for you, or show you the 'tricks' to being faster and together you've received the chocolates that you both enjoy. That's the thing, the hope is in all of us.

I'd like to take a moment to honor the late Senator Breene Harimoto. He was a member of our church community and a leader in my life from afar. I only shook his hand once after a tough topic discussed at the Capitol; however, he came to listen and I was so glad I had the opportunity to thank him for his work, not just for our state, but for His kingdom. I believe he received a huge welcome party with applause and cheers into heaven's gates and God saying, "Well done my good and faithful servant." He, in my opinion, is one of the leaders I've watched from afar, who served with excellence. Thank you Senator Breene Harimoto and family.

My prayer for you, my chocolate friend, is when we love one another and work together to bring excellence to the table, we can cultivate and inspire further excellence in our communities and our world.

With love always,
Your chocolate friend, Erin

"Whatever you do, work at it with all your heart, as working for the Lord...It is the Lord Christ you are serving." -Colossians 3:23-24

"In the same way, let your light shine before others, that they may see your good deeds and glorify your Father in heaven." -Matthew 5:16

— JULY 6—

Week No. 17
Reflection 17: Onward

A lot of people have been asking me two questions:

1. How has COVID-19 affected us as a small local business?
2. What are the next plans for Choco le`a?

As I prepared for a press interview and to speak at a webinar for the HFMA (Hawai`i Food Manufacturers Association) on what our greatest concerns are for our company, I figured I'd share with you the answers to these questions as a look #behindthebusiness and follow up with how we plan to move onward despite these concerns.

How has COVID-19 affected our business?

As a quick recap, we very suddenly lost the following

streams of revenue which totaled up to about 70% of our business: Wholesale (hotel amenities, partnerships with travel & specialty companies), corporate accounts (large retailer gifts, customized client gifts) events (pop-up shops, promotional opportunities, pairings, catering for weddings), in-house events (hands-on chocolate making workshops, tours), export sales, retail sales related to large events (wedding favors, bridal showers, retirement parties,

Client lunches, girlfriend get-togethers, etc.), and retail sales related to travel (your made in Hawai`i omiyage picked up by locals traveling, visitors from the mainland, Japan, and around the world).

When retail shops were required to shut down, we lost the remaining thirty percent of our business - all our retail sales, which meant we had zero income. As a result, we missed being together, growing our chocolate family, working alongside our chocolate partners, and serving our chocolate friends face-to-face with smiles, hugs and tastes in the shop like we were used to and loved doing.

Onward: About thirty percent of our business was and

is from YOU, our locals from all islands, and we are counting on you now and upon our return in order to survive! From the bottom of my heart, I sincerely want to thank you for logging on every week to pre-order and showing up every Saturday to pick up. Even if you don't get chocolates, but you tried, your efforts tell me that there is still a demand out there for us and that you DO want to continue eating and sharing our chocolates, even if you have no parties to attend or trips to take! That was the hope we needed during the times we did this, to push us onward to work towards re-structuring and re-opening.

Rather than waiting for all 70% of our old business to come back, we are taking a leap of faith to start coming back based on the thirty percent, which is YOU!

What are my three greatest concerns for our company? How can I move onward despite my concerns?

1. People - Our Health & Our Economy: My greatest concern is for people because we are in the people business! If people (whether within my team, support system, and customers) are not mentally, we will all suffer together.

It was already financially challenging to live and work in Hawai`i pre-COVID-19, and now this has made it even more difficult. My concerns range from whether our business can make enough to cover costs, to the ability to pay my team good wages and benefits; will there be work for those who do not return to us; worrying that those who worked with us part time won't lose their full time jobs or get the drastic pay cuts that are looming over them; whether all of the other people we rely on can sustain their own businesses and operations as part of the entire sales and distribution channel with us, to concern that our chocolate friends have the finances to shop and share artisan goods!

We're all interconnected. I'm afraid that with the lack of tourism upon which so many businesses rely, even if Choco le`a survives, others won't. All those people will be out of jobs and there won't be enough jobs for everyone living on these islands. When people's mental, emotional and spiritual health decline due to a loss of a job, lockdown, or limitations, then new problems arise and the cycle of giving generously and the culture of caring for one another is at stake. Plus, if those weren't enough things to worry about, there's the physical health concern with the rising number of COVID-19 cases and its ongoing effects until a vaccine or cure is discovered.

Onward: Initially I honestly thought, "No one needs artisan chocolates during a pandemic, when we all need to simply focus on health, shelter, and basic essentials." But I soon realized from YOU and your feedback, that "our chocolates are a necessity." That you "need some kind of treat to look forward to" and most importantly, you "need hope." I then switched my thinking to, "We are needed for our people." We need to contribute to the overall health and well-being of our people however we can. Yes, for some it's chocolate consumption, for others it's gifts to keep giving despite having no parties or get-togethers, and for all it's peace and hope...even if it isn't always in the form of chocolate!

2. Costs & Cash Flow: The cost of doing business in Hawai`i has always been high. From rent and utilities to importing ingredients and supplies unavailable on island, to utilizing limited local ingredients that are available on island and in great demand, to payroll costs in order to pay people well so they can afford to live here. These costs have always been challenging. We work on a very small margin and don't produce large quantities for large profits. Since we are still fairly new, in year six, and started with no capital, cash flow is still an issue as we work from month to month. We are also a very seasonal, gift type of product. As such, we are used to counting on predictable special occasions like Christmas, Valentine's Day, and other holidays that give us the boosts we need.

But with COVID-19, things are less predictable since an anticipated second wave and possible looming shut down is predicted for our busiest month (December). This also prevents us from accepting large orders for that time period or from having a plan in place if those who have events scheduled for that time need to cancel.

Without tourism and our large ongoing accounts that provided the steady income in our "slower" months, we needed to also find a way to ensure we have income throughout the entire year and not just chocolates for gifts during the holidays. Finally, the costs for us to make and store our hand-crafted chocolates, which is specifically a perishable product, increases our utilities and raw material expenses as everything is purchased fresh, which costs more than buying in bulk.

Being on island, if there is not enough demand here, shipping elsewhere is an option, but our temperature sensitive products present yet another challenge to successfully do this.

Onward: I was warned from the beginning by other small local businesses that I would need to be going into this because of my passion. Otherwise I would need to scale up and aggressively grow in order to make the profits. Even with the warnings from business mentors, I didn't realize just how challenging it is to build and sustain a business in Hawai`i. But...it is a choice. And it is the choice I made and will continue to make because for me and my personal values and faith, the platform that chocolates provide to bring joy, hope, and peace to others, is worth it. The opportunities this and any business COULD provide, even if it will take a lot of hard work and time, is a risk I'm willing to continue to take.

3. Child Care: We all had to adapt a lot and all of the adjustments are challenging. But a major one for me to adjust to was having my kids with me full time. I never planned on being a stay-at-home-mom (to all of you parents who do this regularly, my hats off to you...you're amazing!), but I suddenly found myself as one, while also trying to save my business.

It was always a lot to try to grow and run a business while simultaneously taking care of a family before and after school; however, take out "school" and add "teacher," "lunch lady," "custodian," "counselor," "security," and more titles than I can remember right now as a job to your work list - with no income – and it's harder!

Even though I invested time to help my three and five year old become more independent so they can get ready, make their own water bottles, turn on ABC Mouse, make tuna sandwiches, and have "quiet time" paint, playdough, puzzles, and story books on their own, I still have to stop frequently for the numerous random things from *"my baby eagle is missing and we must find him,"* to *"help me sound out this hard word,"* to just pay attention to them for a while.

Great childcare is hard to find and if available, it's expensive. Preschool can also be expensive, especially with the adjustments they had to make in tuition due to their smaller class sizes to follow the health regulations.

As for school, if they are not in session due to a distance learning schedule, or a shut down due to a coronavirus case, then my first job as a parent is to care for my kids which makes it challenging to give as much time and attention to the business. Of course there is also a health concern about sending them to child care or school.

Onward: I will take care of my family and my business the best I can, even if it's not the ideal vision I had in mind. I'd say it's more about integration than balance. The kids come to work with me and they get to see what I do and what hard work is and ask me lots of "Why" questions. Sometimes, they also want to help so I try to let them be a part of it and set a positive example that work can be fun, that work is an important way to help people, and point out some nuggets of wisdom in it all so it's educational at the same time.

171

Our shop is not open for people to come in and browse for one reason: the kids are in it and take up half the space with devices, coloring supplies, paper, a nap time bench, a lunch table, a snack bin, and an open floor to dance around. This is what it has been like for the past almost four months and at least for another month or more as we figure out how to have kids at work while I work and how to keep them learning, entertained, and given the love and attention they deserve. So, the plan for now is to INTEGRATE work and school and fun. Yup...I'll write a whole other blog on this one later so it doesn't get too long. (Plus I'm still figuring it out).

"Trust in the Lord with all your heart and lean not on your own understanding; in all your ways submit to him, and he will make your paths straight." - Proverbs 3:5-6

In closing, I re-write the first question I'm always asked with a different response, from a different perspective.

How has COVID-19 affected our business?
Everyone is looking for peace, hope, and a little

happiness now more than ever, something to make their day, even their life, a little sweeter for themselves and others. That's where we come in. It is our opportunity to live out our mission of "Bringing peace to our world, one chocolate at a time" in a much richer and more meaningful way.

Through deep reflection, I've found myself to be so much more deeply rooted in who we are, our values and our mission, and am able to more confidently and firmly stand up to speak out for what I believe in and hope for. We're making the most of what we do have in this current situation (our Instagram followers @chocoleahawaii and @yourchocolatefriend connections with other businesses, and our stories) to encourage one another and move onward together.

"I press on toward the goal to win the prize for which God has called me heavenward in Christ Jesus." - Philippians 3:4

Lesson Learned: We can't have it all, but we can and must move onward. People need us and we need each other. Though we may feel like no one understands what we are going through, that we are not needed, or not important enough, by talking it out, listening, and writing it down, we find that our challenges are rarely totally unique. We are, by and large, mostly the same as many other small businesses, working parents, concerned citizens, people of Hawai`i, and perhaps around the nation and world. We need to remember that we are still needed - maybe not by many, or not nearly as much as before - but by a few. The few are worth showing up for.

One of you even told me at curbside pick-up this past week with such fervency, "You can never, ever go out of business, okay? You need to be around my whole lifetime." It reminded me that there are people who actually are counting on us. Although we have some specific challenges, each industry has its own challenges and each individual his or her own story.

Opportunity Now: Let's move onward together. Let's share our challenges and not judge, but brainstorm ways to pivot or ways to give ourselves more grace; to have more openness to conversations so we don't feel alone. If you are feeling this way, hopefully this helps to let you know, you're not alone. That I write this weekly for YOU. That I am willing to be transparent and share in hopes that it continues to inspire you and help you move onward, too, together, with me. Share this with another local small business owner, or share your ideas with me.

Hope for Our Future: The continuation and rise of the Aloha spirit gives me hope. We do have something special here in Hawai`i. Our culture of people caring for one another, supporting local, and respecting the changes businesses have to make, have been positively received so far from our perspective. We really appreciate that.

We laugh when you honestly and straight up tell us, "I no like shopping online…I like come in." We can have that exchange with aloha as I respond, "I know aunty, I miss it too. Thanks, yeah. I needed to know that because I was wondering where you went and how come you no stay online or come curbside pick-up?" And you respond, "I give up. I tried online, but everyone always beat me. BUT, I'll be here ready to support you when you pick up the phone again or let me come in!"

Let's keep communicating openly, with aloha, and be an example to the world of how we can move onward together, with the aloha spirit.

My prayer for you, my chocolate friend, is simple...imua! This Hawaiian word translates to move forward and onward. Keep going. God is taking us somewhere we have never been.

With love always,
Your chocolate friend, Erin

"I will instruct you and teach you in the way you should go; I will counsel you with my loving eye on you." -Psalm 32:8

— JULY 13 —
Week No. 18
Reflection 18: Style

"Style is a way to say who you are, without having to speak."

Since the bird in our Choco le`a logo can't speak, I hope her style exudes, "Love, hope, joy, and peace" in whatever packaging, presentation, or point in time others meet her.

Our company logo, a Ko`ae `Ula carrying a cacao branch in its beak is a tropical bird that is beautiful and powerful and can travel great distances. This logo was selected for our company to symbolize our company mission of *"Bringing peace to our world, one chocolate at a time."* Analogous to a dove carrying an olive branch in the biblical story of "Noah's Ark," we believe that through chocolates, we can bring love, hope, joy, and peace to others.

I've learned that to succeed in business that you must build your brand, your logo, and your name. I took to heart that lesson I was taught and visualized the signature dark brown, Tiffany-like teal blue and copper foil tones of our brand and applied it to our packaging and our shop's look and feel. Put together, it's meant to embody a feeling of luxury, with "rustic chic" touches that would be representative of top quality products, the absolute best service, and a sophisticated, but welcoming, environment with that perfect look just for you. We've always loved it and still do. And while it took a lot of time to think about and create the "perfect style" I had an epiphany late Saturday night in the shop after the curbside pick-ups.

Everyone has different looks. So it must be okay if our bird has more than one look too? Right?

Taking myself as an example, I don't just have one style or one look. My style spans the spectrum from a locally designed racer back tank top, shorts, slippers, hair in a high messy bun and a fanny pack or backpack, to a boho soft florally blouse tucked into dark jeans, a pair of open toe heels, hair flat ironed and a long strap leather tote bag, to a solid print professional dress in pumps with pearls and a small cute purse. (Haha! Some of you know me so well that you actually gifted me these items this past weekend during the curbside pickup!)

It all depends on where I am going, what I am doing, and how I feel. Sometimes I am in good old sweat pants that are over 12 years old from somewhere on a sale rack, a buss up t-shirt with holes that are a hand-me down which I absolutely love and can't part with, and hip hop boots going to a dance class. Or on a rare but fun occasion, in a super uncomfortable princess-y dress, a very tiny super hero cape, small bling bling sunglasses, and a hat to go to a dance party in the living room with the kiddos (sorry no picture of me in this...). All looks which are totally different, but all of them, ME. Why do I have to stick to just one?

I am still me, Erin, in all scenarios, in all styles. So why can't our bird, our brand, our company, be just like how we are as people? Sporting multiple looks depending on the situation? Feeling free to soar and fly in what's comfortable and fitting for the moment?

When we began, our packaging had more of a homemade arts and crafts type of a look. It consisted of things I bought in small quantities from retail stores like Ben Franklin and cut and glued and taped together on my own or with a small group of family and friends at home. It evolved as we invested in one designer, then another, and as we grew to know who we were as a company. It continued to evolve when we further defined what look we loved best and what kind of presence we wanted to have on a shelf, in your homes or in the places you took us when you gave us away as special gifts. We were able to confidently pull together our brand "wardrobe"' and our look. We began to find our style and became your party favors, your corporate gifts, and your omiyage from Hawai`i. (Mahalo chocolate friends!)

But in this unprecedented season unlike any time before, the demand for our chocolates were for slightly different reasons. Something more personal and more rustic is desired. What you have been asking for is chocolates to savor and enjoy. Chocolates to share.

With no frills or customizing, but with the same great quality and service. You just want something delicious, comforting, and convenient.

It was so interesting to even hear from one of you that the small imperfections in the chocolates were evidence that the handcrafted artisan products being made are done by real people, who have flaws, and who were in many ways just like you. With my sometimes too thick shells in the truffles, or slightly uneven fillings as I tried to get back into the kitchen with my hair net, mask, and chocolate all over my clothes (another look of mine), we somehow connected on a different level.

You saw me through the chocolates. I'm sure when Christmas comes around, when hopefully we are out and about and safely sharing gifts at get-togethers and holiday parties again, you'll want red ribbons, touches of holly, pictures of pine trees, smiles from snowman, and everything jolly to bring joy to the world through chocolates. And we WILL dress it up, and put on our holiday best.

When 2021 rolls around, who knows what the year

will bring? But I am learning that as we go through different seasons in life, we grow and change as people and as businesses. We learn new things and we improve. We let go of bad habits or things that held us back from growing. Or in the case of right now, we listen more to what others have to say, and we dare to try out new styles, new looks, new ways of doing things even if it feels weird, scary, and out of our comfort zone. Sometimes it works...and sometimes it doesn't make sense to do it anymore.

We would have never thought of offering curbside service if COVID-19 didn't force us to. We would have not thought further about offering delivery services since the demand was never there and people loved coming out to our shop whereas now, everyone stays home. We would have never thought of bringing our kids and their toys to work, but it's what we need to do.

A lot has changed and so I guess what I am saying is, we may be changing too. But please know - no matter what, two things have not changed and will NEVER change: our values and our mission. It defines who we are and why we do what we do. No matter what "style" or "look" we may have on, what remains at the core and heart of our existence will always prevail.

Lesson Learned: Styles evolve and change and that's okay. It can lead to good things. It can actually be fun to change things up, to dress things up and dress things down; play with new, innovative and wild looks and find out what works. Plus, if it doesn't, you can always go back to your signature, tried and true favorites.

Opportunity Now: Find your style for this season. Wear what makes you feel your best. Do things in a way that best represents who you are and what your priorities are right now, what your goals are and what message you are trying to "speak." Don't compare yourself to anyone else's style because God did not create us to all look, dress, act, and do things in the exact same way. What makes everything work is when we embrace the best version of ourselves and the way we were made by our Creator.

Hope for Our Future: Our style (whether fashion or way of life) will continuously change and that's ok! The way we shop, eat, and interact will not be this way forever. But it is this way right now. So for now, let's have fun with our different mask designs. Let's find friendly safe ways to say "aloha" rather than the honi on the cheek here in Hawai`i. Let's get creative and anticipate what the next "new normal" trends may be because of the situation and try it on. Let's look towards the future, but find our style for the present.

My prayer for you, my chocolate friend, is that whatever we do, let's do it in **style!**

With love always,
Your chocolate friend, Erin

"I praise you because I am fearfully and wonderfully made; your works are wonderful, I know that full well." -Psalm 139:14

"Therefore I tell you, do not worry about your life, what you will eat or drink; or about your body, what you will wear. Is not life more than food, and the body more than clothes? Look at the birds of the air; they do not sow or reap or store away in barns, and yet your heavenly Father feeds them. Are you not much more valuable than they? Can any one of you by worrying add a single hour to your life?" - Matthew 6:25-34

— JULY 20 —

Week No. 19
Reflection 19: Simple

We are on week #19! Nineteen weeks of COVID-19! Cases rising, businesses closing, children screaming, parents screaming, fun events postponing, Zooming, Zooming, Zooming, less airplanes flying, rock fever rising, and then a hurricane approaching towards our islands. Feels like life got even more complicated, but in the midst of it all...plain and simple, I'm trying to live a SIMPLER life. I'm TRYING to keep it sweet and simple. Anyone else feel me and can I get an amen?

I began 2020 with 20-20 vision of how the year would be, and let me tell you, it was far from simple. Big goals. Big dreams. Growth. Growth. Growth. Lots to do. People to see. Places to go. Just as I started the momentum of attacking these big goals and dreams for the year, God had other plans: a simple stay at home order that has lasted forever! Well, technically nineteen weeks, and counting, to be exact.

The current state of our world may seem far from simple. With COVID-19 cases rising in Hawai`i, we're asked to wear a mask, maintain social distancing, wash our hands, clean surfaces, and stay home if we're sick. We then found out a hurricane was approaching Hawai`i, and businesses once again closed their doors, boarded up their windows, and we were asked once again to stay home, and be prepared with water, food, and flashlights. As we prepare for our kids to return to school, it's not that simple anymore as drop off times are later, pick up is earlier, schedules are staggered, all on top of figuring out how to do distance learning on devices. Plus, if there's a COVID-19 case in school, we must prepare to all quarantine as a family for 14 days and make adjustments with our work and other commitments.

So how can we simplify things so life can be less stressful? Ironically, it is the simplest things that have been the hardest to cope with. Like having to wear a mask, staying six feet apart, washing our hands and cleaning again and again, finding basic necessities like toilet paper and preparing to stay home again.

But it is also the simplest things that can bring us the greatest joy. For us here in Hawai`i it could be going to the beach and collecting "treasures" from the sand, taking a hike in the mountains and maybe even finding a mountain apple from a tree, or just getting a shave ice which is simply ice and sugar syrup!

Admittedly, I didn't always enjoy these things, but since I was forced to clear my schedule of so many other things due to COVID-19, I had the opportunity this summer, to rediscover and enjoy some of these simple things in life.

Although having my two little kids with me for the past nineteen weeks has been one of the hardest adjustments, they made the most simple things so special. Conner picked me flower weeds and put it in a jar on the table for me. Aubrey drew dinosaurs and taped it around our house as decoration. They both made feasts of plastic food and grass soup and mud pies to enjoy to my heart's content. I watched them pick and immediately eat cucamelons grown in our tiny little new garden and dip anything they could find from their snack stash in our "Dip & Decorate Chocolate Kit."

As for me personally, some of the simple things I was able to accomplish was keeping most of my succulents alive, putting up the lights that sat in a box for months, and finishing one of the many books I started.

I also began reading new books by Emily Ley, founder of the Simplified Planner. I find that I relate to her as a wife, mom of little kids, business owner, big dreamer, and believer. I received her book as a gift from a friend who prayed for me and my "crazy workaholic" life, trying to juggle all the balls and somehow doing it, but knowing it was only a matter of time before I dropped some. I couldn't put the book down. Then I bought and read more of her books.

For 2021, I'm going to buy her Simplified planner. If you were to look inside my 2020 planner, I had something written in it for every fifteen minutes (yes my planner was marked to the fifteen minute intervals) and sometimes forgot to schedule "commute" time or even a "bathroom break" so I constantly found myself about fifteen minutes behind schedule. Yup, I had alarms ringing all day for the next meeting, the next thing. You can ask the chocolate family, they probably had nightmares hearing my alarms in their sleep. It's like God was sounding his alarm to me and warning me to slow down and to stop and enjoy the simple things and be still...at least for fifteen minutes!

On Sunday with the hurricane approaching, after already reading the book, "Spark Joy" and "Marie Kondo-ing" my house a couple of years ago, I found myself simplifying and cleaning again. I packed clothes to give to friends, toys to give to kids in need, and kitchen dishes to donate. Thinking about the hurricane as we prepared, I began reflecting on the things in my house that really mattered. I realized, as I thought about what I would grab if we could only pack up one suitcase and head to shelter as we watched our house "blow away," that not much was needed.

So, I began finding joy that gloomy Sunday while waiting for the storm with the news playing all day in the background, by simplifying one drawer and closet at a time, and packing up things that others would be happy to receive. These items could all bless people that perhaps didn't have much to begin with that could be swept up by the wind. In doing so, I found some peace in that storm in knowing, I had a lot I could give to others.

"But godliness with contentment is great gain. For we brought nothing into the world, and we can take nothing out of it." -1 Timothy 6:6-7

Throughout this past week, we also received gifts, so many gifts! Some extravagant like a rare Yamazaki 12 whiskey bottle so that we can now make the complete Suntory Set again later in August! But the way our generous chocolate friend gave it, was with an ease and simplicity with no expectations in return. He just simply wanted to bless and support us.

We also received an anonymous monetary donation in the mail, letters from folks who never had our chocolates writing well wishes on a legal pad, gifts of plain black, but well sewn face masks, leftover excess mango from your yard (something that may be simple to you, but for others, so hard to get after waiting for mango all summer!), to mosquito patches that work for you because finding a brand that works for me and the kids is anything but simple! It's these simple, little things, that mean a lot.

All the "simple" things we received this week, simply blessed us beyond measure and inspired us to want to do the same for all of you, our chocolate friends. Even though we can't make enough chocolates for everyone to pre-order so we don't sell out or to ship to everyone around the U.S., we brainstormed what we COULD do and realized that even a simple hand-written card, text, uplifting email, or stickers sent in the mail could be all someone needs right now.

As schedules are about to change with the start of school again, or perhaps returning to work, let's keep our plans simple. Things keep evolving and we have to be flexible to allow for breathing room during this unprecedented time. A simpler schedule is the goal, so that we may enjoy the sweet and simple things in life!

Lesson Learned: Less can become more. Just as I read in Emily's book, we can find a lot more peace and joy in the simple things. When there's less on our plate, less on our planner, less in our home, less in our heads, we can make room for more laughter. More fun. More unexpected adventures. More gifts. More moments to savor.

Opportunity Now: Simplify your life. Clean up. Declutter. Donate. Enjoy what you have left and find peace in knowing that you are blessing someone else. As they say, "one man's trash is another's treasure." If you are like me, let's try and reset our schedule too. I actually bought another 2020 planner to start afresh again and got it at 90% off because it's almost August already! Half of 2020 is over guys! But WE CAN DECIDE how we will spend the second half of this year. I hope you spend it by taking the time to enjoy the simple things with me.

Hope For Our Future: With more room in our days, we can actually breathe again! Well, we WILL mess up again and have days where we over-commit, forget about the traffic in our commutes that will start up again, or let the madness pile up in our houses. But instead of waiting for 2021 to roll around, for COVID-19 to go away, or for a storm to pass, we can start making some changes in our schedules and in our lives to start creating new habits.

My prayer for you, my chocolate friend, and myself included, is that we CAN start simplifying and start living a sweeter and simpler life with LESS stress in our homes and our schedules, and MORE peace and joy in our hearts.

With love always,
Your chocolate friend, Erin

"He says, 'Be still, and know that I am God; I will be exalted among the nations, I will be exalted in the earth." -Psalm 46:10

— JULY 27 —

Week No. 20
Reflection 20: Kids

Dear Chocolate Friends,

I thought by now, I'd be done writing these weekly reflections and could possibly put them altogether in a mini journal or book to remember "that time in our lives" of COVID-19 and how we got through it. But here we are, still very much in it with no definitive end in sight.

However, this week I want to "close the chapter" to what I will call the final pages of perhaps book one, a very long "spring/summer break." The end of week #20 was also scheduled to be the week the kids would be on their way back to school and when I had hoped we'd all be back to work and the hustle and bustle of life. But if there's one thing I've experienced time and time again, it is that God always has other plans.

If I could pick one word to wrap up the past twenty weeks, it would be "kids." It was one of the greatest challenges for me to not have my business growing, to not be working and to not have a go-go-go lifestyle.

Instead, everything slowed all the way down to a complete and sudden stop. A shut down. A stay at home with two very little, talkative, and active kids every day.

Then trying to figure out distance learning with them and how to keep their brains active and engaged. Then when distance learning ended and summer break began, it was figuring out how to keep them entertained. In addition to all that, it was learning how to build the business back up slowly with them in tow, all while keeping them healthy and safe.

It sounds like I was doing a lot for them, but really, when I look back on it all, was it the kids who took care of ME the past five months?

I write this from what looks like a perfect little home office, clean and ready for Zoom meetings (something

I set up immediately when this all began). But it's really just one small corner (one desk length to be exact) of our super-hot bedroom. Just one computer screen turn from this angle is a messy bed, clothes on the floor, toys strewn everywhere, cardboard box obstructions that represent the "carnival rides" they built that I must walk around, and two kids playing dinosaurs, roaring at each other, jumping from the bed to the floor and back up again.

They have driven me insane, and yet have kept me sane. They made me cry tears of frustration when extremely overwhelmed and yet tears of immense joy. They have patiently waited for me at the chocolate shop and yet have also eaten the hard work and depleted our inventory.

As we prepare to return to school, I reminisce about my son's preschool's "bye bye window." I remember on the first day of school I dropped him off and said, *"Goodbye. I love you,"* and *"I will come back for you after school."* I remember him gripping my nice work shirt and stretching it as he pulled at it while crying, *"No mommy don't go!"* With all of the strength I could muster up in me, I walked away and didn't look back (which I learned is the best thing parents can do to help the teacher because they actually stop crying in less than five minutes IF you go away).

But then the teacher told me that when I drive out of the parking lot, to stop and wave one more time at the "bye bye window" where he would be waiting. I was reluctant to do it because I had a hard time saying goodbye once already, but I obliged. Every day that first year, I told him "bye bye" a second time from my car with him looking back at me from the window. His eyes barely reached the first jalousies to look out, but I could still see the top of his head and his eyes.

With the classroom windows open and my van window rolled down, we'd yell one last time to each other and I could always make out his little voice saying as loudly as he could on his tip toes so that his mouth would also be visible through the bottom jalousies, *"Bye mommy! I love you!"* Without fail, my eyes would tear up as I'd drive away on my way to work saying, *"Thank you God for these kids."*

Many of us will be saying "bye bye" again soon at school drop offs. A few months ago, I honestly couldn't wait for them to get back in school because I just wanted to go back to my normal busy productive life. Yet here we are and after twenty weeks together, I think I'm going to find it extremely hard to say, "bye bye." (Yeah, yeah I know I'm really emotional!)

I mean, what are those things we need to say "bye bye" to that we still haven't let go of? For me, besides the big plans for 2020 that I have already let go, it's just as hard to say "bye bye" to the season at home with the kids that I had gotten used to. Waking up a little later, home-schooling, baking, figuring out creative safe things to do outside...there's a lot that I will have to let go of. But, there's a lot that I want to figure out how to hold onto, like extra cuddles in the morning. It's crazy how the things I complained about, are now the things I'm going to miss.

Though this is not the end of my story since the pandemic has not ended, to help me transition onward from the past 20 weeks, I write my "bye bye" here in my journal, to serve as the last chapter of my "COVID-19 Reflections." It's time to begin a new ___ and move forward with _____. Not sure what to fill in the blanks with yet, but YOU can help me with that and share what you want to read next! Thank you for reflecting with me, chocolate friends.

Dear Aubrey & Conner,

One of the greatest challenges in this season of COVID-19, was having you with me every day and worrying about your health and safety.

One of the greatest joys in this season of COVID-19, was having with you with me every day and you helping me to not worry about the little things.

You two are such a gift and there are so many moments I wish I wrote down because there were so many blessings through it all. I thank God that He knows me best and knows what I need and allowed this to happen so I could slow down my life, re-prioritize, and take care of the things (or rather people in my life) that matter most. You two, and daddy.

Just for example, today, you both slept in. Really late. You have been going to bed at 10pm and jumping up and down on the bed saying "let's dance" or "let's have a cuddle party" until I firmly tell you both to just lie down and be quiet and you quickly apologize and come right next to me.

Conner, you got up today about 8:30am (this is very late for you since you usually wake up at 6:00am). I saw you rolling around in bed about to get up. I waited for you on the living room couch. I heard you walk around for a bit, then finally appeared crossing our living room carpet to me with a smile on your face and a totally swollen left eye from the mosquito bite you got the day before when we went hiking.

Anyway, you came out this morning with your hands behind your back and just as you got one foot away from me, you excitedly brought it out and shoved 4 marigolds in my face. "For you mommy" you said as you climbed up on the couch. You said you picked them for me from the yard. I don't know where you hid them because I didn't notice them last night and I could tell they were a little worn and torn from not getting water and they were ripped off the stems so just the flower was barely there. But you were so proud to give it to me. You're so sweet Conner. You have a real thoughtful side and I love how you get over things quickly and don't let it bother you for long. You go from mad, to cheery in a matter of minutes. I love that about you. And I love your gentle spirit early in the morning and late at night when you lie on my tummy and whisper, "Mommy, I love you."

Aubrey, not long after Conner got up, as I stood up from the couch and looked at our once again messy house (it's a thing that happens every single day no matter how many times we clean). I let out a loud sigh of defeat, but this time, you stopped and came over to me. You leaned up against my left leg and hugged me and rubbed my back and gently said, "It's okay mommy. I'll help you." Then you began picking up the toys and sorting them in their centers. My dear sweet girl, you know me so well. You know what makes me mad. You can tell when I'm sad and something's wrong. And best of all, you know how to make me feel better.

Throughout this time, we all have gotten to know each other on a deeper level. We've learned the best way to speak to one another, the best way to show love, and I learned that most of the time, the best thing you both REALLY want, is just some quality time and attention. You two have taught me how to be content and to create our own joy. You wake up every morning, trust me and look to me and ask, "Where are we going today mommy?" And I try my best to sound excited for whatever it is even if in my mind, it's the same-old, same old, I try to make it sound fun whether it's "Home school with Ms. Mommy" or "the chocolate shop" you say, "Ok!" and you go about your day ready for whatever I have planned.

Every day I pray that God protects you and watches over us all. I love you with all of my heart and soul. I want to show you the world. I want to give you every experience. I want to teach you everything I know and more and watch you grow and thrive. I'm really treasuring this time as people have suggested. This precious young age and precious time that we have together.

I can't believe it's just about over and you're back

to school and the hustle and bustle of before. I am so grateful that God gave me this time with you. I'll treasure it for the rest of my life and remember it as the summer we spent every day together. Thank you Aubrey and Conner for being the kids God knew I needed.

All my love,
Mommy

Lesson Learned: We will never get this time back! I know, biggest cliche ever! I've heard so many parents tell me this; too many to count. And I said okay, "Okay, I'll treasure it," and I did. But this season, well this season, I treasured it in a way I didn't even know was possible.

"Show me, Lord, my life's end and the number of my days; let me know how fleeting my life is." -Psalm 39:4

Opportunity Now: Reflect on the good in YOUR past twenty weeks. Write it down. Print the photos. Frame it and hang it up. Heck, make your own

Coronavirus journal to share with the grandkids or great-grandkids one day.

For me, one of my longest standing dreams has been to write a book one day. I never had any idea what it would be about, but I guess if I slam the last twenty weeks together, could it be a book? That's what many of you have encouraged me to do. What is the thing you've been saying you will do, but haven't? It has honestly been about twenty years that I've been saying that, *"One day, I'll write a book."* I guess this is it. And as we move into the last five months of 2020, let's start making some of those dreams come true...even if the kids are still constantly around us.

As I've said before, the kids are also our opportunity now. We can help them now to be wiser than us. Stronger than us. More optimistic than us. More inclusive. More loving. More gracious. They can learn from our mistakes as they witness what we do daily and can also learn the good that we instill in them. Kids are our opportunity now! After all, they provided a lot of the content for my "book!"

"These commandments that I give you today are to be on your hearts. Impress them on your children. Talk about them when you sit at home and when you walk along the road, when you lie down and when you get up." -Deuteronomy 6:6-7

"Train up a child in the way he should go; even when he is old he will not depart from it." -Proverbs 22:6

Hope For Our Future: The stuff that sucks the most could become the very things we are most grateful for. Sorry, I couldn't think of a more eloquent way to say it, but basically the thing I struggled with the most became my greatest blessing. So maybe the things we are still grappling with and complaining about right now could be the very things that shape us to become a better wife, mother, daughter, sister, leader, community contributor, friend...it could be the very thing that helps us to become a better human being.

These reflections have really helped me (and hopefully you) to process through the week after week emotions since the start of COVID-19. And since COVID-19 has still not gone away, I think it's time the "reflections" turn into "actions," "routines," or "habits" that can help us journey on in this totally different world we live in. Let's use it to shape us as we continuously strive to become the best versions of ourselves who God created us to be.

Okay friends. I'm a wreck. In tears again and trying to get a grip of myself. It has been an emotional week. The kids make me crazy...but in the sweetest way possible!

My prayer for you, my chocolate friend, is to let the "kids" in your life, bring out the best in you.

With love always,
Your chocolate friend, Erin

"He called a little child to him, and placed the child among them. And he said: 'Truly I tell you, unless you change and become like little children, you will never enter the kingdom of heaven. Therefore,

whoever takes the lowly position of this child is the greatest in the kingdom of heaven."
-Matthew 18:2-4

— AUGUST 3 —

Week No. 21
Routine 1: Prayer

Last week when I said I was closing the "book" on my COVID-19 **Reflections**, it was because I was honestly sick and tired of reflecting and wanted to start *living*! I thought this temporary journaling of reflections would help you and me to process a short season of this pandemic and we would get through it. But seeing that we are still in it, and possibly for the long haul, I am done *reflecting* and want to move into *living* by taking action and establishing new routines

So I introduce you to my next section of this book called, "COVID-19 **Routines**".

This all began with thoughts that turned into words in my weekly reflections. Now, reflections must turn into actions embodied as routines. Our routines will turn into habits as we find our "rhythm." Who else is ready to take action with practical strategies that will lead to healthy habits? That's what I want to focus on next. As we continue life's journey, I pray we will reap the rewards when we choose to take control of what we can (our thoughts & actions) and leave the rest up to God. HE is still, and always will be, in control even in a world that feels so out of control.

If you are an organized control person like me, these past few months have been hard because COVID-19 frankly messed up all of our plans for this spring, then summer, now looking like the year, and basically, our life. (Well truthfully, is everything ever completely in our control? Nope.) I want to start focusing on what we *can* control. What I want to work on together is what we *can* do. I will begin to share with you the new sweet and simple routines that are working for me, to live life past reflection. And although I will continue reflecting because it is an important part of the process, we won't stop there.

I realized in my writing I share so openly and strongly about my faith. I know we all have different beliefs and values, and that's totally okay. For me personally, my

216

faith has been my source, my comfort and my joy. I only share in hopes that you will also experience God's love, because I care for you. I am grateful for you, my chocolate friends...no matter what you believe and where you come from.

In week #21, we received the announcement that schools would be doing distance learning for one month, pushing back the return to school once again to mid-September (at the earliest). We also had a second "shut down" possible and as I braced myself for the news of what this would mean for our family, business, and fun in our lives, we received the "Act With Care - Do Not Gather" order. The free, fun things - including beaches, parks, and gardens that I had been occupying my kids with to balance towing them to work with me - were now all closed, among other things.

I literally dropped everything I was doing and took chocolates and my kid and picked up my favorite curbside coffee from our neighbors at Morning Glass Cafe, then headed to Manoa Park down the road and we picnicked in the shade, climbed the trees, raced in the grass, and said "goodbye" to the park.

Then...I broke down. I cried for what felt like the thousandth time in the past 5 months. This week, I got down on my knees and cried out for help. How much longer is this going to last God? How much more worrying will we be burdened with, for our health, our community, our finances, our kids, our work, even our hobbies? The life we knew and had a routine for changed so much and then we got a glimpse of it slowly returning to "normal," only to be changed back again.

God must have heard my prayers because thank you, Jesus, for grandparents! My mom and mother-in-law both texted me to offer help again and today I sit alone and uninterrupted to reflect and write week #21.

"And I will do whatever you ask in my name, so that the Son may bring glory to the Father. You may ask me for anything in my name, and I will do it. If you love me, you will obey what I command."
-John 14:13-15

So let's not only reflect, but start **Routine #1: Pray**.
Pray daily.
Pray for anything.   —
Pray for everything.

Pray for everyone.

I used to pray every morning during my one and a half hour commute of traffic and drop-offs. Now that this commute is no longer part of my routine, I found that I began praying much shorter prayers. I realized I needed to **pair prayer** with something that I do daily to remind me to turn to God. So what is it that you feel like you are doing over and over again?

For me, I chose washing the dishes and doing the laundry. Having little kids at home means breakfast, snack, lunch, snack, dinner and dessert. I feel like if I'm not working, I'm cleaning. And so it was the perfect fit to bring back prayer into my life as a routine with a much larger load of dishes, clothes, and now masks.

It's my reminder to remember to pray when I pick up the dish towel and pump the soap again or pour the laundry detergent into the washer; that it's time to ask God to help me with this. All of this. Even the small stuff. To help our world. To wrap his arms of grace and love around us all as we try to rid ourselves of the dirt and grime stuck on our plates, clothes, and in our minds.

It is the constant negative things we say in our heads that are the most detrimental to our mental and emotional health and wellness. Prayer helps to change our frame of thinking and refocus on Who is in control and what we can control.

Another time that I've begun to plug prayer into my routine is before our Saturday curbside pick-ups. Before each curbside pick-up begins, I pray with my chocolate family for our chocolate friends, everyone's health and safety, for the orders to be correct, for pick up to be smooth, for it to be fun and full of smiles behind our masks, for the chocolates going out to bring love, joy, and peace to those who receive it, and for God to receive the glory. It is our new routine at the shop that we do together and it really reframes our thinking for the day: what we are doing, why we are doing it, and the impact our chocolates can have in the lives of others.

Prayer is such a big part of my life and I want it to be a constant in our constantly changing world. It is the first routine I want to make sure is set in place because even if COVID-19 all suddenly and miraculously went away, or everything went back to "normal," prayer would still need to be a part of my life because life never was or will be super smooth and perfect. There are always things and people to pray for and I have personally experienced the power of prayer time and time again.

In just the past five months alone, I have truthfully witnessed the answered prayers of requests in my prayer journal...some several years old. Couples finally conceiving and having their first baby; much needed finances for a family came in a very unexpected way; the miraculous healing of a loved one with cancer; the strengthening of a marriage almost lost; the hope and purpose for living found again, and the courage in one's heart to take the place of fear and anxiety in this COVID-19 world.

"Ask and it will be given to you; seek and you will find; knock and the door will be opened to you. For everyone who asks receives; the one who seeks finds; and to the one who knocks, the door will be opened." -Matthew 7:7-8

Lesson Learned: You can control some things like how often you pray, what you pray for, who you pray for and who you pray to. There truly is power in prayer.

Opportunity Now: Pray to God every day. To make it a routine, pair it with something you do every day. For me, it will now be whenever I wash dishes or clothes. And if I don't know what to pray about, I just talk to God like I'm talking story with my best friend over coffee and chocolates. We will talk about anything and everything. Nothing fancy or rehearsed, just sharing what's in our head and hearts. Anyone can pray and you don't have to be a certain person or act a certain way to do it. In fact, as you are right now, you can simply say something like this:

"Dear God. Thank you for loving me just as I am. Thank you for listening to me right now. Thank you that I've been blessed with dishes and clothes to wash. I pray that you help me with _____. I pray that I can _____. I pray for _____. Please let me experience your power through prayer. Amen."

Hope For Our Future: God answers prayers. He still does! Sometimes it's a *"Yes."* Sometimes it's a *"No."* And sometimes it's a *"Not now."* But he does hear them all and he does answer them all. We might as well keep praying and asking.

When I do it out loud throughout the day at home, my kids hear me too and they start to pray and thank God for the little things. Like parking so we could go on a hike or for "coronavirus to just go away." We have more prayer warriors in our house now and we need as many as possible to fight this battle that we are all in.

To encourage you as an example of a recently answered prayer, I have prayed about having a blog for YEARS for Choco le`a. But I never "had time" to write or had "nothing to write about" or believed that "no one would care what I had to say." Quite honestly, I also didn't know how to put a blog on our website or connect it to a blog platform. Even for the past couple months, many of you have asked me to put all of these emails together in one place so you could revisit them and share them, but "I didn't have the time. I didn't know how. It was too much work."

Yet, through this season, COVID-19 provided content. The business shut down gave me the courage to write and share. Just last week, I received an email that our point of sale system made an easy add-on tab to create a blog page. How's that? So here it is! My prayer answered and for some of you, your prayer answered too!

Pray
Until
Something
Happens

Let's P.U.S.H. through, friends!

My prayer for you, my chocolate friend, is that your heart remains open and that you don't stop praying and that you don't stop *living*. Establish the new routines in your life and ask God to help you with them. Thank you for pushing me to keep writing and sharing with me how these emails have impacted your life and encourage you week after week. It is why writing has become a new routine in my life and that I have you to thank. You are my answered prayer for a community of readers and friends I had long hoped for.

With love always,
Your chocolate friend, Erin

"Take delight in the Lord, and he will give you the desires of your heart." -Psalm 37:4

— AUGUST 10 —

Week No. 22
Routine 2: Mornings

I have a confession to make: I eat chocolate before breakfast.

Yes this statement is true. I still like to start my day in a sweet way. Literally. If it's not a muffin, donut, or some other locally made fresh pastry, it's our chocolate. It also helps me get up in the morning when I just want to hit "snooze" over and over again.

As we transition from reflections to routines to help us LIVE through this challenging time, for week #22, routine #2, I'd like to share with you my most important routine. My morning routine.

It is said that, *"Every day may not be good, but there's something good in every day. And we will not have every day again. So make this day count."*

My morning routine is the longest standing routine that WAS a habit, but was broken during the shut-down, stay at home, chaos. I had to start it back up again as I mentally and physically prepared myself for going back to work and school. But even if things aren't "going back to normal" for a long time, I have discovered through first-hand repeated "research," that when I don't have this morning routine, I am a whole lot GROUCHIER (my husband and kids can confirm this).

When I set myself up right in the morning, I feel like I get chance to conquer the day! It sounds so cliché, but I know this to be true. I have more patience for my kids the moment they wake up. I can remain calm in traffic. I can walk into work with a positive attitude and give my best to whatever needs to get done.

I'm not talking about a morning routine of eating breakfast, brushing teeth, and changing clothes. That is already a habit for me and is done without a thought AFTER my intentional morning routine. What I'm talking about is being in control on how I want to start my day before this "out of our control" world wakes up.

Because of my morning routine, I like getting up early. Prior to this pandemic, I would be up at 4:30am. Now it's more like 5:00am. This early morning time is so precious to me and I like to be up before the world starts emailing and messaging me and definitely before the kids are up and asking me for everything.

I discovered through my morning routine, that I am a morning person. If you know in the depths of your heart that you are NOT a morning person, not to worry. Your "morning routine" can be a "late night routine." We all have to find our flow and time of day.

So here's a glimpse of my morning routine. My house is a mess. Daily. No matter how many times I straighten up and organize (and yes I am still simplifying like I said I would weeks ago...slowly, but surely I'm chipping away at it) it is still a mess. This is not a part of my life I have mastered or found contentment yet with a three and five year old. However, there is one tiny corner that I can control on a portion of our dining room table. This is MY spot, where I begin my morning routine.

Steps:

1. Make good quality coffee and let the aroma fill the room.

2. Turn on my 'random twinkle' white Christmas lights because they make me happy and remind me of my favorite time of the year.

3. Ask Alexa to play 'spa music' at a very low volume to set the mood.

4. When the coffee is ready, I pour it into one of my favorite mugs (I'm a sucker for cute dishes on sale).

5. Put something sweet on a little plate. It's usually chocolate! And when available, it's either Crunch a le`a, dark chocolate nuts of any kind, chocolate covered Oreo, or whatever we have. Now it's going to be the Reverse Dark Chocolate Crunch a le`a...my new love!

6. Sit down at my corner of the table with a fresh flower or plant, my Bible, devotional journal, gratitude journal, planner, pen and pencil (I'm also a sucker for cute stationary).

7. Read the Word. No particular order, I usually read one to two chapters per morning and go in order of

the Bible.

8. Underline what stands out. Something new always stands out each time I read through the entire Bible. I usually also post it on my personal Instagram account's Stories to encourage family and friends.

9. Journal about it.

10. Write 5 things I am thankful for from the day before in my gratitude journal.

I don't write the big things I am thankful for like health, family, friends, a house, etc. I try to find the small and simpler things unique to the day. For example, just this past week I wrote things like:

- Taught Aubrey how to make meatballs and she was impressed.

- The feedback from "Mrs. B" to my e-newsletters and how she has been encouraged and finding purpose and hope again as she now watches church online.

- Conner started giving me a thumbs up at dinner when he likes my cooking. (I never used to get thumbs up!)

- Received another bag of second hand clothes from a

friend at curbside pick-up as she's "simplifying" and cleaning up too (read week #19). From just a peek, it looks like stuff I will love to wear to feel cute!

- Visited my parents and saw the stars clearly outside in the sky as we waved goodbye after some dinner and dessert.

After I write my five things I am grateful for the day prior, I make five bullet points to prep me for the day ahead to remind me to keep my eyes open for things or people to be grateful for to journal about the next morning. This helps re-align my heart with gratitude for even the little things and changes my perspective as I start looking for things to be ready to note down the next day. If you are a list checker-off-er, you'll love this exercise! It's one I learned from Rachel Hollis and her gratitude practice and began doing it every single day from October 2019.

"Give thanks to the Lord, for He is good; His love endures forever." -1 Chronicles 16:34

"Above all else, guard your heart, for everything you do flows from it." -Proverbs 4:23

Finally, I look over my schedule for the day, and the

three most important things I need to get done.

Just like that, the day begins and the kids start stirring in the bed, the noise of car engines roar outside, and the sunlight peeks through the windows. I get ready with my well-established habits of brushing teeth, changing clothes, eating breakfast before I get the kids started on their morning routines.

Morning routines are great for kids too because they know what's expected of them and makes them feel proud when they get it done. Actually, I think that applies to adults too! We all feel a sense of security in knowing what comes next. Even if something always throws us off, it's nice to know there's a routine in place.

This morning routine of mine may not be perfect, but this WORKS for me. If you don't have any routine, feel free to try mine, or make your own! Don't forget to give yourself some grace too if you miss a morning or can only do a part of your routine. As we continue to progress from reflections to routines, I want to share real, authentic, straight-up, practical steps that have helped me to set myself up for 'success.' Even if that 'success' is getting everyone seated at the dining room table on time for distance learning to begin and work at home to begin. #godhelpusall

I've heard the quote that *"Systems and structure like this alleviate some of the stress."*

I pray that as I share my routines with you, it will help you to alleviate some of your stress and eventually lead to good habits as you find your rhythm in this season. Remember, we're in it together chocolate friends! I'll share with you and you're always more than welcome to share with me so we can learn, grow, and LIVE right now!

"Greater love has no one than this: to lay down one's life for one's friends." -John 15:13

Lesson Learned: I am a better person for everyone, when I make a little time for myself every morning. When I know I will have the opportunity daily to refresh and enjoy the simple things I love, I am better for myself and therefore better for everyone else I interact with. Lord knows the madness can start the moment the kids wake up or once I drive out onto the road. When I know I can read the Bible for HIS guidance, understanding, and grace, then I know I am filling my mind with the right things.

When I write out my thoughts to process what I am reading or feeling, I can give it up to God and also make sure my head is thinking clearly. When I can reflect on the day prior, and find gratitude plus look ahead to the priorities for the day and anticipate the things to be thankful for, I am guarding my heart. When I follow my morning routine, Not only do I set myself up for success, but I set myself up to give my best to everyone and everything for the day.

Opportunity Now: Establish your morning routine. Start by waking up just 15 minutes earlier than you do right now. Try the gratitude journal or read one chapter per day in Proverbs and pair it with one thing you love. Try it out for at I have a morning routine, tweak it if needed for the changing times. I added plants to my little morning routine spot since I'm working from home more. It was a worthy investment to bring my space some life. It also has a better chance of surviving as I try to get better as a plant owner. I also added some of my 'hard brain thinking' kind of work to my early mornings since it is so much harder to concentrate with kids around during the day. It will take practice to intentionally repeat the routine until it becomes a habit, but let's get started right now.

Hope For Our Future: When we wake up and we're given another day, let's be grateful and happy about it. I recently learned from my almost-ninety eight year old grandma who has been stuck inside her assisted living home and has not left for five months, that she wakes up every morning and says, "Ooooooo...I'm alive?! Thank you for one more day!" Then she repeats to herself over and over as she gets out of bed, "I am happy. I am happy."

Then she goes and gets a cup of hot chocolate, something sweet like a pastry or chocolate (can you guess where my sweet tooth comes from?), and reads the newspaper. I understand how much that little morning routine means to her like it does to me so I like to make sure she has those sweets to look forward to in the morning! Her mention of this routine, was the answer she gave me when I asked her how she was getting through all of this.

My prayer for you, my chocolate friend, is even if we have nowhere to go, not much to do, or on the flip side

237

have so much to do or a stressful job to go to, we can prep ourselves to be the best we can to be ready to serve and love others around us.

With love always,
Your chocolate friend, Erin

"Love one another. As I have loved you, so you must love one another." -John 13:34

— AUGUST 17 —
Week No. 23
Routine 3: Value

I re-wrote "routine #3" probably three times and am finally finishing it after devouring three Reverse Dark Chocolate Crunch a le`a pieces. #forreal

I really felt on my heart that I wanted to talk about "values", but that's a noun and not a routine and so changed the word again and again until I came back to the message I really valued and wanted to share. Then it hit me. I Googled "value" and realized it is ALSO a verb. It's actionable. It's when we consider someone or something to be important or beneficial. That action is a routine that I continuously try to live out.

To help me do that I write down the things I value and post them everywhere in hopes that I can add value to my life and the lives of those around me. So week #23

239

brings routine #3, **Valuing your values.**

We all have favorite sayings, quotes, or scriptures that we routinely go to, encouraging us to live our best lives. Last week I told you about my morning routine. Well, when I brush my teeth, I routinely read what's posted up on my bathroom mirror:

"What is the lesson I am supposed to learn in this?"

"Where's the opportunity now?"

This and more words of encouragement are there for me to reflect on whenever I look in the mirror.

When I put on my makeup, I am listening to John Maxwell's Leadership Podcast and his emphasis on valuing others and how I can do the same. He is one of my greatest mentors and one message he repeatedly shares in his podcasts is to "Add value to people."

Listening to him over and over again has ingrained in me this same value.

My secret routine that I share with you, is that I leave little notes EVERYWHERE that remind me of my values, how I should think, feel, and act. They are written on big yellow Post-its, squeezed into the corners of my calendar, typed in the notes on my phone, and in various other places for me since to be honest, they are sometimes so hard to remember and don't come naturally.

When I sit down at my desk, I have sticky notes with my goals related to business, reminders about my communication, and encouragement in leading a team. In my car are scriptures to memorize as I drive.

In a couple of places at home and at work, framed in our home hallway, written out on a large poster board in Sharpie in our kids' bedroom and printed on white typing paper and taped up in our closed shop and kitchen, are the values which I try to live by:

Be...

...Faithful

...Grateful

...Humble

...Respectful

...Joyful

...Honest

Again, why do I have these notes everywhere? Because I need them. I forget what I read or heard. I get distracted. I get discouraged. I need visual cues to remind me to say my values out loud as I go about my daily routines. Hence reading these reminders, valuing my values, are a routine.

We live in a world of information overload. We see things good and bad. We hear tons of different opinions. We are constantly consuming something from a TV, computer, or phone. What we allow to enter our minds, our thoughts, and our hearts influences our emotions and moves us to action...or inaction. So we must be conscientious of what's coming in, what we allow in, and how we respond.

This week I felt a weight of negativity. Negativity from news all over the world and also right in my inbox. Harsh criticisms and comparisons and the utter frustration of chocolate friends who can't get online pre-orders quick enough and our small team that can't make enough. Believe me, we hear you and feel for you! We are always thinking and trying to adjust weekly to make as many of you as happy as possible. Or at the very least feel heard and valued for your feedback.

When we grow weary, we need to remind ourselves that we can't make everyone happy, but we CAN live a life that we value. We look to our values to guide us. We look at our mission, and we ask ourselves again and again what CAN we do? What do we want to do? What should we do? Then we do our best.

Can we do what every single person wants? No. Can we let the negative comments dictate our lives? Yes. Will we? No. But can we still value their opinion and respond with gratefulness, humility, respect, and honesty? Yes.

It is often in these moments of negativity that we get the opportunity to put our values into action and value even those that can hurt us. (Though to be honest, this is easier said than done.)

Critical feedback is key to push us repeatedly out of our comfort zone so that we don't become too complacent or lose our humility and stop listening to great ideas others might have to share. So the feedback is always welcome, but the action that follows needs to align with our values.

This is why having this routine of reminding ourselves of our values, intentionally seeing them, hearing them, and declaring them out loud helps us to LIVE them. We can easily get confused about what's important and who we are without reminders of what we value most.

It is also a reminder that not everyone has the same values as us, but that they are valued the same by OUR same Heavenly Father.

"Love your neighbor as yourself." -Matthew 22:39

One routine to remind myself of His promises is whenever I first get into my car for the day I recite a scripture or two out loud. I have never been one who memorized scripture, so I decided to start saying one at a time until it was memorized and simultaneously witnessing to my kids in the backseat. If you ever see me driving and I look like I'm talking to myself, there's a good chance I'm reciting these five scriptures that are now also a routine for my son and daughter.

"Be joyful always; Pray continually; Give thanks in all circumstances, for this is God's will for you in Christ Jesus." - 1Thessalonians 5:16

"I can do all things through Christ who gives me

strength." -Philippians 4:16

"For God so loved the world, that He gave his one and only son, that whoever believes in Him, shall not perish, but have everlasting life." -John 3:16

"'For I know the plans I have for you,' declares the Lord. 'Plans to prosper you and not to harm you. Plans to give you a hope and a future.'" - Jeremiah 29:11

"Do not conform to the pattern of this world, but be transformed by the renewing of your mind." - Romans 12:2

Let me tell you that nothing realigns your heart faster than saying scripture as soon as you get moving in your car. Especially when the first words out of your anxious, rushing, usual-late-self are, *"Be joyful always."* Boom! Puts you in your place and reminds you to lighten up a little and value what and who really matters.

What matters most to me is people and relationships. I value my time with God, with family, with friends, with my chocolate family and with you...my chocolate

245

friends.

I truly hope you feel valued as I write and type this out loud. It is as if you're sitting six feet away from me on my couch. Even if you can't get your online pre-order in, I want you to know that I write these notes for you. Because it is my hope that they are adding value to so many of your lives and if I can't get chocolates into the hands of every single person that wants them, I can at least get the same intentional love and joy that goes into the chocolates, that ALSO goes into these stories, to you! The best part is, this is absolutely FREE for everyone AND zero calories! Plus, you can easily share them with multiple people, safely, to add value to their lives from the comfort of your home.

Plus, in doing something as simple as forwarding these stories, it lets the other person know that you thought of them and they were worth taking the time to share with. I pray that the words you hear may be sweeter than chocolate, and that chocolate is just the extra sweet something to go with this weekly message.

Speaking of feeling valued, thank you ALL for voting us Hawai`i's Best Local Chocolate Store! Since our opening, we have been recognized year after year. Even in the year that our actual brick and mortar store is closed and we have even less chocolates to share, you still voted for us. It is an honor and we are truly humbled that you value us this much! We value this award, because 100% of the votes authentically came from you...the voices of the friends we value.

We are all yearning to feel valued and to find meaning in our lives, but it starts with us. I myself must constantly tell myself this when I feel undervalued or hurt by someone. (Let's be honest, sometimes it's totally not a big deal and I do it all to myself). We can't keep looking to someone else or something to fix our problems and our thinking, but must look deep inside and declare what we value. Though there are sweet sources of joy that can fill a void temporarily, nothing else can truly fill us like the undeserving favor and love that comes from our Lord and Savior.

Lesson Learned: Others will not always value you, but you should continue to uphold your values, AND you can still value them. People may not have nice things to say to you, but you know what you are doing. You know what effort you are putting in, what care and thought you put into what you do; your intentions behind what you say. Only you know what else is going on in your personal life and what your capacity is. They don't. And you don't know what's happening in their life or what wrong information they may have received. All we can do is simply value them as people. We can't control everyone and everything, but we are in control of what we value and how we live out our values.

Opportunity Now: Think about your values to live by. Write them out. Post them somewhere where you will see them daily. When you do, check yourself. Ask God to help you live them out. Ask your trusted family and friends to hold you accountable to those values. It is a routine that you can add to your day and either tape it up to your bathroom mirror so you can see it when you brush your teeth, stick it on a post-it on your computer monitor while you wait for it to boot up every day, write it on the bottom on the inside soles of your shoes so you see them as you sit down to sock up and put them on, or leave it in your car on the radio dial. Seeing your values again and again will help you remember them and will help you to intentionally live them out.

Hope For Our Future: God already values us. He wants to be with us just as we are, where we are, and to live this life WITH Him. NONE of us are perfect and living righteously day in and day out. So if you feel far from getting this or any of the prior routines down, it's totally okay. We are building routines into our lives together and you and I CAN live a more meaningful life from here if we intentionally add value to it. Add value to others and ourselves. Don't look over at what someone else is doing and compare. You don't know their whole story, and they don't know yours. If we can all start by continuously working on ourselves first, there will be a lot less blaming, fighting, and pain that steals the joy from our lives.

My prayer for you, my chocolate friend, is that as you go through this next week, you recognize the value in who God created you to be, value others around you, and write your values down. Post them up, say them out loud, declare them and live them. Add value to our world!

With love always,
Your chocolate friend, Erin

"Each of you should use whatever gift you have received to serve others, as faithful stewards of God's grace in its various forms." -1 Peter 4:10

— AUGUST 24 —
Week No. 24
Routine 4: Prepare

"Tired" was the word I was feeling this week, but then realized I am working on developing routines and "being tired" should not be a routine. One of the reasons I was tired this week was because I was making a lot of preparations both at home and at work. Because things change on a daily basis, our preparations change and preparing oneself mentally again and again gets very tiring.

Distance learning began for our household and for many families throughout Hawai`i this week, while a second stay at home was also implemented. On top of an added extension on distance learning, it meant that many of us had to adjust to working at home, work while distance learning, or working a "second shift" after school.

For school, we were prepared and had all of our supplies ready to go, but now we had to prepare for a different kind of school. Enter tech support, EA, lunch lady, yard duty, etc...I could not stop yawning all week! But I don't want to just dwell on the feeling and feel sorry for myself and drag into next week thinking I will just be "tired" forever. Instead, is there something I can do to better prepare for this craziness?

As for work, prior to COVID-19, we already had procedures in place for phone orders and pre-order pick-ups in our shop; however, throughout this pandemic we had to learn to shift and prepare for online pre-orders and curbside pick-ups.

I found that preparing for distance learning AND preparing for Saturday's curbside pick-ups were similar in many ways.

John Wooden once said, *"Failing to prepare, is preparing to fail."*

I did not want my daughter to "fail" in finding joy through distance learning with a new teacher and new friends. I also did not want my chocolate family to "fail" in finding solutions to keep working safely through this season. This week, I'll share with you the 6 routines that helped me **prepare at home for distance learning and prepare at work for curbside pick-up.**

1. Mental Preparation

Home: Distance learning was going to be different and we knew that so we talked about it as a family so that our now Kindergartener, Aubrey, knew what to expect. We previewed her curriculum calendar, practiced logging on to the different apps and websites, and taught her how to use her device. We also visited Aubrey's school, saw the physical classroom and desk she would eventually sit at, and met a couple of the really nice educators that would help her learn in her new school. Of course, we also prayed.

Work: As a chocolate family, we sat down together or virtually met at least once a week to plan ahead and get visual and mental preparation for what's to come. We discussed feedback from you, both good and critical, and made decisions after weighing the pros and cons. We decided to continue with once a week online pre-orders and curbside pick-up, but now with a different work schedule.

We then went through our routine of what we would be making, what we needed to purchase to prepare, what boxes we needed to fold and have ready in advance, labels printed, verbiage posted, counts we needed to hit in production, etc., etc., etc. We went through all of the details and planned what to strive for while keeping the mission, our values, and our goals in focus. Once again, we prayed! Prayer was an ongoing thing!

2. Preparation of Supplies

Home: All of the brand new school supplies purchased earlier for the start of the year were ready to go, and patiently "waiting" in my closet. They were in big bags ready to be delivered to the classroom that Aubrey was still not in.

I watched my daughter start day #1 with the supplies we had at home left over from last year. Her crayon box was full of broken pieces, some too short to hold comfortably, multiples of the same color, some favorite colors missing, and a mess that took Aubrey time to sort through. I watched her get frustrated looking for a color, then needing to pull back the paper to sharpen it, then getting frustrated again, then giving up and choosing one color to hurriedly just fill in the whole picture.

I went into the closet and pulled out the new box of crayons and replaced the old. Aubrey started to smile. One of each color was sharp and ready. Now, she had the properly prepared supplies to finish her picture. It was a good selection of colors (not too many to be overwhelming) and sharp enough to get into the small details in her picture. (This is why teachers are so smart to ask you to get two sets of 24 and not 104). They understand the importance of preparing a child for success. A big part of that is having the right supplies so they can focus on the content and the lesson.

Work: As for our weekly chocolate sales, we too were making brand new products fresh, week by week. Therefore, our supplies had to be ready, we needed to have all the right ingredients on hand, checked the dates, did quality control inspections, taste-tested, and prepared all the different components for each product. (Example: We temper our chocolate, hand-craft our truffle shells, make the ganache filling, and separate paper cups to pack the finished product). We aim to have a nice variety of about 3-4 products so that it's not overwhelming, but a sweet assortment carefully

257

crafted in detail to standard, so you will find it satisfying.

3. Set Up Preparation

Home: With supplies ready to go, now we needed to set up. I had to find the furniture that worked in our house and the best spot for her to stay focused, cool, and comfortable, all while I could still keep an eye and ear out for her while trying to get other things done too. We also wanted a nice, clean and non-distracting backdrop so I didn't have to worry if the house was a mess or I needed to walk into view, and I definitely did not want to distract the other kiddos.

That spot for my daughter was the dining room table right next to a window and with her back up against a white wall. Because we needed the table for breakfast before school and then after school for dinner, I had to figure out how Aubrey could get in this spot and prepare to set herself up each day.

Keeping everything labeled, color coded (especially for kids still learning to read), and all together in one bin made it easy for Aubrey to have everything in one place for a quick set up and clean up. Her website were bookmarked, only the apps needed were on the first page, with all pass codes easily accessible. Her device was charged from the night before and hooked up to the Internet.

Other physical items in her set up were a water bottle, comfortable headphones to block out noise and distraction (primarily me), and a clock with a timer to keep her accountable when she went on breaks. Before you give me all of the credit, I credit the teacher who helped to label and color code all her folders and laminated her pass codes. I also credit the other parents who shared with me their tips for a successful set up.

Work: When we prepare our weekly chocolate orders, besides actually making the chocolates, preparing the packaging and putting the chocolates in the packaging, there was a lot more preparation that needed to take place prior to the pick-up. As online pre-orders came in, two of us checked each order, one by one. One person read the order, the other person wrote it down. The one reading checked the one writing and the one writing checked the computer. It was a double confirmation.

We then alphabetized our order signs and counted

them. Next we typed out a backup, alphabetized order list of each chocolate friend who placed an order. Two of us then read the list, matched it to the order signs, and packed the finished chocolates.

Finally, the orders were organized alphabetically with a final check on the number of bags per order if all of the chocolates didn't fit into one bag. These multiple checks and back-ups helped us to reduce the human error prior to curbside pick-up, and better set us up for success.

4. Break Preparation

Home: Aubrey's teacher would tell the class to get out of their chairs, use the bathroom or grab a snack during breaks. I did prepare snacks and some lunches ahead of time, but I guess because we were home, we found ourselves wandering to the refrigerator more frequently to look for something to wake us up between breaks. As a result, we were eating more.

I prepared all of the healthy fruits, veggies (and yup chocolate) for her breaks, packed it into little containers and placed them into an easily reachable drawer in the refrigerator (which happens to be below the chocolate drawer, which is just out of reach for the kids LOL! Anyone else have a chocolate drawer?)

The best snack tip was one I got from my mom. Freeze your Gogurt! My kids love Gogurt, but when it's frozen, it's now a popsicle and very refreshing on these hot days AND it takes them ten minutes to finish one. Ten full minutes of silence and keeping them occupied meant peace and quiet for me.

However, by the end of day #2, she (and her brother) had gone through all of the snacks I prepared for the week. So although this helped and I planned to do it again, I thought I needed to plan other things for her to do in those multiple 10 minute breaks, besides eat. It's not quite long enough to go outside and walk, so maybe we needed to come up with some quick fun indoor exercises to get the blood pumping so her brain keeps working (and mine too). Stay tuned since we have not completely figured this one out yet!

Work: For our Saturday curbside pick-up team, our breaks felt the opposite of distance learning at home. We were up and moving most of the day and sitting down during the short breaks. We had our huge water bottles, sometimes a refreshing drink (like Cowcow's

Tea) and music! Hip hop music! It's the one day of the week we listened to this genre and turned up the volume to pump us up! We usually dressed in our soft comfy t-shirt, pants, shoes, hair back, mask, and shield. When there was a break between texts and cars, Ally yelled at us to "drink water" like a varsity team coach. Christine and I drank and caught our breath between "laps."

Sometimes Ally said, "Go, go, go" as she told us the make, model and color of cars that we repeated to ourselves as we grabbed the bags and headed out to the beat of the music pumping. As Ally responded to texts, Tori pulled orders and quadruple checked them. During the breaks, Tori quietly gave us a thumbs up and said, "Good job guys!" as she sanitized and wiped things down. It honestly was very fun!

5. Safety Preparation (aka Sanitizing Stations)

Home: Even though we were staying at home, pretty much anytime we went out and came in, went through a new safety and sanitizing routine to help us do our part. This sanitizing station, as I liked to call it, was something I prepared as a result of kids not liking the masks I chose for them to wear and them leaving their dirty masks on the floor by the door when they came home. So to help prepare them (and save me time and excess talking), we created a sanitizing station. In seconds, I put up command hooks to hang clean masks for the kids and adults to choose from daily, a basket for the dirty ones, a laundry basket for dirty clothes, the spot where everything must go to be wiped down (monster trucks and such), and the "don't touch anything, walk straight into the shower" routine for a rinse off.

Work: At the chocolate kitchen and shop, it was the same. We had multiple sanitizing stations and sanitizing routines that were done daily. We also added routines like daily temperature checks and supply deliveries were left outside in a designated area, wiped down before they were brought in.

We cleaned, before, during, and after everything. Six feet markers were on the floor to remind us to keep our distance. Masks were worn at all times. We even had designated work areas spread apart, and hand-washing was done as usual throughout. It's something we were used to doing in the food manufacturing business, being regulated by the Department of Health; however, we were being even more mindful to not socialize like we used to. We adjusted old routines like throwing air fist bumps instead of our usual "Cacao" (good job fist bumps)!

6. Work In Progress

Home: Lastly, there were some preparations that were still a work in progress. For distance learning, it was mainly related to technology. Aubrey knew how to navigate the microphone mute button and video (although she did sometimes tell the teacher and her whole class what she was thinking when she was actually just talking to me!)

But then windows popped up asking questions. She yelled to me with her microphone on, *"Mommy something is wrong,"* while simultaneously another five-year old said, *"Grandma, I don't know what just happened,"* when a screen froze, or another kid said they couldn't hear a question because someone's radio was blaring in the background. These were all tech issues that we didn't smooth out in week #1, but we will figure it out. It was only the first week so we needed to give everyone some grace as we worked towards progress together.

I am so grateful to have been part of a class with parents and grandparents who were trying their best to support the kids. I knew this since we all saw each other's heads peering in from the corner as we tried to stay out of view and look at the screen to make sure all the right settings were on, as we typed to each other in the chat box how to "adjust the layout view."

Work: As for our curbside pick-up, you got into the routine of "no line", and parked in any of the three designated areas. You texted the needed info, and waited comfortably in your cars with your masks on. We learned to do the final check on orders as we checked the note with the bag's contents and confirmed your name when we got to your car with your order. The only thing I personally was still trying to learn was the make and model of cars. I sure learned a lot about cars!

For the most part, we did pretty well. One exception was on a Saturday when two white Honda Odysseys pulled up front at the same time and both of you texted *"Honda Odyssey white parked right out front of the shop."* Then two gray Audi SUV's also parked right outside of the shop at the same time. Are you guys doing that on purpose to have a little fun with us? Just kidding!

Anyhow, we made it fun. We laughed and gave ourselves some grace when this happened. We had to take a fifty-fifty chance by asking the person in one car if she was "Kristen" or "Christine" since sometimes, those with same or similar names also came at the same time!

I shared all of these preparation routines that worked for us for distance learning and curbside pick-up, in hopes they could help you too. By having implemented the things we did for our kids, my hope is that it will work in ourselves and our work teams as well. We have prepared to set one another up for success, so we could do it, too!

My kids were on distance learning, but I was sure they learned a lot about preparation - not by being distanced, but rather by being very close at home. I saw what made her frustrated, what got her excited, what she responded well to, and how mental preparation helped her. Having had the right supplies, set up, breaks, sanitizing, and grace for the works in progress were preparing her for success, and prepared me to feel a little less "tired".

Lesson Learned: Preparation takes a lot of work in advance, but it is well worth it. The benefits allow for margin and breathing room if there's a mistake, something unexpected, or for fun when you get into the flow of what to expect and how to be prepared for it. I have experienced this both at home and at work and have seen that as we came up with these preparations together, made little checklists to help us remember what we needed to do, and then followed them, edited them, adjusted, and got better with each day or each week, we slowly built the confidence and capacity for something new.

Whether it was more challenging supplemental work, or more play time during breaks, or another means to offer chocolates besides the once a week online pre-order and curbside pick-up, we have determined to get there as we are nailing one routine down after another.

Opportunity Now: Set up your distance learning or your work for success. Pick one or two of the preparation routines listed above and try them in your home or work place. Discuss it with your family or team to decide what you want to try, prepare and adjust it as you see fit for your situation. A simple one to start with is having a safety and sanitizing routine at home the same way businesses have. Plus, NOW is the time to do it if you haven't been already, so we can crush coronavirus by doing our part.

Hope For Our Future: These changes are forcing us to prepare as best as we can for the things we are unprepared for. Thankfully, our kids are probably more adaptable than us. At least that's what most of my friends and I have noticed as we exchanged notes on week one of distance learning.

We know most kids would rather be in the classroom with their friends, but they are learning to change and they are trying. They are figuring out the buttons on the computers and iPad. They are learning how to angle their cameras and be mindful of their facial expressions in response to others as they can now see themselves on the screen. They are learning new programs that are able to self-customize to the child's level based on the answers they provide.

As we the adults in their lives get to be with them and learn from a close distance what distance learning and school is like for them, we can even better support them and see the areas they struggle and need encouragement in. We can see the areas they thrive in that we can hone in on. Our kids are showing us that with a little bit of our help and preparation, they will soon be on their own and we will have greater time and energy to work on other preparations in life.

My prayer for you, my chocolate friend, is that whatever you are experiencing in this world of distance learning, work at home, or shut down number two here in Hawai`i, I pray that you prepare for abundant blessings.

With love always,
Your chocolate friend, Erin

"But in your hearts revere Christ as Lord. Always be prepared to give an answer to everyone who asks you to give the reason for the hope that you have. But do this with gentleness and respect." -1 Peter 3:!5 "The horse is made ready for the day of battle, but victory rests with the Lord." -Proverbs 21:31

— AUGUST 31 —

Week No. 25
Routine 5: Celebrate

To cry or to celebrate?

As the pandemic continues on and on, crying has sort of become a routine, but I want to balance the tears with cheers and start a routine of celebrating...even the small stuff!

We need to find reasons to celebrate. There is a lot to cry about, but I want to cry more tears of joy. I want others to cry tears of appreciation and gratitude. I want to cry tears of relief as we become friends with technology. I want to watch our kids cry tears of satisfaction as they learn to accomplish one thing after another.

Crying several times a week feels like a "new normal" routine for me (yup I am a crier). Celebrating, on the other hand, doesn't come as easily for me, but this week, I stopped to celebrate the little things because September is here and it's our birthday month! In September, we are usually picking up balloons, plating our chocolates on silver platters to serve, breaking open a bottle of Dom Perignon champagne, and having a potluck party. Even though we are not able to do all of that this year, there is still a lot to celebrate!

Here we are, still standing in a world of so many challenges, costs, and uncertainty, and yet we continue on as we fight to stay in business with our local community. Thanks to you, our online pre-orders have been selling out week after week and we're surviving week after week. We actually tried online ordering over a year ago and designated a bunch of products for the online platforms that sat, got old, and never sold. It was sad because it flopped, but here we are trying it again in different times, and this time, it's working!

As Oahu wrapped up our second "stay at home order" that was then extended, and with cases still present everywhere in the country, we knew parties were still possibly months away. We honestly thought that September was the month we'd have our shop open again and we would be able to honor all of the birthday truffle coupons we sent out for our April, May, June, July and August babies to come in to redeem.

For now, we don't see the shop opening again anytime soon, and so we are re-planning and re-purposing our space, our plans, and some of the beautiful things we did enjoy (even if alone) in the past 5 months.

For me, I finally had my dream "window office." After years of sitting in the back in our old ingredients closet turned office, I longed for a day that I would have an office window. I ironically got what I wanted when the shop had to close! During the first shut down when I found myself feeling down and alone in our shop, I rearranged the furniture, decorated, and eventually created the perfect set up for me to be right up front in the shop to welcome chocolate friends when we re-opened. I visualized having you all sit across the table from me and we'd talk story over chocolates and coffee as I helped you create custom packaging, favors for your parties, and gifts for your clients and loved ones, through a very personal, in-person experience.

Instead, over these past months, that space turned into a daycare filled with kids, toys, devices, and blankets spread out on the floor. Now as we find ourselves in another work at home order, which is becoming a very common thing, there is a need to expand our production space so that we can make more chocolates.

I am taking one last look at this beautiful space and although I feel like I'm going to cry because I have to "give it up," I am choosing to celebrate the beautiful "window office" I had for 5 months. I'd rather trade it for more workspace, more opportunities for my team, and more chocolates for you.

Week #25 was filled with tears which I chose to turn into cheers. First, I cried on camera as I had the opportunity to share a little testimony with my church, Pearlside Church and Pastor Billy Lile, about how I am still living with purpose in this pandemic and how our business continues to be a platform to share God's love and blessings.

We talked story and recorded it for all services and it played over the weekend. I wish I didn't cry and could articulate my point better, but the feedback received from so many people who tuned in was so encouraging! Others are also trying to figure out how to keep going when it feels like everything is just shutting down and how to stay the course of His purpose when we are ordered to stay at home. I celebrated as I realized that what we are going through is continuing to help others, and sharing it with our community is part of the important work we have to do.

Also, an article came out featuring us in the UH Alumni Small Business Spotlight. This article made some people smile, send a few messages of congratulations and emails of appreciation. When asked in the article, "What do you love most about your work?" I responded with, "What I think I love the most is my ability to connect with many different people, because many different people love chocolates! This work has become my platform to share my faith and the lessons I've been learning, the opportunity now, and our hope for our future."

Right there and then I was reminded to celebrate. To celebrate right here in the NOW and use my opportunity to write this all down to connect with YOU! Choco le`a has overcome a lot and in the process, we have been able to help others as well. There are still many obstacles ahead and it's never all good and perfect so we might as well celebrate along the way through our years of studying, learning, growing, downsizing, and building again.

Then, only two weeks into distance learning, the tears really started to follow. First with Aubrey, then with me. She turned off the video because she didn't want her friends or teacher to see her and I muted the microphone because I didn't want anyone to hear me crying either.

We love technology and we get frustrated over technology. We miss being with people and adjusting can be hard. We know it will get better, but for right now, it's tough. So that day, at two p.m., I started our own pau hana happy hour in our house. We call it the "Choco le`a Happy Hour!"

I think I am going to keep this up with one fun video or cute photo of a #chocoleakid once a week on our Instagram account. I need a happy hour and so do the kids. What better time to be "happy" than in the hour when school is pau?

As incentive, I told Aubrey that when school was over, she could do her chocolate taste-testing (which she now loves to do for the videos on Instagram). When school was done and Aubrey threw down her headphones and glasses on the table where I was setting up to do the weekly photo shoot, I got the idea to dress the chocolate up to cheer her up and put the glasses and headphones on the Reverse Crunch a le`a and added a smile. She laughed. I laughed. Then we ate chocolates. We needed to celebrate another day done and needed a cute and sweet happy face to cheer us both up.

Later, after school, we celebrated at work. We celebrated when some of you who have been trying for months to get an online pre-order in were able to do it! After numerous messages from you about your frustrations that you can't do it and us continuing to encourage you that you can do it, after yet another video made about how to order, and after you "practiced," your orders finally came through!

We literally celebrated you in the shop as we went through the orders and we celebrated as we sold out everything in about twenty five minutes. We are extremely thankful for your support because being in business for one more week, is reason alone to celebrate in these tough times!

I cried again as I struggled to figure out how to fit a 40 hour work week into a week also filled with distance learning. Although I had made a lot of preparations to set my daughter up for success, I couldn't just leave her alone on week two. I wanted to so I could do my work, but quickly realized I couldn't. She still needed my support. We still had to figure out some sound and visual challenges and I still had to figure out how to get things done and not be a distraction when her mic had to stay on. I still had to figure out how to work while being distracted with her school since her headphones don't stay on.

So we celebrated the little wins like the fact that she was trying, she was participating and finishing her work. We celebrated by spending her break with some short sprints in circles and spinning with our arms out while walking, and doing "jumping jacks." (Her choice, not mine!)

That's when I realized Aubrey couldn't do jumping jacks! I couldn't stop laughing as she tried to coordinate the open and close jumping movements and then she laughed because I was laughing and we both just gave up and looked up at the clouds It was the most beautiful day in Hawai`i nei.

She looked for shapes and I daydreamed and asked God for more moments to celebrate. Not necessarily for more reasons to celebrate, but that I make it a routine to celebrate the little things and find joy in jumping jacks and that kind of stuff.

By Thursday, I was straight up tired and took the afternoon off after school to just spend time with Aubrey. My family and I have been encouraging her to ride a bike since April, but she refused. I told her again that parks, beaches, playgrounds, and hiking were all closed and we are only allowed to swim and ride bikes for outdoor fun.

As soon as she realized she had to get it if she wanted to do something fun with me outside, that girl got on her bike and told me, *"Let go already,"* (verbatim)! And she rode her bike! It brought me to tears, but this time tears of joy and not frustration, though there was a lot of that at the beginning. I started to wonder if she was just messing with me and holding out! Grrrrr!

That girl took off! She rode her bike for a really long time. It started with a small voice saying, *"This isn't so hard,"* which turned into *"Mommy, I'm starting to have fun!"* (with a little shock in her voice that this could actually be a good thing), to a shout as she pedaled her bike faster while yelling, *"I am so happy!"*

She changed her mind and attitude and just like that, she was able to ride. The feeling of riding must have felt like a celebration for her, too, as she felt the breeze on this hot day and cooled herself off by going faster. I jumped on my dad's bike and found I never forgot how to ride after all these years and rode beside her. We rode in circles on the street for a very long time as I tried to soak up this moment of celebration watching her accomplish something and that she realized what she was capable of.

On Friday, refreshed after a fun Thursday, we celebrated the end of the second week of distance learning by brainstorming how we could make it even better, then sharing our ideas with our teachers for an even smoother third week. We also launched our first Instagram giveaway for the month with some special "Happy Birthday" chocolates for each week's winner!

We picked up some special food to drop off to loved ones from a place we always had on our restaurant wish list to try, but had no reason to go. We went, for no reason at all, to celebrate nothing in particular ... well, maybe, to just celebrate life, health and family.

Then, on the first **Saturday** of September, our sixth birthday month, we kicked off our first curbside "celebration." Honestly, we forgot the party balloons and hats, but we felt like we were having a party in our hearts. We celebrated by throwing in a sixth birthday gift into EVERY single bag because we knew the sweet extra surprise was going to make you smile! It made us smile just thinking about that, and seeing the bright colored birthday cards pop against the brown chocolates.

We also celebrated by throwing six random Birthday Surprises into the bags of six chocolate friends! We danced by a couple of cars at pick-up and celebrated several of YOUR birthdays! A mom who celebrated the birth of her first daughter now was at curbside just a couple of days after being released from the hospital. A dad who came to pick up chocolates for his wife and their son to celebrate his first birthday after we celebrated their wedding with them a couple of years ago.

We also celebrated the birthday of a seven year old who wanted mochi truffles for his special day. Thank goodness for the timing on making it and mom getting her online order in! He and his family have been enjoying our chocolates for a couple of years now. The next generation of #chocoleakids are looking sweet, thanks to their sweet parents, aunties, uncles, and grandparents!

Finally, the day ended with a dance delivery to the last curbside car of the day. Seeing all of you, even if just your eyes for a few seconds, really makes us happy and sometimes we can't help ourselves and you catch us doing a little celebratory dance!

Our shop is blessed with six years of being in business and although we are still closed and we can't have a party, we still wanted to celebrate. So there in the back of our shop, in the original little kitchen where it all started, as we cleaned up, and looked at the food, cakes, cupcakes, cards, and well wishes that YOU surprised us with to help celebrate six years, we stood six feet apart and sang a little "Happy Birthday" to Choco le`a and our entire chocolate community!

As we read your cards and your memories on how you

284

"first met us" at our pop up in Shirokiya over six years ago, before we established our brick and mortar shop, flashing back to way back then and how far we've come together, we realized that's reason to celebrate! But even more so the fact that we stayed in touch all of those years and kept connecting through chocolates. We celebrate with YOU loyal chocolate friends! Thank you for your years of friendship!!!

So if you are crier like me, let's try a new routine and change our tears into cheers. Find things to celebrate and celebrate them!

Lesson Learned: Life itself is worth celebrating and we shouldn't wait for a reason! There are a lot of things worth celebrating if you stop to acknowledge them or choose to make them a big deal. There are also a lot of people in our lives worth celebrating if we look around us! We don't need to throw a party, or give expensive gifts, or do it all of the time. But when we stop and look for reasons to celebrate, it continues to add value, joy, and fuels our purpose in this pandemic.

Opportunity Now: Start a weekly celebration routine! It's hard to find reasons to celebrate unless you begin looking for them. You can make a list of the good things that happened during the week and then order take-out from an eatery you want to support, sit around the table with your household, eat, and go over that list. This is sort of what I do in my gratitude journal in my morning routine, but in terms of actually celebrating the good things done and moments accomplished with a reward, I think I need to add that routine right now!

Anyone else down to celebrate? For our family, we just decided that we will get take-out food or dessert from a new restaurant or cafe we want to try, once a week. This is our celebration for doing our part in wearing our masks, keeping our distance, staying socially apart, finding fun, distance learning, working while at home, and keeping a good attitude.

The best feeling is when we celebrate with others. We can have a team celebration with our household, or if we can't physically be with others, the beauty of technology is it does allow us to let them know we are thinking of them and we celebrate them! Small celebrations for now until we can party again and also support our event industry friends.

Hope For Our Future: Celebrating doesn't only make you feel better, it makes others feel better too! So a little self-celebration can turn into a cycle of celebrating with a community! You all say you are so thankful to get chocolates from us and that you know how good it feels to share our chocolates with others. But you also are helping us celebrate that we have work to do and a way to support our families. When we order food or purchase gifts from another business to celebrate, it supports them, too.

Lastly, kids are literally our hope for the future. Little kids...wow, their pure young hearts and wild imaginations believe everything, literally everything, is a reason to celebrate! If I bring home chocolates they say, *"Let's have a chocolate party."* If I bring home fresh produce, we have a "fruits and veggie party!" If we get gifted a new movie, like "Mulan", we have a "movie party!"

I'm sorry I keep mentioning kids, but I am around them all of the time and I see their zest for life and their cluelessness on just how massively COVID-19 has affected the world we expected for them. They, however, are still expecting a lot of fun and are finding their own reasons to celebrate. Their childlike faith reminds us that we have a God so big, so powerful, and so loving that we can expect a life of eternal celebration with Him.

In COVID, we really have built a stronger chocolate community and we celebrate our birthday because of friends like YOU!

My prayer for you, my chocolate friend, is that you find little reasons to celebrate throughout the week, for every week we get to live this life. I pray God helps us change our cries to cheers and transforms the reasons behind our tears.

With love & celebration always,
Your chocolate friend, Erin

"The Lord has done it this very day; let us rejoice today and be glad." -Psalm 118:24

— SEPTEMBER 7 —

Week No. 26
Routine 6: Move

Do you have a routine to de-stress?

Each week, depending on the experiences I have during the week, I select a "word" as the topic for my email blog. This "word" is what drives and connects everything I write. This past week, I honestly had a lot of "not so positive" words for how I was feeling. Words like "frustrated" "defeated" "tired" (again), and "stuck" resonated with me.

As I shared this truth at curbside pick-up with my extended chocolate family, chocolate friend and volunteer blog content commentator, Shandis, she responded with, "Write about it."

"What!?" I responded. "No one wants to hear me grumbling." To which she said, "Then tell them how you manage these feelings. What's your routine to de-stress?"

So for week #26 and routine #6, I am going to do what Shandis suggested, and share with you a routine that I have to manage all those "not so positive words" that I experienced. So how do I manage stress? I "**MOVE.**"

I MOVE my body. Some of you may not know this, but prior to Choco le`a, my full-time job was as a Dance Director, Instructor and Choreographer. As a child, I grew up dancing ballet, tap, jazz, lyrical, and hip hop first with Rosalie Woodson Dance Academy, then with 24-7 Danceforce.

Although I never pursued dance as a professional career, I always found a way to dance: I started a dance team for fun while I was a school teacher at Leihoku Elementary in Waianae, which was then turned into a part-time job at my friend Mandi Scott's hula studio, Na Maka O Pu`uwai Aloha, which then turned into my full-time job with hundreds of students ages five through sixtyfive.

I danced for hours every week at the studio that felt like home and at various schools under my business

292

license, "Embraceology." For seven incredible years I had the greatest opportunity to dance for work. Along the way, I danced for fun too. I took classes all over the islands at the University of Hawai`i, Studio 808, Funkaerobics, Honolulu Classical Ballet, and even right before the pandemic shut down, I was in a class that I absolutely loved with Jose Silva at Infinity Movement Studio. (Shout out to ALL of my dance teachers, friends, students and parents! #workit #fierce)

Dance has always been a part of my life, and has shaped me into who I am today. It has served as an avenue for me to build my confidence, express how I am feeling, de-stress, and move my body for exercise.

I haven't taken a dance class since early March before this all happened. Six months without in-person classes meant that I returned to one of my other loves, hiking the great outdoors.

Then when hiking got shut down too, I honestly got really sad because I felt like I lost not only one, but now two activities that I had built from a routine to a consistent habit that I loved to do to help me de-stress, in a very stressful time.

Now that I am "repeating" Kindergarten with Aubrey and doing it via distance learning, the mornings feel like they go by so slowly as we say our letters and the sounds they make and practice our basic counting. Business is still far from booming as we navigate on a week to week basis, dreams and big plans are still on hold, and it feels like small businesses are either slowly shutting down or just surviving.

A lot of the world feels like it's moving too slow at times…especially for people like me who can't move at the pace we were once used to and when spouses, friends, and others are going about work, business, and life as usual.

Life can get hard and the game of comparison can sneak in if I sit and just dwell on it and watch as other people continue moving on. Instead, I needed to get up and find new ways to "move." I jumped on my bike and started taking short rides again, even if it's twenty minutes in circles on the same street with Aubrey.

I also actually started swimming a little in the ocean with my family. I'm much more of a mountain and land person, but with everything shut down, I considered, for a second, taking up surfing! I keep my mind moving forward by reading, learning, dreaming, and journaling.

I have to move not only my body forward, but also my mind, too. It sometimes feels like we are stuck waiting for coronavirus to go away. Stuck waiting for our health to get better. Stuck waiting for the opportunity to come. Stuck waiting for the kids to go back to school. Stuck waiting for the positive case numbers to go down. Stuck waiting for the nation to come together. Stuck waiting for the world to heal.

But in a world of "waiting," there ARE still people moving. There are people working on vaccines and caring for others. There are people out exercising. There are people still chasing dreams or creating new ones. There are people learning online and adapting their lessons and style to make it work. There are people moving about at safe distances and doing their part. There are people coming to the table to talk. There are people trying to change their little part of the world, wherever they are.

I want to be one of THOSE people - moving!

Some of my best ideas, inspiration, and personal growth lessons come to me during hikes way up top of the mountains, in the quiet stillness and in long conversations with God. Some of the worst feelings I had inside were expressed in a healthy way through dance and movements when the lyrics of a song helped me "get it all out" safely.

But for now, a weekly swim, a bike ride, or walks around the neighborhood will need to suffice as a way to move, gain some inspiration and de-stress.

"Walking is boring," is what some of you may be thinking, and what my kids will always say, but I know they need to stretch their legs and re-energize from sitting down in front of a computer screen all day. Aubrey thinks walking is boring so we started doing scavenger hunt walks looking for things that begin or end with a certain sound, or we observe and make tally marks and count the number of geckos we see (ewww); or go on a treasure hunt to find a new flower in someone's yard that we might like and never noticed before.

It makes the walks more fun and the kids don't even realize that they have agreed to "move their bodies," which is what I tell them they have to do every day. One of my friends even moved into the neighborhood and I told her to send me a photo of her house so when I go walking, I can keep an eye out and look for it as my own scavenger hunt. I told her that when I find it, I will send her a selfie of me outside. These are just some ideas to turn your neighborhood walks into games that will help you move.

The best part about this routine is, whenever we are finished moving our bodies, we never seem to regret it, but always find that we feel a little better afterward.

As for this Kindergartener, she had her first articulation day of school, rotating between subjects like music, Hawaiian studies, and computer. She discovered that P.E. is her favorite subject! In P.E., she got to get up and move and learn "step jacks!" Earlier I mentioned she didn't know how to do jumping jacks…well this was a move in the right direction.

Seeing that spark light up in her during P.E. reminded me that we all get tired and bored and need a routine to de-stress and re-boot and get back to it again. Moving my body and mind does that for me.

A couple of months ago, Tori, our amazing Chocolatier and CEO, helped me set up her video

297

game, "Just Dance," in the shop so we could do quick three minute song breaks to re-energize! Being with her in the kitchen and quickly moving between the tasks of making chocolates, tapping moulds, drizzling sprinkles, and bagging products felt really good.

When I come in late after school feeling tired, our other amazing CEO, Ally, turns up "work out music" on Pandora and sometimes (sometimes) even dances with me for a whole 3 seconds! Running to cars at curbside with Tori, Ally, and another amazing CEO, Christine, to see your smiling faces really pumps us up to see what we are able to do and the little hope and joy we can bring to others during this time.

Making the move to keep our small business going however we could with our local chocolate friends is something we're so glad we did! Yes, we are all CEO's in the company. It means that we all agreed to be a "**C**hocolate **E**verything **O**fficer" and are willing to try and do Everything needed to get through this together.

"Moving" happens in forms other than physical as well. As many challenges continue on, we must make moves that we think are best for us and our families for this season. Sometimes it's a move to not return to work, stay home and focus on the kids or start a family. It could be a move to close a business and try something new, or a move to go out, get work and take a chance on a new opportunity even if we're not sure if we will like it; a move to a different position in your workplace; a move to try a new activity or way to manage stress, or a move to tell someone how you really feel and be completely honest so you can share your deep concerns and come up with a common goal to work towards together. Someone has got to make the first move.

During this pandemic, with heavy hearts, we had to watch some business friends and partners literally "move" out of their business and off island.

Sadly, some moves are to leave this life too soon. As we cried for another chocolate friend who passed away this week, we prayed as a team that she moved into heaven with no pain, and for her family and friends to find peace as they figure out how to move on in life without her.

In especially hard times like this, I need to remind myself and those around me that God is always moving. He knows what comes next and He is here to guide us and help us carry our burdens if we make the move to trust Him, ask Him for help, and walk with Him daily.

"And I am sure of this, that he who began a good work in you will bring it to completion until the day of Jesus Christ." -Philippians 1:6

"But one thing I do: forgetting what lies behind and straining forward to what lies ahead, I press on toward the goal for the prize of the upward call of God in Christ Jesus. " -Philippians 3:13-14

So even though I do sometimes feel frustrated, defeated, and stuck, I move out of it by moving my body and my mind. Honestly, I literally paused right HERE and went outside for a 15 minute walk since I was starting to space-out while proofreading and returned to wrap this up.

Moving is a routine that I may not feel like doing, but it always makes me feel better afterward. Also, the less we move now, the less we are capable of moving in the future. After all, our ability to simply move is a gift from God.

Lesson Learned: Keep moving! If moving my body and my mind has always helped me to feel better, why should I stop now? Even though the activities I prefer are not available or not the same at the moment, I can explore other ways to still move and try something new. We all need ways to get inspired, energized, and de-stress. Sometimes we find new inspiration and new energy with a new activity.

Opportunity Now: MOVE! Get off the bed, couch, or perhaps floor, or even the mental pit that you dug and threw yourself into. Climb out of it! Do something that moves your spirit and your soul. Something that makes your heart feel like dancing or as I always said, "Dance to the beat of your heart."

Get up and just turn on your favorite music and move your body. Who cares what it looks like. Remember that song with the lyrics, "When you get the choice to sit out our dance, I hope you dance!" Do that! Heck, I might even finally try TikTok even though my team asked me repeatedly not to do it since before this pandemic!

Take walks, go on treasure hunts, do yoga, pilates, run, or if you're brave, swim or surf! Move your mind into a new place or just move positions for a different perspective, from parent to teacher; teacher to grandparent; business owner to consumer; unemployed to employed; helpless to volunteer and from stuck to unstuck. Make your first move.

Hope For Our Future: This book, emails, my blog, and posts on Instagram accounts are some of the moves I am making in my life to create a community with others who want to keep moving forward together. The stories you share with me move me to tears. When you let me know the impact that this is making by encouraging you, inspiring loved ones, and helping us all through this, I am reassured that this is a move in the right direction.

Let's keep moving together and along the way we may discover things we never knew we loved, an energy we haven't felt in a long time, and a lot less stress on our shoulders.

My prayer for you, my chocolate friend, is until we can physically return to dance classes, to the mountains, to some of the old routines we once had, or move into the arms of loved ones we miss being with, let's just keep on moving forward and letting God direct our paths.

With love always,
Your chocolate friend, Erin

"Your word is a lamp for my feet, a light on my path." -Psalm 119:105

"He replied, "Because you have so little faith. Truly

I tell you, if you have faith as small as a mustard seed, you can say to this mountain, 'Move from here to there,' and it will move. Nothing will be impossible for you." -Matthew 17:20

— SEPTEMBER 14—

Week No. 27
Routine 7: Connect

As I reflect six months in, the hardest thing about this pandemic is that I am no longer able to physically connect with people the way I once used to. I am a hugger. I am a talker. Some of my favorite things to do was to have conversations with friends over chocolate in the shop, or coffee in a cute cafe, or share a meal in the homes of family members jumping from couch to dining room and squeezing the cute kids running around.

The hardest thing to think about for those who are suffering from COVID-19 is suffering alone. Not being able to connect one last time with loved ones, and loved ones not being able to sit by their side and hold their hand.

It is why during times like these, I am more than ever connected to the One who never leaves us nor forsakes us. God longs for connection and a relationship with each and every one of us and He is always with us. We are never truly alone. I just want to reassure you, and myself, if you are feeling lonely or longing to be with the people you love, that God is with us.

I personally long to connect with so many people again. I guess that's why I quickly shifted when our shop closed and immediately started jumping on Zoom meetings, finally started doing FaceTime, picked up the phone and made real phone calls, started writing letters again, wrote journal entries to share, and posted on Instagram @chocoleahawaii & @yourchocolatefriend. It is my way to stay connected with loved ones and feel connected to the world.

When I actually see people face to face at curbside pick-up or in my weekly adventures alone to the market, it's a major highlight!

Connecting with people is a very valuable routine in my life. It is routine #7 in week #27. So for this week, I not only want to talk about connecting, but I actually want to CONNECT you to some very important people in my life and this business.

You already know my kids Aubrey & Conner because they always make their way into my writings and are the only two non-camera shy people in my bubble, hence why they love to do taste-testing videos! Yup...everyone else, literally, my husband, parents, family, friends, chocolate family team members....all prefer to stay behind the scenes or incognito. That's why you see me all of the time! I am the only non-camera shy one to let you know that this company is made up of real humans!

Choco le`a is a locally owned and operated artisan small business built by people, crafting chocolates with their hands, and using those chocolates as a way to connect people and sweeten relationships, thus fulfilling our mission of "bringing peace to our world, one chocolate at a time."

Connecting with people is how Choco le`a really got started and became a part of my life. The most delicious and beautiful chocolates were the hook into a conversation with a long-lost family member, Uncle Colins & Aunty Joan Kawai, that then turned into learning to make chocolates together as a family along with my husband Chris, so we could spend time together and build our relationship. Today, we continue to connect and build relationships through sharing chocolates, even if only through a quick pick up or drop off.

The one blessing I have seen through this pandemic for our business is this: Financially we are not at all close to where we once were nor do we have the space, accounts, time, and team to perform like we were this time one year ago; but although financially it feels like year one for us, relationship wise, it feels like year ten!

During this stay at home time, we've been able to connect with each other as a chocolate family and with all of you in a much richer and deeper way. Though it may not be with hugs and long conversations in the shop like before, we've shared similar pain, struggles, and hardships, as well as moments of joy and celebration! We've been swapping stories and a lot of you mentioned that by living through this pandemic together, you now feel a lot more connected to me.

Well, today I want to connect you to the other people who make up Choco le`a, my current chocolate family. Small, but mighty, their hearts are huge, skill sets gifted from God, and are the reason why we are still going and can celebrate six years this month!

Even though we can't have our usual birthday party which would be the last week in September with chocolate friends and family, I'd like to celebrate by connecting you to the people in my life, particularly in this company, that make it all happen. Even if they are completely content not to be featured, I want to introduce them because they ARE the business and knowing and working with them is such a joy!

CEO & Chairman – God

First and foremost, our ultimate CEO and Chairman is our Lord & Savior, Jesus Christ. He's the one that called me into this business. He provides guidance for the direction of the company through His Word. We make decisions that align to Biblical principles, take action in faith, and He ultimately gets the last say! If you don't know Him, I'm happy to connect you! He's available to meet every single day, at any time during the day, right where you are, and you can basically talk to Him about anything and everything and He will always listen to you and love you. And He can run all businesses simultaneously! He's quite an amazing boss!

I knew that in addition to having God lead us through this pandemic, I needed a team where everyone would perform as a CEO. You see, to be totally transparent, just one year ago in 2019, we had a team of seven full-timers and eight part-timers. In early 2020 just before the pandemic, we began building up for a large expansion and had a team of eleven full timers, nine part-timers, and two interns.

We went from a very large team of 20+ to a tiny team of CEO's. That is the title every single one of us hold, **C**hocolate **E**verything **O**fficer. It means that we are willing and able to do everything required to get this off the ground, survive, build, and thrive together. That means all of us are folding boxes, packaging, making chocolates, cleaning, answering questions, running out to cars, planning, etc. These three jumped in with their heads, hearts, and attitudes ready for the job and they genuinely care about every single person we connect with through chocolates. We hope to connect with more CEO's in the future!

CEO & CIO (Chocolate Inventory Officer) - Tori

If you love our chocolates, let me connect you to Tori! She is honest, optimistic, respectful and trustworthy.

Tori takes care of InvenTORI. She makes sure we have all of the components necessary, from packaging to fresh quality ingredients and she makes all of the chocolates! She strives for and only accepts top quality, oversees health and safety standards, and keeps track of everything!

It's a lot to do, but somehow with just a can of Coke, and that fighting spirit in her petite body, she moves like a ninja: silent, swift, and steady. Sometimes we will yell *"Ninja Chocolatier"* because we can't find her as she moves effortlessly around our tiny kitchen always in action, always aware of the temperature and texture of the chocolates, and only disappears to get a cheeseburger and French fries from McDonalds.

When not at work, Tori loves relaxing at home, playing Animal Crossing, and doing crafts that will take an average of seven-hunded hours to complete. Her love language is words of affirmation and quality time. She may have few words to say, but I love spending time with her in the kitchen, watching her in her element, trying to keep up while I poke fun at myself. She silently laughs, and is learning how she is always improving the efficiency and quality of chocolate making over and over again.

311

CEO & CSO (Chocolate Service Officer) - Ally

If you appreciate our follow-through, friendly service, let me connect you to Ally!

She is compassionate, faithful, kind and honest.

Ally makes sure everything flows. She follows through with the best possible service and care for everyone. Regardless of what it is, with all of our chocolate friends, partners, and pretty much any person or thing that we come into contact, she makes sure it's taken care of. That's a lot! She's a mama to many. The many apps, inboxes, messages, voicemails, emails, deliveries and pick-ups are all taken care of by Ally. It's wiped down. It's answered. Everyone is helped as best as possible.

Our goal is for everyone to feel connected, valued, and heard. Oh, yes…she throws in a lot of fun too! She pumps up the music, brings the snacks, makes us laugh, makes up contests, adds all the graphics and boomerangs to IG, and can do it all after getting to sleep in, have a Diet Coke during the day, and going to some exciting local bento spot to try after. When not at work, Ally is making jewelry, baking, cruising with her cute pup, or somewhere with friends (pre-COVID) exploring the islands. Her love language is acts of service and quality time. I love watching Ally's attention to service, her huge heart for others, and spending time with her is always filled with jokes, laughs, and learning tons of new, random, helpful information!

CEO & CFO (Chocolate Fiscal officer) - Christine

If you are grateful we are in business, let me connect you to Christine!

She is loyal, persistent, honest and respectful.

Christine makes sure we are doing all of the behind-the-scenes stuff that keeps this business alive and rolling! She pays the bills, the taxes, more bills, has the right documents updated, signed, in order, and ensures that we are operating within budget. Christine also makes sure the goals and direction of the company are progressing forward.

She's a very grounded person, which complements perfectly a visionary like me who thinks far ahead. She keeps us grounded in the present. When I shoot out crazy ideas, Christine makes sure that what I say is communicated properly, makes sense, and puts the data and the feedback to the ideas to connect everything together. She does this brain-wracking work calmly over a bottle of San Pellegrino Blood Orange, and whatever new food you introduce her to because she's down to try it all and likes it with a side of fries!

When not at work, Christine is hiking, dining out (pre-COVID), and going anywhere fun with friends, so she is also missing her connection with lots of people right now too! Christine's love language is quality time. I love spending hours and hours talking with Christine strategizing, planning, re-planning, and working together to make ideas come to reality.

If you noticed, all three of these ladies share the value of honesty and I honestly couldn't be more grateful to have them in my life.

CEO & CCO (Chocolate Connections Officer) - Erin

Hello! My job is to connect everything and everyone. My role is to connect chocolate family with chocolate friends, with chocolate partners with chocolate suppliers, with our community, Hawai`i to our country and to our world. I connect our values and mission to everyone's ideas, goals, and vision. I connect each family member to our company culture and to their lives outside of work as well to the people they love.

When not at work, I am at work continuing the same mission under the same values, but with different goals, and a different group of people since my life work is to, "Live a life of faith, leading and learning with others, through God's love." I'm constantly connecting with people, with the Word, with the outdoors, and up close with my family since my favorite thing to do is cuddle with my kids and talk my husband's ear off.

This is why my drink of choice is my 36 ounce Yeti bottle of iced water filled at least three times per day and no matter what I'm eating, I always end up having something a little sweet too. My love language is quality time and words of affirmation, and so I hope by taking the time to write these words to you, conveys my love and connection to all of you.

We are a small, but mighty, team and we are looking forward to growing with more CEO's. Through Choco le`a, I have been blessed to connect with such kind-hearted, talented, and willing people over the years. I love being able to give work and benefits to others, while learning from them as they help build this business. We have a very LARGE extended chocolate family, with what we now call our hānai or extended chocolate family, made up of family members, subcontractors, volunteers, suppliers, prayer warriors, neighbors, partners, and others who help us along.

Every single one of YOU and every little thing you do is truly appreciated. I am beyond blessed to be connected to so many generous family and friends. Only with ALL of you has the past six years been possible. Choco le`a with its white picket fence is what we always visualized it would be: a place to call HOME for many.

I've always loved the quote, "You are an average of the five people you spend the most time with." Well, the people I spend the most time with in and out of work, are some really incredible humans whom I credit for my personal and professional growth!

The people you let into your lives, who you spend time with, and what you allow them to say to you, is all a choice. Who you connect with is a routine. Especially now more than ever as rules kept changing and we were forced to shrink our bubbles to ten people, then five people, then just our household, it becomes clearer who the people you most spend time with are.

I choose to routinely keep the positive people in my "bubble." As for the downers, the haters and the constantly negative folks who try to bring us down, I make it a routine to learn from them, but not to spend too much time with them. We are all given the same amount of time in a day. Not only how we spend that time, but who we spend that time connecting with, says a lot about what and who we value in our life.

Lesson Learned: We can choose who we want to connect with outside of our "bubble." Since that's a term we've been using in this pandemic, I'd like to suggest that this "bubble" contains the people you include in your lives even if without physical connection at the moment. I've learned to keep the people close who love me for me. Those who share in my dreams, but keep me humble, let me live in faith, but remind me to be grateful, who have taught me respect by how they live and who are straight up honest with me.

These family and friends that I surround myself with make me a better version of myself. They make me want to strive for more and be content with who I am. They are the reason why I love to connect with people, lead people, learn from people, and have found my purpose. I choose to connect with these kinds of people.

"As iron sharpens iron, so one person sharpens another." -Proverbs 27:17

Opportunity Now: Hug the ones you love tightly and hold them close. Staying-at-home has given us more time to connect with those in our household. As we re-connect with other family and friends, let's let them know how much we love them and how much we appreciate them. Don't be afraid to connect beyond your bubble. You never know who could be another Tori, Ally, or Christine in your world - all of whom I didn't know before Choco le`a - unless you believe the best in people and give them a chance.

How can we do this? Through stepping out of our comfort zone: for now through Zoom meetings, FaceTime, phone calls, letters, and having the conversations to really learn others' love languages.

Get to know what they love and value and that's how we can best connect differently with each other. I like to call it "customized connecting" with each person.

Hope For Our Future: We will hug again!!! I am still believing and praying for it! When we do, the hugs will be so much tighter and longer and our hearts will be filled with so much more gratitude for the super sweet and simple things. Like sitting side by side, sharing a cup of coffee and chocolates, walking and talking closer than six feet together, without a mask. We will be together again and this time right now will be a thing of the past, a time well spent when we strengthened our spiritual and emotional connections to one another.

I hope you feel more connected to Choco le`a and the real people behind the business that make this work. Although I may be the face of the company that you see, there are a lot of other faces, heads, hearts, and hands tirelessly beside me making sure that we can get chocolates to you to connect with you, help you connect with others and sweeten the relationships in your lives. I choose to connect with you here because of the last words of Jesus to His disciples:

"Therefore go and make disciples of all nations, baptizing them in the name of the Father and of the Son and of the Holy Spirit, and teaching them to obey everything I have commanded you. And surely I am with you always, to the very end of the age." - *Matthew 28:19-20*

So let's stay connected!

My prayer for you, my chocolate friend, is I hope you can re-connect with the people you value and your loved ones very soon. Until then, air hugs.

With love always,
Your chocolate friend, Erin

"And let us consider how we may spur one another on toward love and good deeds, not giving up meeting together, as some are in the habit of doing, but encouraging one another—and all the more as you see the day approaching." -Hebrews 10:24-25

— SEPTEMBER 21 —

Week No. 28
Routine 8: Change

Are you a "yes" person? I can be. Yes to everyone and yes to everything that sounds good. But I heard a great quote that if it's not a "hell, yes" then it should be a "no."

Well, I forgot that quote this past week and said "yes" to everyone and everything and even added on my own things to say "yes" to. All of those "yes's" resulted in so many changes that it threw off many of my routines.

Sometimes change is good. It's uncomfortable, but even routines need to change, especially if they aren't working anymore or can be improved by taking a risk to step out of our comfort zone. Sometimes when we change our routines we also find that some changes are not good and confirm that we should stick to what was

323

working.

There were different types of changes taking place in week #28: **Good Change, Bad Change and Better Change.** Some changes were small stuff just for fun to shake things up, a.k.a. **Change It Up!**

Good Change

To start, we decided to end our birthday month strong with a killer Secret Stash Birthday Bash, which meant a LOT MORE product, a lot more orders to process, a lot more to pack, a lot more free gifts to make, a second curbside to run, and a lot more correspondence and questions. It was a super-duper, great opportunity that we were so glad to give our chocolate friends, but it did throw off a lot of our weekly routines.

It threw off our newly established "normal" and that meant with the same team, space, and time, we had to figure out how to do a lot more. We were forced to find even more efficient ways of doing things, a better use of our space, and ended up moving furniture again, moving stuff out again, and moving our minds to see opportunities differently.

Some of the simple examples of things we changed

were how many steps we take from the refrigerator packed with orders to the door for curbside. We moved out furniture and brought different pieces into the kitchen to give us a more practical working space.

We brought back Carol, a friendly familiar face that some of you may have seen as she helped us run to cars for curbside.

We read through A TON of direct messages on Instagram about which products you love most and would like to see back. We read through countless feedback forms and learned your frustrations, joys, and questions about online pre-ordering and curbside pick-up. We kept refining the process and making more and more tutorial videos to help share so you'll get the hang of it, and so many of you have! We are seeing chocolate friends in their eighties figuring out how to use their gift cards and putting in online pre-orders in time before they sell out, then texting when they arrive while they wait comfortably in their car! We're so happy for you!

We watched the joy it brought so many of you who had a full three and a half hours (as opposed to thirty minutes) to shop our Secret Stash Birthday Bash on a

Sunday morning since you can never get in on Tuesdays at noon. The main thing we hear the most is *"I always miss it because I am at work on Tuesdays at noon."* So, we're changing our online pre-order date to SATURDAYS at noon! And that means all of the little details of the things we do throughout the week to prep will be changing too. We're a small business. We have to be constantly changing to stay in business!

This birthday bash week served as a test to see what we are made of, how we can pull together even tighter as a team, and what our Christmas season could feel like. We all decided that we don't want a hectic holiday season and would rather focus on our health and overall happiness. So that's what we're working on after some of the bad changes experienced this week.

Bad Change

I had to say "no" to so many of my good healthy routines this week because I said "yes" to so many other things. Those changes were not good.

I didn't get out to move as much, exercise, or get enough sleep. That made me very grouchy, tired, and unpleasant to be around. I couldn't think and function very well and couldn't make decisions. My inboxes got super full, I didn't drink enough water, and I got headaches. Then I broke my eating routine too and did a bunch of emotional eating of greasy fried fast food, ice cream shakes, and late-night binges that made my stomach hurt and resulted in me curled up in a ball, wondering why I did this to myself.

I didn't ask for prayer. I didn't sign in online for my grace group. I didn't really sit and read and reflect and dive deep into my devotion. I rushed through it all just to check it off my long list of things to do.

I overworked myself and missed almost all of our family dinners. I came home so late that I wasn't able to put the kids to bed, either, which disrupted their routine of reading the Bible, prayer, talk story time, and making shadow letters with our hands on the ceiling to practice spelling. They missed me. I missed them.

I'm also pretty sure I had a slight panic attack and felt that I wasn't good enough for anyone. A cry again to God that, "I don't know how I'm supposed to do all of this!" Yup, I'm being super real. I even cried thinking about how far we are from world peace and how would I ever make enough to start helping all the kids around the world that felt alone, didn't have a parent figure, felt hopeless and had so many less opportunities than my own children. I felt the weight of the world on my shoulders and a need to take care of it all.

Just about every weekly thing got done late. Our weekly email campaign went out on Thursday instead of Wednesday. We posted it to Instagram on Saturday instead of Thursday, and then to top it all off, we made an announcement that we will not be doing any pre-orders online or curbside pick-ups for next week.

I totally made a change and called a one week "break." I needed to breathe. I needed to use the "bad" I was experiencing this week to make changes. This break would not bring us back to good, but would get us to better.

Better Change

This break was more of a "pause" to plan. A pause to catch up and gather some of the fallen pieces and move forward to continue doing it well through the end of this crazy year, as best as I can. What does that mean? What does that look like for me both professionally and personally? That's what we needed to figure out after the reminder this week's madness brought; how things can feel even more out of control if we can't stay in control with our routines and have the margin and capacity to make some helpful changes along the way.

And so that's what this week was. It was nuts. Maybe you wouldn't have known from the outside since we of course post the good moments - and yes there were some on our highlight reel - but on the inside, my brain was foggy. I was overwhelmed. A little sad. These feelings are not new... honestly, this is a chronic cycle in my life.

I hate to admit it, but you already probably figured it out from reading this: I am a people pleaser and a chronic over-achiever. I am a "yes-er". There I said it. I love to make everyone happy and want to figure out how to do everything, and it comes at the expense of not taking care of myself until I am overwhelmed. This is a bad routine, a bad habit, that has got to CHANGE in my life.

The lock downs and limitation as a result of coronavirus actually helped me to snap out of this as I was forced to stay home and not see as many people. I had to shut down the business temporarily. Plus, my little kids were back in the home with me to constantly care for them. I had to figure out even more how to stay healthy and that meant mentally healthy, too. I had to care for what I had in front of me and that meant caring for myself as well.

The pandemic naturally put the boundaries in my life and told me "no" to all of the things I would normally say "yes" to. It sucked to not have family gatherings, to not be able to go out and see friends, go on trips, build the business more, etc. But I guess I took this as God's way of telling me to slow the heck down.

"Be still, and know that I am God; I will be exalted among the nations, I will be exalted in the earth." - Psalm 46:10

As the expectation of things opening up again grows, and as things actually open back up allowing us to say "yes" more again, the temptation to return back to how it was is very real. As the holidays creep in right around the corner, it reminds me of the absolute busiest time of the year for us. A stretch from November through February is always NUTS for Choco le`a! It's Thanksgiving, Christmas, New Year's & Valentine's.

It's the four hardest months in the year for our company every year.

It's a lot of hard work because we bank on the increased sales from the holidays to make up for deficits we may experience in the slower seasons. It's the time of year where more people want chocolates and more people want to ship our chocolates and we don't want people to be unhappy.

It's coming up so fast and it has started to feel all so overwhelming already. Don't get me wrong, we're extremely grateful for so much business this time of year, but I do need to better prepare to make sure we maintain the good and accept that we can't and shouldn't do every and anything.

So, do I really want things to go back to how it was before the pandemic?

Or am I yearning for change? Real-life, lasting change? Such as boundaries that are not put on me by pandemic restrictions, but boundaries that I choose and set up myself, so I can better control how I feel and what I do. So I can be the best version of myself for the things and people that matter most.

It's something I've been trying to learn for years and this one week, week #28, reminded me of all of the feelings I've known to be familiar and was able to "handle". I'm just not sure I want to anymore. It's time to change up some of those routines.

Change It Up!

To change up long established routines that have become bad habits can be super hard. The hardest part is accepting the fact that as times change, we change as people. That's not necessarily bad, as long as the change is for better.

Just to snap myself out of it, I had to get out of my comfort zone and change some things up this week! I agreed to a video shoot without the usual makeup, dress, heels, and a polished background, but rather a mask, sweating, with no eye makeup, and running to cars in slow motion at curbside. I had a speaking opportunity for On Da Rock podcast to share my thoughts and our business, but did not prep. No questions reviewed ahead of time, no idea what to expect, and I even let a little non-professional language slip as I forgot that I was being recorded. It felt like I was just talking story with Nate.

I put my hair in a ponytail for the first time in over four and a half years since I haven't been able to cut or color my hair in over eight months. I used a different type of pen when I wrote. This sounds so trivial, but even using something other than my favorite Pilot G-2 black ink 0.38 ultra-fine are the little changes we sometimes need to shake us up; to show us that we can and will survive, so don't fret about the small stuff.

And since running outside for recess with friends is still not a thing yet, I let my daughter try FaceTime with a friend who is much more tech savvy than us. It was actually pretty hilarious to watch two five year olds figure out what to "play together" on a screen, while in their separate bedrooms. They had to try to work out playing dollhouses and figuring out how to prop their moms' devices up so they could see one another's rooms. Aubrey also discovered the emoji button which resulted in them having some kind of secret code conversation.

One thing that never seems to change is the cost of doing business in Hawai`i increasing year after year - even in a pandemic. So, we are looking at possibly changing some of our packaging for 2021 as our costs continue to go up; not only do we try to make changes to stay in business, but to prepare for the future.

With many restrictions still in effect on Oahu, some of our routines that we've made peace with are slowly starting to drive us insane unless we change it up! Even the little stuff to make a three and five-year-old think it's "fun and funny" - like having breakfast for dinner - was one of the good moments in the week. When the weekend started, we announced to them that with the change in restrictions, we would have a change in plans and would go out to hike as a family AND sit on the sand all in one day for a change in pace since we haven't been able to do that for the past month.

All of these little things to change it up, can be the little spark that ignites the bigger changes that need to happen to turn the bad to better and to remember to hold onto the good.

Lesson Learned: We must create boundaries; give ourselves more time; don't do it all; say no, or not now – or suffer the consequences. I was reminded this week just how overwhelming my schedule used to be, how easily it can become that way again, and that I was the one that allowed it to happen. I don't have to help every single person, volunteer for everything, go to every meeting, speak at every opportunity, answer every message myself, do it all alone, do it right now, post it all, and work at things until they're perfect.

Setting boundaries for myself and being okay with changing how I do things now, as opposed to how I used to do them, is okay. I need to keep working on not being such a workaholic! Can anyone else relate … or am I just a "weirdo" as Christine calls me?

Opportunity Now: Get back into the good routines and change the bad ones. For example, a friend, or maybe two or three, actually told me I need to literally schedule in my planner "fun time." I need to pre-commit to exercise time, me time, or whatever I need, whatever fuels me and gives me energy, so that I am able to continue to operate as my best self and block it off in my calendar. So better planning and getting into the routine of thinking and looking ahead at the big picture is what I'll be working on right now as I write this at the start of week #29. I hope you can join me in a better planning routine as well.

Hope For Our Future: Just imagine how much better life can be right now if we just change out more of the bad for good in our lives? I know for myself I can make people truly happier (maybe not all, but a lot) and still achieve a lot if I have my own act together first. I've heard a quote that "A company's greatest asset or liability is the owner." Well, I definitely don't want to be a liability. If I can change the bad routines to good, the good to better, and change it up every so often to keep caring for myself now, it will save my future self!

As I practice what I preach, you will see a lot of changes this holiday season for Choco le`a. It's hard for me to make the change since the holiday season was always so profitable in the past, but I need to remember that times have changed. My team is smaller. Our space is smaller. Our resources are less. Our capacity is less, and that's okay as long as our hearts are still BIG, our values still at the core of what we do, and our mission still the focus. We want to do our jobs well, but we also want to live our lives well both in and out of work. This way we can keep doing this for a long, long time…for our chocolate family and friends and our non-chocolate family and friends, for everyone and for ourselves.

That's what you will see from here on out. I'm writing it down for some accountability so call me on it if I get out of hand! Some of you already have! Changes for "yes" to fun in October! "Yes" to gratitude in November! And "yes" to joy in December so we will not have to say "no" to peace on earth, starting within ourselves.

My prayer for you, my chocolate friend, in this last quarter, these last 3 months of 2020, let's change up our routines for GOOD!

With love always,
Your chocolate friend, Erin

"Do not be anxious about anything, but in every situation, by prayer and petition, with thanksgiving, present your requests to God. And the peace of God, which transcends all understanding, will guard your hearts and your minds in Christ Jesus. Finally, brothers and sisters, whatever is true, whatever is noble, whatever is right, whatever is pure, whatever

is lovely, whatever is admirable—if anything is excellent or praiseworthy—think about such things. -Philippians 4:6-8

— SEPTEMBER 28 —

Week No. 29
Routine 9: Plan

Can you believe it is already October? Just 3 months to go until the end of 2020 and the start of the new year! Who is ready to plan out the last 90 days, the last quarter, of this crazy year to be the best it can be based on what we can control and for what matters most? I know I am!

I promised I would take the opportunity to plan ahead, block off exercise and me time, and plan for good routines. I said I would take time to look at the big picture, then break it down in my planner and integrate more fun. I did, and it felt GREAT!

Coincidentally, the week kicked off with me receiving my 2021 planner in the mail from Simplified by Emily Ley. Ever since receiving her book, "When Less

Becomes More," I have since read the rest of her books, started following her on social media, and have learned some great tips on simplifying life and reaffirmations that self-care is not only okay, but necessary. This planner came with little notes and reminders to plan for "what matters most."

Routine #8 for week #28 is to **plan**!

How do I plan? I start BIG and work backwards. I start with a word for the year, an overall vision, broken down into quarterly focuses, monthly goals, weekly tasks, and daily 'to do's' that little by little, with time, consistency, and discipline, will fulfill the overall vision. Ironically, the word that God gave me when looking back on my journal to January 1, 2020 was "peace." I planned for peace, and God challenged me to find that peace in the chaos of this pandemic!

Here's an excerpt from my personal journal (pre-COVID-19):

"I'm a little scared going into 2020...but I have incredible peace about it too. The same familiar Holy Spirit kind of peace and trust. That's the word God gave me today...January 1st 2020. 2019 was a year

of of go-go-go. Accomplish this. Do that. Everything was about efficiency...Today, God tells me to switch focus. Looked up "peace" scriptures and it all confirmed what I need to do. Seek and pursue peace..."

"May the peace of God, which transcends all understanding, guard your hearts and minds in Christ Jesus. -Philippians 4:7

I did find a lot more peace this year with who God created me to be, but I did lose myself here and there. I filled up my schedule to the brim and it overflowed with no margin to really rest and care for myself. I can plan and get a lot done but planning for "self-care" has been something I felt guilty about for a long time and sticking with it was even harder. However, after a crazy non-peaceful week last week, I promised I would plan for more of this, and I am happy to report that I did. I hope this will inspire you to take some time for yourself too.

Here's what I did for some self-care: I took a twenty minute bike ride alone. I processed life with my small group, and we prayed for each other. I had pizza and pasta with my chocolate family for at least four meetings during our quarterly "break" week to plan for the upcoming holidays, plus all the things we never have time to talk about. I did a short hike and walk with my chocolate family after work. I had date time with my husband Chris, with take out from a really good restaurant. Mahalo Livestock Tavern! Finally, we had our usual #familyfundaysunday which now-a-days is mainly either beach or hiking together! Here in Hawai`i, we are so very fortunate that we can plan to enjoy the beautiful outdoors year-round. This pandemic has forced us to go outside and do free and safe fun things together as a family.

Now let me record how I felt so I don't forget it...it felt GREAT! Absolutely GREAT! And you know what? Having a plan and knowing I was going to have this time for myself in between work and chores made me even more efficient in doing work and chores! I focused better. I washed the endless dishes and laundry with a little less bitterness. I felt more in the moment, more present for everyone around me.

All of this self-care break time was super productive too! It was time well spent while exercising, investing in relationships, planning, and eating.

I did say "no" to many things this past week that I would have been inclined to say "yes" to. In addition, as a chocolate family, we also decided that we will say "not this year" to many of the things in the past that we did when we had the capacity to. This included no custom orders, no last-minute add-ons, no wholesale, no delivery, and no shipping. I felt badly, but they were all things we knew we wouldn't be offering during the holiday season.

Truthfully, it was hard to say "no", but we also knew we physically and financially couldn't anyway. I really wish we could do it all, but as we planned out what we could do, we wanted to make sure that whatever we committed to, we could do our best, continue the same top quality and service, and live life well all around.

So what we were expecting was the absolute best that we could give in this season of life. We thought long and hard, talked about everything and are happy with the results. We will say yes to a great variety of small and large chocolate favorites based on your input, yes to different price point options, yes to ready to-go hassle free gifts everyone will love, yes to promos and fun for you for each month, and yes to making it sweet and simple for you, too, in this crazy season, so that

345

you will not feel frustrated if you didn't plan and can easily say, "hell, yes!" The best part is, mostly everyone loves chocolates so these gifts will work to connect with almost everyone on your list and we know it can help you sweeten those relationships!

As a side note, though we made all of our plans, they are never foolproof since a lot of what we do, is dependent on others' plans, too. We are all interconnected. This pandemic has magnified this fact even more in our economy. Our packaging, our ingredients, our communication through technology...so many things are tied to one another. As we plan the best we can (and we are honestly planning well into January, February, and March 2021 right now), it is inevitable that plans will change as we work with our supply chain, the demands from YOU, our chocolate friends, the changes in restrictions, and all of the things that we can never really perfectly plan!

I also said "no" to some good opportunities which allowed me to say, "hell, yes" to some really exciting opportunities!

I love planning and although I can plan for "work" no problem, planning for my personal life takes a little more effort. This time last year was the first time I took a vacation since starting Choco le`a. I mean a REAL vacation where I'm not checking emails daily, texting with the crew, or traveling for work. It was also our first family vacation and the first time our kids went on an airplane.

It was chaotic, as I never had imagined taking a two-year-old and a four-year-old to Japan, but we didn't want to miss the "four year old magic" other moms told me about. They said I needed to do it or would miss it. That "four year old magic" is when they see everything with wonder and amazement and magic.

That's exactly what every sight, sound, and thing was for Aubrey. Starting with us spending our first night after arriving sleeping in the airport since we were stuck there during a typhoon. Remember, not everything goes according to our plan, but we plan the best we can as things happen!

We planned it out, but thankfully being married to a non-planning, go-with-the-flow guy, we also adjusted when things went awry. But that magic that moms told me about, that was real! We experienced it in both our planned and random unplanned adventures. Yes,

Disneyland and seeing princesses in a parade was unreal, but so was trying ikura and all kinds of new foods, with the kids discovering they loved it. It was pure magic visiting light, science, history, and technology museums and seeing the real deal of their favorite thing: dinosaur bones!

Riding a rollercoaster for the first time and falling in love with the thrilling speed, spending time in a Japanese family's home and experiencing the subtle daily differences while asking ten million questions about it all was so amazing. It was such an incredible experience! I am so glad I took other moms' advice and as a result, our hope is to plan a family trip every several years to give our kids these kinds of experiences in different places around the world.

This real vacation, or just a really long break, was so refreshing, that I pre-committed to another vacation immediately after. I planned one year in advance so I would be sure to take another big break this time for myself in 2020. Because who are we kidding? Taking a two- and four-year-old on their first trip to a foreign country most often doesn't feel like a break at all, but just results in higher anxiety for us parents!

2020 was going to be my first girls' trip, my first trip to new countries, all planned by an expert traveler friend who finds great deals. This one was pre-paid for air and hotel to Dublin and Lisbon. Honestly, I didn't even know where those places were on the map when I said yes, but agreed because it was a, "hell, yes" to go on vacation!

But as you know and as we have all experienced, not all plans go through. We will not be going this year but hope we can plan for a future time. That's the thing about plans. They change. Some things are out of our control. In the midst of it, we need to learn to trust God and His plans.

"For I know the plans I have for you declares the Lord. Plans to prosper you and not to harm you. Plans to give you a hope and a future."
-Jeremiah 29:11

I do believe in the importance of planning, but I also know it is just as important to be flexible to change plans, go with the flow, and trust our Heavenly Father. The big vision for 2020 was "peace." I've found that for me, I have to plan in the goals, tasks, and daily-to-do's that bring this peace in my life. God also stretches me to search for His peace through His own plans…the things we totally didn't plan for!

Lesson Learned: Make time to plan the things that matter most. If you don't, everything else will make its way into your day and take up all of your time that you can never get back. Some things are ok and even good, but they are not great. If you always say yes to the things that are just "ok" and "good", you can also miss out on the GREAT.

But you will not regret that you planned for the things that fill you up, bring you the most joy, peace, fun, energy, or care. Even if things don't go according to plan, at least you tried to get it in there and probably got more of it in your life than you would have if you didn't plan for any of it.

Opportunity Now: Plan backwards. Take the big vision, the peace you are searching for, or whatever it is and break it down into quarterly plans, monthly goals, weekly tasks, and daily priorities to do while also being sure to plug in those much needed breaks, fun, and self-care before your planner fills up! Get it in there and commit to it. Again, I am far from being an expert in this, but it is the opportunity I am trying to establish as a routine and hope you will do it with me too!

Hope For Our Future: We don't know what the future holds but as we plan for the best, we are setting ourselves up for the most optimal opportunities. Even if they go differently or not exactly as planned, at least we had a goal and a plan to get there and we're working towards something meaningful. Something that really matters. The best is when you align your plans to be the same as God's plans, for His plans never fail. Yours may, but His won't.

My prayer for you, my chocolate friend, is that you take the time to try and figure out what God's plan is for you, and build your plans around that. If you're not sure what that is, check what the Bible says. It says to love God and love others. That's what He wants for all of us and that's a great plan to start with. Figure out how you can love Him and love others...including yourself.

With love always,
Your chocolate friend, Erin

"'Love the Lord your God with all your heart and with all your soul and with all your mind.' This is the first and greatest commandment. And the second is like it: 'Love your neighbor as yourself.'
-Matthew 22:37-39

— OCTOBER 5 —

Week No. 30
Routine 10: Learn

What have we learned in this pandemic?

Did you experience a great **loss**, or discover an even greater **strength** inside of you?

Did you give up **exhausted,** or did you learn to get **focused**?

Did you hold onto **hope,** or did you **forget** who you are, your purpose, and where you came from?

Did you change your **perspective** and find **gratitude** in everything around you?

Did you realize life is a series of different **seasons** and that you should hold onto your **faith** constantly through it all?

Did you find that going through this **movement** was a challenge you weren't ready for, but still managed to treat those around you with **kindness**?

Did you have **fun** or were you straight up **uncomfortable**?

Did you **persevere** through it all and strive for **excellence**?

Did you just move **onward** however you could, but did it in **style**?

Did you keep it **simple** and focus on the little things that you realized are really the big things in life, like your family or **kids**?

These were the twenty **reflections** that I personally processed through during the first twenty weeks of the pandemic. I learned a lot about our God, my family and friends around me, my business, our community, our leadership, our country, and our world. Mostly, I learned a lot about myself. Through journaling these reflections and vulnerably hashing it all out, there were many lessons learned.

After the first twenty weeks, my hope is that you have

started to take those things you learned about yourself and created routines to help live IN this pandemic. For week #30, routine #10, I know that there is still a lot to **learn**. We should continually learn how we can grow and improve, using what we are experiencing.

How

How do I keep on learning?

1. Find the lesson learned in everything.

2. Surround myself with people and experiences I want to learn from.

Having a mindset that there is always something to learn has made experiencing the not so good stuff that just seems to keep "happening" be a little more bearable, and a little more meaningful. This mindset has helped me to get through the hard stuff as I reflect on it and search for the lesson learned as we have done together here.

Some learning we can set up and do intentionally for ourselves. The people and experiences that I learn from, I find mostly come from one of three things:

1. Events & observations

2. Conversations with people

3. Reading books & listening to podcasts

1. Events & Observations

The most common way to learn is to attend school, an event, or be in an environment that is intended to teach you something. A lot of the things I learned to grow Choco le`a was done this way. From signing up for online courses on chocolate since I couldn't go to Europe, to attending community events with resources on how to register and start a business in Hawai`i. These are great opportunities to learn a lot of information, in a short amount of time.

I learned a lot about the importance of product packaging and presentation at a trade show in Japan, about the importance of paying attention to our finances from a business seminar, about the importance of mentorship through a professional development conference, and how to do various other things like export, trademark your business, and food safety and certification through workshops.

Learning the regulations for operating a business in Hawai`i was critical. This week was kicked off with an inspection from the Department of Health to renew our food permit and receive another green pass to continue on. As a food manufacturer, if we don't make the effort to learn how to do things right, it may cause a lot of detrimental mistakes, and could cost us our business.

Observations outside of our business that have nothing to do with chocolates can also teach us a lot. Going to a restaurant and watching the prep process or going to a retail shop and experiencing the displays, the service and how you feel as a customer provides great experiential lessons. Trying something new and kind of scary like modeling, wakeboarding, or judging can teach you what you are made of and that if you face your fears, you can survive and maybe even discover that you're good at it, or that you enjoy it!

Thankfully with the internet, a lot of the "events" that we can learn from are in the palms of our hands. Definitely not the same, but still something you can immerse yourself in to search for little golden nuggets. I've had to do that with shopping online or pre-ordering take-out food online for pick up. From these little excursions, I have learned a lot about this new way of business and sometimes just experiencing it helps you get over the uncertainty of how it all works. I always say we would have never done curbside if we weren't forced to learn how and now we love it! Especially because you love how convenient, quick, safe, sweet and simple it is.

2. Conversations with People

We can learn a lot if we listen, observe, and ask lots of questions in our conversations with others. Pre-pandemic, one of my favorite things to do was take team members with me to see the behind-the-scenes of other businesses, watch everyone at work, and ask questions about what everyone is doing and why. It's fascinating! It's how we can learn from others' years of experiences and the tips and tricks they figured out along the way. It can also be very helpful even if the businesses we observed had nothing to do with chocolates! We would also be inspired to hear the same responses everywhere. It takes a lot of hard work, mistakes, a good attitude, perseverance, and consistent learning to improve and get better.

With visiting other businesses not being an option

now-a-days, I try to have more conversations with different people outside of my usual scope of work to learn their current challenges with the pandemic, their work, and how they are overcoming it. This includes conversations with employees at both ends of the spectrum within the Department of Education, other local small business owners and a friend on a brand new entrepreneurial journey; a stranger who quickly became a friend over the start of her new leap of faith assignment; a family member in a health crisis; and a store clerk about how sales are, what has changed, what feels different, and how are they adjusting to the changes.

As a team, our time together to talk during our "break" week of planning for the holidays really helped me to reflect on past frustrations and successes; what we learned from them, what we are learning about all of YOU and what you like, plus how we can adjust as a business to think and operate differently. These discussion times of sharing, listening, and asking questions with a diverse group of perspectives, experiences, and skill sets really helped us! It's enabled us to come together with what we can do to bring joy and peace to as many people as possible and keep this business going and growing.

3. Reading Books & Listening to Podcasts

With a lot of my time spent at home currently, reading books and listening to podcasts are probably some of my favorite things to do to get inspired and learn. I read everything from business finance to parenting, home organization to leading large corporations, going boldly after big audacious dreams to living very simply. I also enjoy reading books with personal stories such as the memoirs of world leaders, as well as a local church member's experience of the sudden and tragic death of his spouse, raising two girls alone, and learning to forgive and find hope again. Of course, reading the Bible daily is the truth I always return to.

As I read the books and listen to the podcasts of these high performing, high achieving, yet very real, honest, confident, humble, and inspiring people, there are two trends I notice that almost all of them have in common:

1. They love the Lord

2. They make their own health and wellness a priority

I've learned that to be able to do the work they are doing and live the lives they have with their families I have to be willing to put in the work that they have put in as well.

I started expanding my horizons and am learning more about what wellness means and how to make it a priority. To help me get started, I picked up "Body Love" by nutritionist Kelly LeVeque several months ago and finally finished reading it this week. She teaches us about our bodies, hormones, chemical balances, big science words, and things that I usually don't read about; however, I wanted to expand my horizons since I have been trying to figure out how to get more energy!

Back in June, I started drinking her smoothies every single day and started cooking some of her recipes, especially since we were running out of food to make other than the weekly tacos. Though I really did not like the smoothie for the first two weeks, now it has become a steady routine that I do almost automatically and find it refreshing on these really hot mornings here in Hawai'i. As for what I am learning about wellness…well I still have a long way to go.

For me, the ultimate goal is to live a well-rounded life with good routines turned into healthy habits so I can accomplish all of the things that God put in my heart with the people that I love. And boy do I need more energy to teach the kids and keep up with their non-stop energy! Also, to change and start up this business again with my chocolate family and all of you, as well as exploring brand new adventures that I know nothing about.

In terms of wellness, I do the same things I do when I am trying to learn. I listen. I observe. I ask questions. Only I do it to myself. I listen to my body. I observe how I feel and what I did and ate before and write it down. I started to question why I did something and if I was happy with the effect. I looked for patterns.

Coronavirus has made me hyperaware of hygiene and health. I want to ensure my family and I are at the most optimal health - physical, mental, emotional, financial, spiritual - to endure this virus and others. So this week, I have spent a lot of time on this routine of learning new information. Researching new resources. Observing my own patterns and becoming aware of my routines and habits, good and bad.

362

If you'd like to join me on this journey too, heck we will go through it together as friends. I am no expert in it, but the more we can learn from each other, the better. I am not a good cook and I already made everything I know how to in the past 30 weeks at home and need new recipes and ideas for fuel that are quick, healthy, and simple.

I am slowly learning to make things with ingredients fresh from our little garden, just like the online show during this pandemic for my family has been "Li Ziqi." Since we were introduced to her by my sister-in-law and started watching her on YouTube this May, my daughter and husband have been obsessed and started a garden. They want to grow everything in nature and cook with it. I love how Li Ziqi makes all of the food look so good with an incredible presentation for just her and her grandma to enjoy at home!

Anyhow, I am now finding myself reading more recipes and learning about new ingredients as I search for information to expand the scope of what I know and can do. Thank you to those of you who have already shared your favorite books with me!

I'm still learning!

The reason I wrote this book is because I want to touch and inspire people I will never have the opportunity to meet. There are so many people around this world that are looking for something. Perhaps how to do something with what God has given them, or who are searching for His peace, joy, and love. I really want to be a friend to them in their journey and share what I have learned! I want to be able to put a book in their hand, or give you the opportunity to put a book in their hand, so we can pass on a love for learning and growing in life together.

Learning is a lifelong thing, if we decide to make it a routine. It is a choice. We can simply decide that "we know it all" or "don't care" and just be, but I believe God created us for more. We need to invest in ourselves, our body, mind, spirit, talents, and resources He gave us, and do even more with them, rather than just sit on them. One of my all-time favorite quotes is: "What you are is God's gift to you. What you make of yourself, is your gift to God."

"His master said to him, 'Well done, good and faithful servant. You have been faithful over a little; I will set you over much." -Matthew 25:21

Lesson Learned: There is always a lesson to learn. We can learn from our experiences, events, observations, conversations with people, listening to others, asking questions, and through books and podcasts. Some lessons are harder to grasp than others, but as long as we are continuously striving to grow and be better, we are making progress and moving forward. And the more we learn and know, the better choices we make, and the better lives we can live.

Opportunity Now: Pick up a book to read or find a podcast to start learning something new. To give you a start, some of my favorite recent books have been "Grace Not Perfection" by Emily Ley; "Girl Stop Apologizing" by Rachel Hollis; and "The 15 Invaluable Laws of Growth" by John Maxwell. Some of my favorite podcasters include John Maxwell, Andy Stanley, Trent Shelton, Oprah Winfrey, and Craig Groeschel. But my all-time favorite book is the Bible. Make it a goal to finish one book by the end of this year. Perhaps even the one that you started multiple times.

Hope For Our Future: If we can take the lessons learned from other people and apply them to our own lives, we can avoid the mistakes, the hurt, the pain, the costs that they endured, learn from them, and choose better for ourselves. It's almost as if we can skip past what others had to go through, by simply listening and learning from them.

My prayer for you my chocolate friend, is that you continuously learn more about yourself and the world around you to find ways to make it better. I'm right here with you on this never-ending journey to keep learning and growing.

With love always,
Your chocolate friend, Erin

"I will instruct you and teach you in the way you should go; I will counsel you with my loving eye on you." -Psalm 32:8

— OCTOBER 12 —

Week No. 31
Routine 11: Try

First and foremost, thank you. Thank you for giving our chocolates a try, this book a read, and our business the opportunity to continue "Bringing peace to our world, one chocolate at a time." #companymissionstatement

These real, raw, and personal reflections that came from my heart began as my attempt to stay in touch with you during the shut-down, to feel connected even though our shop had been closed for seven months, and to deepen our relationships through sharing these stories.

I tried to do this, even if it was a little scary, because I believed it could bring you the joy, love, and peace we had always wanted our company to bring through chocolates, in a new and different way.

And it did, week after week.

We have become closer chocolate friends and so many of you have shared how much our weekly emails and blogs have helped bring hope in this unbelievable time. So far, we have shared a total of thirty weeks here together - the first twenty weeks were reflecting on what was happening in our Choco le`a world, then we continued and shared ten routines to help us start LIVING IN this pandemic.

I am going to try and write ten final routines that I genuinely feel are helping me through this time. That means we will end up with 20 reflections and 20 routines to wrap up the year 2020! I did not plan it to be that way. It's so God! This is what HE said…

"…Write in a book all the words I have spoken to you." -Jeremiah 30:2

After that, I will try to continue and write shorter emails about something else. Something free I can continue to share with everyone. Something positive that I hope will bring hope. Something helpful that will provide information and tactical tips like lessons learned in owning a small business. Or perhaps something that is purely "for-fun" entertainment like #behindthebusiness of Choco le`a. I'm not sure of the specifics just yet, but I am going to try something different in 2021.

We have learned a lot and our last chapter was the routine to "learn." This week #31, routine #11 is to **try**. It's great to learn but growth happens when we take action and try to implement what we learn. After we are equipped with new knowledge or have experienced something we want more of in life, we must go for it! We grow when we try new experiences, try to look at things from different perspectives, try to be with others, try to get out of our comfort zone, and try to live a life in faith.

I tried a lot of new things this past week. It solidified just how important it is, to make this action a regular routine in life rather than wait, make excuses, run away, or hide.

Some of the new things that I tried this week were cooking new recipes. I tried eating healthier, tried a different hike with a different friend; tried signing up for a new commitment with a coach; tried teaming up with an accountability friend to help me meet some of my new goals. I tried modeling. I tried new foods, tried wearing my first pair of fins and snorkeling with fish (Eeeek...way out of my comfort zone, but not as bad as I had imagined. It will get better! When I came back to shore, I also found out from my husband that I had been wearing my fins backwards!).

I tried changing up some of the procedures behind the scenes that would best fit my team's needs and the big picture vision of where we wanted to take our company. We ended the work week trying our absolutely scrumptious new truffles for November in our Fall flavors: Pumpkin Pie, Caramel Apple, & Maple Pecan!!!

Some of the things I tried may not seem big to you, but each of us have different commitments that scare us, adventures that thrill us, and obstacles that challenge us.

A quote that really helps me to get started and try new things is this: **"You're never good the first time."**

This simple quote almost seemed to have set me free! Like I was excused to suck at something and just do it, and no one would care! I didn't need to worry about comparison. It was simply stating that as expected, I wouldn't be very good. That provided some strange relief, that I might as well just do it.

In fact, that was the exact quote I heard that gave me courage week after week to write. Even when I wasn't completely happy with my work, or I felt it was coming across the wrong way and was too much about me. I still hoped it would touch lives and make a difference for people, allowing me to connect deeper with them, since the drafts did no good just sitting there.

One person that I connected deeper with through this was Allison Izu Song, a local clothing designer who empowers women to embrace who they are and #liveyourletter. This week, I had the opportunity to be a brand ambassador for her and her small local business which I absolutely love!

Allison asked me to model and promote her new "elevated basics, work from home" collection and although I am no professional model, I respect this leading momtrepreneur, love her team, the quality of her locally made pieces, style, comfort, and fit and so I went for it! I discovered it was so much fun! Modeling was actually a lot of fun, especially knowing I was helping to support and promote her company in some small way.

Giving our own Choco le`a Allison (Ally) a chance to see the behind the scenes of THIS Allison with her team was an incredible collaborative field trip. We were able to exchange notes, tips and honestly, we've been in our own bubble for so long that getting out and interacting with others pivoting in the pandemic was refreshing. I'm so glad I said "hell, yes!" because it was an answered prayer that I hadn't even realized at the time.

I was journaling one morning (week #22, routine #2: mornings). I came across my goal list, which I had written a while back, "Goal: To become a chosen ambassador to brands I love, modeling their products and helping them promote their business, while learning from them!" I didn't even realize at that moment, that thing I was being asked to try and do was the thing I had been hoping and praying for!

"Thy word is a lamp unto my feet and a light unto my path." -Psalm 119:105

374

What's similar between Allison Izu and us at Choco le`a, is that we are both trying to figure out what our community wants and likes and how we can meet those needs. So chocolate friends, please don't be afraid to speak up and share! Make suggestions and the best we can do is try and continue to build on the business as we learn what the demands are and improve in what could be possible blind spots for us. Tell us what you have always wanted us to try, but never have! The crazier sounding your idea, the more we welcome it!

Another local entrepreneur we love, Colin Hazama, is someone that we have worked with for years at various big special events, first at the Sheraton Waikiki then at the Royal Hawaiian Hotel where he was the Executive Chef. When this shut down first started, I noticed how Chef Colin took action and began actively sharing his cooking from home on social media.

This week, I tried his new dishes that were well presented for friendly take-out service in his new adventure on his own, C4 Table. We've seen him among many other chocolate friends in the tourism, events, and hospitality industry, try and find other things to do and Chef Colin recently took the leap of faith to try his own business and I know he will do really well. Congratulations Chef Colin and the C4 team on your delicious upscale comfort cuisine!

After we try something for the first time we can get better. Each time we try is an opportunity to build our confidence. To paint a picture of this in a very simple and tangible way, I will reference my personal weekly supermarket trips.

I am not the best cook. In fact, the first few times I cooked for my husband, it sucked. I quickly learned how much better and faster he was at it and thankfully, he also loves to cook, so he took on the majority of this responsibility in our home. But during this pandemic I tried to cook more and find quick and simple healthy recipes that everyone would love. True story: I often brought home the wrong spices or vegetables or wrong type of meat for what my husband wanted to make when I did the grocery shopping and he had to change things up on the spot!

It would also take me quite a while to find things as I walked back and forth across the store trying to go down recipe lists. Now, I research recipes prior, discuss requests with my husband and kids, and make my list before I go. I list ingredients needed into sections of where I know I will find things in the market. Then I go in and work from left to right, with the goal to never backtrack and get in and out within so many minutes gathering everything needed for the week.

To make it fun, I even make it a game and time myself before going in to see if I can get out faster than the week before. It's how I take weekly routines and try to make them "fun!" If I could get things done in time and under budget, I would reward myself with flowers as a way to "celebrate." (week #25, routine #5: celebrate) *I hope you're still incorporating some of the past routines we've been trying!

Trust me...it was a process to get to this point and be able to confidently whip up a meal and get a thumbs up from everyone. It took a lot of trying again and again, but it did get better and easier every time I did.

Taking calculated risks and trying again and again in business can also result in improvements, opportunities opening up, or lessons learned. Some things we tried recently that we really had no idea if you'd like were our bulk Crunch a le`a bars; baking and snacking macadamia nut bags; unrehearsed and unscripted chocolate tasting videos that were video bombed by my kids, and online tutorials of how to place a pre-order.

We have learned just how much some of you really appreciate step-by-step instructions, visuals, explanations, and behind-the-scenes of what we do on Instagram, so we're trying to share them more on Facebook and via YouTube links. In the past, we tried other things we weren't sure about like our Choco le`a Kids' Club, Dip & Decorate workshops, coffee to pair with chocolates and so much more. Everything we do whether, it became a long-lasting success, or a "here today and gone tomorrow," was something we had to try to find out.

What things will **you** try this week?

I encourage you to try. Be better. Live better. I encourage you to try and lift up those around you with loving words, a smile, a helping hand, a generous gift, an air hug, a random act of kindness, or by sharing a new experience together. I encourage you to try and get out of your bubble and safely explore something new.

Lesson Learned: We probably won't be good the first

time we try something new and that's totally okay!!! Sometimes just taking the first step and trying is the hardest. But once you do and realize it's not that bad, you will learn, know better, perhaps get better, and carry on. Or, you may actually discover something fun, something you're good at, something you want to learn more about and you'll be glad you gave it a try!

"They were all trying to frighten us, thinking, 'Their hands will get too weak for the work, and it will not be completed.' But I prayed, 'Now strengthen my hands.'" -Nehemiah 6:9

Opportunity Now: Try something new! Not sure where to start? Try and place a pre-order online! If you're someone still reading this and still feeling like you can't do it, we are here to help you learn how you can with an updated video tutorial. Watch how to order online, how curbside pick-up works, and how you can feel confident that you can get your chocolates in this new way! Some of our friends refer to it as "shopping Choco le`a from the comfort of home with sweet and simple curbside pick-up." And if you're already comfortable with ordering online, try something else totally new that has been tugging at your heart, but you have been hesitant to try.

Hope For Our Future: We never know what we're capable of and what we're missing, until we try!

My prayer for you, my chocolate friend, is that you try. Try whatever God has placed on your heart that you're scared to say or do but know that if you can get over your fear and step out in faith, you will experience something so big and so exciting! I'm doing it right alongside you as you read this. I am trying a lot of new things in my life that are scary for me too and may make me look far from perfect. I'm not here to live a perfect life. I'm here to live a life with purpose and sometimes trying things will help us further discover what that purpose is.

With love always,
Your chocolate friend, Erin

"For the Spirit God gave us does not make us timid, but gives us power, love, and self-discipline."
-2 Timothy 1:7

— OCTOBER 19—

Week No. 32
Routine 12: Choose

Ok, I feel like this is a pep talk to myself, straight out of my journal. I did after all say these are real, raw, and personal reflections as I process this pandemic and how to live in it with routines that help. Well, this is THE routine above all the others because for each routine to work, we must choose to do them.

The word "choose" seems to be appearing everywhere more and more...at least I'm noticing it more. Choose to vote. Choose joy. Choose how we want to live. Choose how we want to think. At the root of it, we have a choice.

But that's just it. We - you and I - HAVE to choose. If we don't, things will be decided for us, which made me realize that even after we have routines like "learn" and "try" we still need to have a routine to "choose" to do so. Choose to continue. Choose to improve. Choose to change it up. Choose to stop.

When our alarm rings in the morning, we choose to snooze or get up and do our morning routine. When we come across tough times, we choose to pray and keep on trying or complain and give up. When it rains, we choose if we still want to go out and move or make an excuse. In my weekly emails and blog, I have to choose what I want to share. Often times, I'll start with a negative attitude as the words flow and I start to vent, but as I continue to write, I choose to find the good in it. The lesson learned, the opportunity now, and our hope for our future.

Our world has become a place with so many choices that it is sometimes hard to choose what is right. We start to look to the media, our friends, our leaders and influencers to make the decisions for us. For me personally, when all of the noise and voices get loud and confusing, I choose to go to the source, the Bible, for the answers. I always find it helps me to make the right decisions based on the commandments, the way Jesus did things, and the way He says for us to live our lives which is pleasing to Him. I am FAR from perfect and don't always get it right for sure. But when I do choose to do it His way, I always gain a peace about my decision, even if it's not conventional, expected, or what the world wants of me.

"Do not conform to the pattern of this world, but be transformed by the renewing of your mind." - Romans 12:2

I've been thinking a lot about Choco le`a's future, but someone asked me a question this week that was worded with a different perspective and it made me really think.

"Where do YOU want this business to go Erin? What do YOU, Erin, want for Choco le`a?"

Lately, I've been thinking a lot about what other people want: what makes the most business sense? I have been trying to take our best guess about what will happen and when, based on predictions about this virus and the recovery of our economy. What would be in the best interest for my chocolate family and our chocolate friends. What's the most comfortable future everyone expects for this little local chocolate shop?

But when asked this question, "What do I want for this

business?" I turned back to my devotions, my journal, and focused on God. I had honestly relieved him of this "responsibility" (as if I didn't want to burden Him) and took it on myself to think through all these things. So I found myself asking Him again, "Geez...what do YOU want me to do with this business?"

The funny thing is, even though I'm asking God what HE wants for my business, He knows the desires of MY heart! When I think I don't know what I want, He reveals what is deep in my heart. He wants us to experience joy in our lives. He wants us to prosper AND have peace. That sounds almost impossible to me when I start to think of how I can accomplish all of that, but then I am gently reminded that Matthew 19:26 reads, *"With man this is impossible, but with God, all things are possible."*

Right then and there, I found that the same dream He put on my heart a few years ago was still inside of me. It was just buried down deeper by the weight of the changes in economy, lack of resources, time, skills, space, etc.

I started scribbling, writing, and letting the ideas flow from my pen onto the pages as I envisioned Choco le`a's future, both the big picture along with some small details. We will continue to use Choco le`a to be a platform for God's glory. To "bring peace to our world, one chocolate at a time." The dream is the same, but the thing that is very different is the how and the delayed timing. That, I feel as though I didn't get to choose. I guess the only thing I can choose right now, is my attitude towards it.

What am I trying to say? Well, with all of the routines we have explored together, you have to choose what works for you and what doesn't. Tweak the ones you love and have found a rhythm in. Let go of the ones that don't serve you and the purpose for your life. These are just my routines that I share with you. You need to choose for yourself what you value, and make sure you focus on doing those routines again and again.

This past week I did choose the good routines that served me. I also tried to think of the final eight routines that I consider most important in my life right now, to share here with you. Truthfully, there are a lot of things I really want to learn, try, and do, but am limited by time, energy and resources.

So I must make a choice. It's frustrating to have

sacrificed so much to grow a business in the past six years and then watch as you lose so much, so fast, so unexpectedly to return to what feels like year one. I want to build it up again and want to do it all right now, but at the same time, I am "held back" with so many things out of my control.

But even as I write this, I have to choose to stop whining right here and now as I feel my emotions swelling up and getting the best of me. I cannot compare. I cannot get distracted. I cannot be discouraged by how slow this is all going. I need to choose to change my perspective and have a more positive outlook.

These talks I have with myself are ongoing! It is in difficult times like this that I find myself throwing my hands up in surrender and asking God to help me choose what's best. I myself sometimes don't know what that is!

"For we live by faith, not by sight."
-2 Corinthians 5:7

But the most amazing thing is, that when I open my heart to let Him in, He's always there. This week, I heard Him through someone else. To be super real with you, this is what I heard Him say, *"Start small. Everything starts small. Grow gradually. Consistently. Fight. Keep fighting for your dream."*

What will you choose this week? What will you choose to start? What will you fight for?

Lesson Learned: The one thing usually holding us back is ourselves. Our minds are a battlefield and we're making ten million decisions a day hoping that we make the right ones. We battle to choose what we should do versus what we want to do and choose what is right versus what is easy and self-serving. Choosing to take action or choosing not to take action is still a choice. Choices need to be made or they will be made for us.

Opportunity Now: Choose what works for you and start implementing routines in your life that will help you to be the best version of yourself and who God created you to be. Choose not to do the things that don't serve this purpose. Figure out your routines and then choose to do them over and over again.

Hope For Our Future: We have a choice. I choose to start small. Build slowly again. But keep dreaming impossibly big so when it happens, people will ask how, and I will respond with the same verse that spoke to me, *"...with God, all things are possible."*

My prayer for you my chocolate friend, is that you choose a better outlook and live life to the fullest. That you choose to be the best version of yourself possible. Believe me, I totally understand and know it's not easy. Remember, these are my own journal entries and I share them openly with you in hopes that it will help you to reflect and live your life too.

I felt like I sacrificed so much to grow this business to get it to where it was. To have to start all over again can be discouraging, but I choose to look at it as a fresh start to start dreaming again. Connect with God again, and enjoy where He will take all of us slowly, season by season.

With love always,
Your chocolate friend, Erin

"Do not despise these small beginnings, for the Lord rejoices to see the work begin." - *Zechariah 4:10*

— OCTOBER 26 —

Week No. 33
Routine 13: Break

Notifications off.

From the events at the very start of this week, I knew that this week would need to include "re-st." But it wasn't really resting. For me it was more about a break for re-freshing, re-flecting, re-setting and re-connecting. Taking a **break** was my routine for this week.

Taking a break doesn't mean doing nothing and letting go of all of your responsibilities and obligations. Rather, it's about taking short little breaks here and there for yourself; taking longer breaks for bigger chunks of time away, or a break away from things you're unwittingly spending too much time and energy on or worrying about. It's letting the universe continue without you and guess what...it will! The show goes on and it's ok to allow myself some breaks!

Whether you are a business owner, employee, wife, mom, distance learning supervisor, friend, or a number three on the Ennegram test...you get it. We don't take breaks often, until we are forced to. We like doing, not waiting. We like problem solving, not sitting and complaining. We like progress, not slow-moving results. And whether we like to admit it or not, we need breaks.

This week, as part of my routine, I took short breaks here and there, and one long 24 hour break away from everyone. I'm so grateful I was able to because it was the kind of break I needed. Ironically, taking a break actually takes some planning! I started by doing what I could. I turned off all of my app notifications. I silenced my phone and left it in my purse for stretches of time. I simply needed a little break. Not a "tune out the world," but a re-centering with myself without a "ding" sound every few seconds!

If you follow me on Instagram @yourchocolatefriend I was MIA, so maybe you thought the routine was to "unplug." I did that too. I have already turned off my notifications long ago on IG, but this week, I logged out of my accounts. Ally took over the business feed and did a great job! I definitely didn't check my Facebook or LinkedIn, gave the team a heads up that I was going to try to not do the daily grind stuff and emails for 2 days to which Ally, Tori, and Christine were like, "Of course, no problem. We got it!" #Godblessthem they're amazing! They called in the help of some of our extended volunteer chocolate family members who happily jumped in.

I gave myself a pass on one of the many monthly meetings I have been Zooming in along with for months, postponed a podcast, rescheduled a couple of online meetings, and actually shut down my desktop. It never shuts down. A bunch of windows are always open ready to jump from task to task. You know how that dreaded "spinning rainbow of death" comes out (that's what I call it), and everything takes so long to open, or it seems like it's taking so long to think. I guess it's because it never gets a break and too many windows are simultaneously open and running. Kind of like us! Ha! I think even my desktop was re-lieved to go dark for a bit.

For two days I completely put away the TV remote.

On other days, I did turn the TV on to, ironically, finally watch "The Social Dilemma" #soooointeresting, and also watched part of the series "The Last Dance" with Michael Jordan. #soooogood. When I needed a mental break, I watched these shows which funnily enough, made me reflect even more if I had any bad addictions or obsessions that I needed to break away from!

Taking breaks is a routine that I need to actually schedule because I naturally love doing, and not resting. The funny thing is, for the time that I was on a break, I got a lot of stuff done! Different stuff. Not the usual emailing, cleaning, answering this and that, and checking off to-do lists, but the things that really move the needle! We hired another full-time team member back to our chocolate family. We entered a national competition and wrote a reflection about how we pivoted during this pandemic and are keeping the business moving forward, bringing hope and peace, starting in Hawai`i. As a chocolate family, we discussed the really big challenges, both personally and professionally, that we are facing and not going away anytime soon, and how to not just push through them, but really use it to fuel us to do something better and find a better way. Taking time to think through these things felt good. No, actually, it felt great!

While on break, I also opened some books. I wrote in my journal. I floated around in the ocean. Like actually floated on my back, looked at the clouds slowly moving, accidentally swallowed some salt water, and listened to the sound of waves in the distance. I took a walk in the mountains and sat in a garden (Even Aubrey seemed to benefit from this break. Like it was good for her soul too and a much-needed rest from the school screen). For me it was like my way of re-centering, re-aligning, and most importantly, re-connecting with not only myself, but with God.

I get frustrated when I can't hear Him. But often times, it's because I am too busy listening to everyone and trying to do everything. That's when I miss Him. It sounds weird, but I miss our talks. I miss our intimate time together where I ask a question or make a request or throw some cry out to the sky and wait a long, long time before talking again to just listen.

What does a conversation with God sound like? It's like venting to a best friend and our Heavenly Father. This week I told Him I really miss going out. I miss my kids having more interactions with other kids, their friends and playing. I miss meeting friends for coffee. I miss romantic dinners with my husband. I miss traveling. (Ironically though, I took 5 work trips last year and was exhausted and asked God if I could travel less this year and be home with my kids more. I didn't expect a full stop of no traveling and home with the kids all of the time, but I guess I need to be more specific with my prayers! I digress.)

I miss so many things. And I just cried and cried. It was one of those weeks of crying. With so many things happening, health struggles amongst numerous challenges, I honestly just started to feel a little depression sneak in. I felt darkness. Thankfully I recognized it and knew it was time for a major break.

"Come to me, all you who are weary and burdened, and I will give you rest. Take my yoke upon you and learn from me, for I am gentle and humble in heart, and you will find rest for your souls.
-Matthew 11:28-30

As you can see this is an ongoing journey. This is not a "cry week" and be done and accept where we are, or a "cry out to God week", get the answer and all is well.

It's ongoing. And the reason is because we are constantly evolving. With every experience, we are changing as people.

Our perspectives are changing. Our minds and hearts are changing. Our plans have to keep changing and the priorities have to keep changing. With so many constant changes, we need to take frequent breaks to re-evaluate. Re-align. Re-fine. Re-prioritize. Re-_____ whatever!!! I guess you could argue the routine would be "Re" instead of "break!"

"And he said to them, "Come away by yourselves to a desolate place and rest a while." For many were coming and going, and they had no leisure even to eat." -Mark 6:31

I'm taking a break as I type this from the balcony of the beautiful Kahala Hotel! Nothing but the sound of the waterfall below, my fingers on the keys, and some planes flying overhead. It's a ghost town with occupancy at eleven percent. This is an incredible resort that we've partnered with for several years providing some of their chocolates. I used to walk through the loading dock and to the meeting rooms off the beautiful grounds.

This time, I am here in a room for the first time on my semi-annual staycation "break" which is way overdue (something I love to do and would like to do more frequently). This time I am actually not walking around talking to the workers like I normally would, fitting in meetings, and doing photo shoots with the chocolates. I'm literally taking a break!

At check in, the long-time loyal employee somehow recognized me by name and thanked me for the years we had made those delicious chocolates for them. That was so sweet. And then that was the end of a chocolate conversation - the shortest one I've ever had in a hotel!

I booked myself here at the Kahala for a full twenty four hours (well actually twenty six hours with their current early check in and late check out special) of no kids' voices or cleaning or helping anyone get anything. I just made myself coffee, slept alone, woke up when I felt like it, and sat in my pajamas feeling refreshed! And I don't regret it! I took a shower alone. I went to the bathroom with no one following me in or banging on the door. I know right now some of you with little ones are nodding and saying, "Yes sister I get you. I know what you mean." I just really wanted to be alone for a little while.

"And I say, 'Oh, that I had wings like a dove! I would fly away and be at rest.'" -Psalm 55:6

It is important that I share here how I felt after this experience. I am re-charged and I'm ready to work and get back to reality with a fresh perspective. That short, but luxurious break really made me feel special, made me feel cared for, and the distraction took away the darkness long enough for me to re-set and get re-focused on what mattered. It reminded me what I needed to do, and of His truth and His love for me so I can really keep on living life to the fullest.

When I got back home, I found little daily "breaks" I could continue to allow myself to have since the reality is, we can't "run-away" to a resort for breaks anytime we feel like we want one! So for long term maintenance, I started to really develop something I didn't have set like a morning routine. Meet my nightime routine:

Nightime Routine

I am trying to get my seven hours of sleep every night and am striving for seven and a half. I am going to try putting my phone away in another room at least one hour before bed and not check the emails, the messages, the texts, and the things that can wait. I will make sure I rest my eyes as I learn more about screens and blue light. (Yikes! I need to buy an old fashioned alarm clock I guess). I will slow down the stimulation before bedtime and fill it only with the things we do now, like stories to the kids, Bible, family prayer, shadow puppets on the ceiling, cuddles, and a book for myself to read to sleep, but with no digital distractions.

Eventually, I will build it up to enjoying a cup of chamomile or de-caffeinated tea out of a cute mug for 15 minutes alone outside under the stars or a string of those cafe lights I always wanted. For now, I'll take what I can get and take breaks as much as I can to have the energy needed to keep living the life God calls me to.

After all, even God Himself took a break!

"And on the seventh day God finished his work that he had done, and he rested on the seventh day from all his work that he had done. So God blessed the seventh day and made it holy, because on it God rested from all his work that he had done in creation." -Genesis 2:2-3

Lesson Learned: We all need breaks. I need to stop feeling guilty about taking longer blocks of time off (like a full 24-48 hours) to break away from the daily grind to re-calibrate, re-energize, re-focus, and re-connect, because I find it always makes me a better person when I return, and I can actually do more things that matter.

Opportunity Now: Take a break! Plan for it, then do it. Book a one-day staycation at one of our local hotels that you always dreamed you could check out beyond the lobby or actually enjoy it for one day rather than work in it. I highly recommend the Kahala if you can! The Kama`aina deals are the best they will ever be, cleanliness is at an all-time high, the occupancy is super low, and the business is very much needed and appreciated. If you can't yet book a stay away, start saving for one. Put a little away at a time for YOUR time. In the mean-time, you can create your own daily breaks and nighttime routine too!

Hope For Our Future: With regular breaks, we will survive! For real, I wasn't sure about this and actually questioned everything and went off the deep end early in the week. However, I am refreshed and focused and realize that we've gone through so many different challenging and painful experiences in our pasts. We will get through this one together too.

My prayer for you, my chocolate friend, is that you will take breaks too. I've come close to giving up hope, but moments like this when I return to the Word, to His love, to listen to my body, refresh my soul, rest my mind, pray, and quiet myself, I find gratitude all around me in the little things.

With love always,
Your chocolate friend, Erin

"Therefore do not worry about tomorrow, for tomorrow will worry about itself. Each day has enough trouble of its own." -Matthew 6:34

— NOVEMBER 2 —

Week No. 34
Routine 14: Work

Let's get to work.

Let's work together.

Everything takes work.

Building a business takes work. Marriage takes work. Raising kids and parenting takes work. Staying in touch with friends takes work. Staying socially distant, clean, and safe takes work. Keeping up with daily routines takes work.

It's a constant routine in our life and, many times, the word "work" itself can have a negative connotation. It depends on how you look at it. Some people see work as an opportunity they'd love to have, a way to pay the bills, something to be thankful for, an opportunity to problem solve, or something that gets them excited and they're ready to do. As I heard Pastor Tim Ma say, "If you're comfortable, you're not working in your calling."

"Therefore, my brothers and sisters, be all the more eager to make your calling and election sure. For if you do these things, you will never fall, and you will receive a rich welcome into the eternal kingdom of our Lord and Savior Jesus Christ." -2 Peter: 10

When we at Choco le`a have work to do, we are very grateful. It took a lot of work for us to get to where we are. We consider it a privilege to continue to have work to do for you every single day. For this week's routine of "**work**," I thought it fitting to share with you the thought process and work behind our jobs to give you a #behindthebusiness look at what we are doing to close out 2020 strong.

Here we are in November and the start of the holiday season! These next two months always go by the fastest. Preparation began months ago because we wanted to be sure that, as a chocolate family, we had taken the time to discuss what our focus and goals were to be for November and December. We agreed that

November would be about showing **gratitude** and December would be about sharing **joy;** all while continuing to provide the highest quality hand-crafted products and authentic, meaningful service.

We thought long and hard about how we could share **gratitude** with all of you for your continuous support and adapting to this new online and curbside chocolate business. We thought about the various encouraging Scriptures we could slip into your bags to help you keep a grateful heart too. And we created gifts that we sincerely fell in love with: Pumpkin spice chocolate bars, our annual pumpkin pie truffles, caramel apple, and oh my gosh maple pecan! These flavors would be appreciated by anyone who received them. We hope that through these products and our continual efforts to be of service to you, you feel our gratitude for the work you've given us in the years past, and especially in these last months of the pandemic so we can remain in business.

Spreading **joy** for December means making sure as many people as possible can get our favorite holiday products. Thus, the "Choco le`a Christmas Bundles" were created. We sincerely love every single item in each bundle and know that they each have something for everyone! We did it this way to make your holiday shopping easy with an assorted gift set for the whole office or a whole family to dig into and choose their favorites, or a variety for one or two very special people to enjoy a little of everything. #sweetandsimple and convenient so you don't have to think!

You can also split up the bundles and give various gifts to different people (what better way to share the joy?), and even maybe save your absolute favorite in the bundle for yourself. We will even have limited ala carte products available if you can't quite afford a bundle, but want to experience the joy!

Of course, like every month since this unexpected coronavirus, we will throw in an unexpected little note or surprise to bring you an extra smile during such a challenging time. It's a little extra work, but so worth it! This is our way of bringing you some "peace to our world, one chocolate surprise at a time."

For December, the extra joy you will find in your bag will be FREE gift tags for you to stick on the bags and boxes for easy gifting! No wrapping needed. But if you really want to SPARK joy, then be sure to snag one of our brand new, custom, rose gold cooler bags that we brought in just in time for the holidays! It can serve as a keepsake to remember this time. Break up your bundle, separate into cooler bags you can purchase separately, and make this season really sparkle! Honestly, just looking at this bag really brings us joy!

No matter when you buy these holiday specials, you can simply refrigerate them and they will keep through the end of this year! (No, the chocolates will not turn white.) We put a lot of thought to try and ensure it is as fair as possible, to serve as many people as possible, with the smoothest opportunities for everyone to experience Choco le`a joy safely this holiday season!

Finally the most exciting thing we'd like to announce is our partnership with The Salvation Army to Rescue Christmas! If you are **grateful** for our business, our products and service, show your gratitude and bring **joy** to us by providing **joy** to another keiki or kupuna in need.

We don't add on or ask for tips with our online purchases or at curbside delivery. Instead, we'd love for you to join us in a cause that will help "bring more peace to our world." There are so many people in our local community who need your help. We have been

411

voluntarily working closely with The Salvation Army for the past four years and this holiday season, we have pre-committed to 20 Angel Tree tags as a company, to bring gifts of joy to those in need this Christmas.

With your help, we can fulfill these gifts (and possibly more) and may also have the opportunity to deliver the gifts directly to the recipients to see the joy on their faces on the same day as our final Saturday curbside pick-up. It's hard work to ask for donations during this season, but we are doing what we can to help one another out. After all, we want everyone, even those who are not yet chocolate friends, to experience God's peace and love on Jesus's birthday!

Behind the scenes, we continue to work on refining our processes, our inventory system, our best use of space, our rising costs, and do as much as we can to benefit you. We are in the works of the next phase of re-opening our business targeted for early next year, which will be in shop appointments to give you the opportunity to shop safely and privately, for us to clean thoroughly, and to avoid waiting in lines outside the shop.

We are working on all of the details of what to bring

you in 2021, down to predicting if we will be in gatherings of 5 or 10 in January and so determining which size truffle box makes the most sense. So much to think about, but we're ready to do the work to keep innovating, adjusting, and bringing you our absolute best work!

Our chocolate family has really grown into our roles as CEO's (Chocolate Everything Officer) in addition to our specialized roles. We work in our God given skill sets where we can create the biggest impact, and that's what makes work feel like a calling more than a career. We know what we are here to do and how we contribute to something so much bigger than ourselves, for the good of others. We work together and because we are so different, we can do things better when we work as a team.

At this point, I really want to express my gratitude for my chocolate family who works so extremely hard all year long. They take their work seriously but do it with such a positive attitude. They problem solve and look for new opportunities while respecting one another, keeping our mission in mind, and our values at the heart of everything. They do all of this while having fun! A lot of why we love our work is because we love the people we work with and the people we serve...all of YOU!

We're also continuing to work on all of our routines: preparing, planning, changing, connecting, trying, learning, choosing, breaking, etc. to make sure we practice what we preach in and OUT of our work environment. This is week #34 of COVID-19 and there are just six more routines together to work out before we wrap up our 20 Reflections & 20 Routines. Thank you for being on this journey with us as storytelling has now become a lot of the work that we do.

What do YOU want to work on in these last two months of 2020? How can you make your work feel less like a job, and more like a God given purpose, platform, or place to share His love, through utilizing the talents and resources He gave you? Whatever it is, don't work at it alone. Let us work together. Let us press forward working hard. Let us work on the right things, and in the right way, to be our best and make this state, nation, and world a better place for us all.

Lesson Learned: Everything takes work. Work never stops. We should not be discouraged by work; rather than complain, we should view it as an opportunity. Be grateful for the ability to work and be a part of using what God gave you to better the lives of those around you, wherever you are. And remember, *"I can do all things through Christ who gives me strength." - Philippians 4:13*

Opportunity Now: Get to work. Find a way to contribute your talents, resources, and time to someone or something. Even if you don't have a job at the moment, there are always opportunities for volunteer work or opportunities to donate. Start by working on yourself so you can identify what you have to contribute and be prepared when your time comes to join a team, step into a new role, start a project, mentor someone else, lead a district as a Representative, a city as Mayor, or a country as a Vice President or President.

Hope For Our Future: If we all give our best where we are, *"...we know that in all things God works for the good of those who love him, who have been called according to His purpose." -Romans 8:28*

I am so grateful that my parents, grandparents, and my family before them, worked so hard to give the next generation the best opportunities possible. A lot of who I am and what I have, I owe to them. Knowing their sacrifice and commitment to provide also gives me strength to do the same for my kids and the future for all of our children. Again, let's show gratitude to our kupuna and bring joy to our keiki, by being a Chocolate Angel this holiday season!

My prayer for you, chocolate friends, is that you embrace the opportunity to work. Find the good in what you have to do, as something you have been given the ability to do. We also really want you to know that we appreciate the work you give us! We all rely on each other and we find gratitude in knowing that even if no one sees or understands the work that we do, God sees it all and is proud.

With love always,
Your chocolate friend, Erin

"The Lord is my strength and my shield; my heart trusts in him, and I am helped. My heart leaps for joy and I will give thanks to him in song." -Psalm 28:7

— NOVEMBER 9 —

Week No. 35
Routine 15: Give

What's something that lights your heart on fire and gets you really excited? For my husband and I, it's the ability to **give** generously. We get an absolute thrill and it bonds us even closer together, when we have the opportunity to bless others, by giving them something they don't expect. This ultimately gives God the glory. It could be something small, from a fresh caught fish shared with friends, to paying for a stranger's dinner across the restaurant, or little snacks for our coworkers to fun experiences for our team to give them a boost during the week. It really excites us as a couple and our dream is to be able to give a lot away, to a lot of people, and include our kids in the experience of the joy of giving.

I share this because if you are in a place of feeling really down, really junk about yourself or where you are in life, you can help yourself get out of this rut by simply giving something away to a person who you know needs it or will love it. Look around for something special you can give to a family member or friend, something to donate to a stranger, or even give of yourself and your time and talents in service to someone else. You will find that you will almost immediately start to feel better. That's the magic and joy of giving! One of my favorite quotes is: *"We are blessed to be a blessing."*

As we approach Thanksgiving, I keep thinking about what I am grateful for and am content in, yet I am simultaneously unsatisfied by how there are still so many others here in Hawai`i alone, that are struggling so much. You may be thinking, "What do I have to give?" Well, everyone has something to give! **Giving** can be a regular routine in your life too and this week, we will review many different ways we can give. For example at Choco le`a, we started a new routine in this pandemic to give a little something unexpected to every chocolate friend at our curbside pick-up! These were our promos, notes of encouragement, scriptures in bags, personal gifts, an extra trick or treat, extra time to connect and talk story, or something extra sweet!

2 Corinthians 9 sums up the idea of "giving" so well and is one of my favorite scriptures. In verses 6-8 it says:

"Remember this: Whoever sows sparingly will also reap sparingly, and whoever sows generously will also reap generously. Each of you should give what you have decided in your heart to give, not reluctantly or under compulsion, for God loves a cheerful giver. And God is able to bless you abundantly, so that in all things at all times, having all that you need, you will abound in every good work."

It goes on to say in verse 10-13:

"Now he who supplies seed to the sower and bread for food will also supply and increase your store of seed and will enlarge the harvest of your righteousness. You will be enriched in every way so that you can be generous on every occasion, and through us your generosity will result in thanksgiving to God. This service that you perform is not only supplying the needs of the Lord's people but

is also overflowing in many expressions of thanks to God. Because of the service by which you have proved yourselves, others will praise God for the obedience that accompanies your confession of the gospel of Christ, and for your generosity in sharing with them and with everyone else."

Time and time again, my husband and I have witnessed first-hand that when we allow ourselves to be a conduit and let things flow in and through us, God uses what we give, to do abundantly more AND continues to provide for us as well.

Beyond giving of finances or physical possessions, the gift of service is honored by God. With Veteran's Day recently celebrated, I shared with my kids what this holiday meant and tried to explain the sacrifices families have made for our country in order for us to live the lives we have here today. My own dad, who served in the U.S. Army, serves as a role model to me of how he gave up a lot for his country and his family so that we are cared for and provided for. I think again about the generations before myself and my parents and how much they gave day in and day out working in the plantations, washing laundry by hand for field workers, and doing whatever they could to get by in order to give future generations the opportunities that are within our reach today. Happy Belated Veterans Day to all who served!

Within the walls of Choco le`a at our team meeting, we experienced each other's giving through food (breakfast and lunch purchased), service (work effort and ideas shared), time (volunteer hours), and more. This chocolate family gives their hearts to everything they do and I am so grateful for them. I hope you can taste it in the chocolate and feel it in the service that we are giving it our all because we appreciate every single purchase and every single Saturday you sacrifice to spend with us.

The great news is we are also able to GIVE YOU MORE CHOCOLATES and time to shop, as we grow our team!!! We are making more weekly products with our expanding team and faithful holiday volunteers who are jumping in with us!

And speaking of giving, we're so grateful for your generosity as we launched our Angel Tree campaign less than a week ago and shared how you could all be a part of showing gratitude by spreading joy with keiki and kupuna in need this Christmas. Within a couple days after the email went out this week, we received $700 in donations!! Your selfless giving and quick response to become a "Chocolate Angel," got us excited to start our plans to go shopping for these individuals who will be overjoyed to receive a gift this holiday season. At the end of the week, we received our Angel Tree tags from The Salvation Army and will be taking you along for the journey with us via Instagram @chocoleahawaii with videos on Stories to purchase bath mats, a frying pan, and bath towels for our kupuna and sports items, dolls, and backpacks, and other requested gifts for our keiki.

It is so exciting for us to have the opportunity to give and live out our mission of "Bringing peace to our world" not only one chocolate at a time, but also one gift at a time outside of work as well. The constant balance to give our best and live our mission not only during our work hours and within the walls of our shop and kitchen, but more importantly in our every day lives, is something we have really begun to focus on more during this season. We are striving to give our best to our families and friends. For me, I see the joy in my little kids more clearly now than ever, that when I give them some time, not even a lot, but real quality time, with no work phone calls, texts, or checking emails, just designated time for only them, they are truly, truly happy. I also see the little sweet things (and sometimes crazy hilarious things) they say and do that I would have missed. I'm definitely savoring this cute little age that all parents tell me, "you can never get back again."

I honestly did miss some of this precious time with my family pre-COVID. I hate to admit it, but I worked harder, not smarter. I confessed this to a customer, (turned chocolate friend) during a walk around Manoa literally the day before this pandemic hit us and our world flipped upside down and then again this week, 8 months later. I told her that I gave my everything to work in order to grow the business and the team, but this time as we grow it again, I want to make sure I also have enough time and energy to grow my family and friends around me outside of work.

I am trying it a different way. It seems to be the way God has been telling me to do it for a while. A little slower pace this time, with more fun, family, friends, and self-care time included. It's not my timing and everything is taking longer than what I want, but I'm learning that His timing is never the same as mine, but

His timing is always perfect and I need to give it up to Him. Having more breathing room daily has allowed me more breaks, opportunities to move, celebrate, pray ... and all the other routines I have been incorporating one week at a time since my world suddenly slowed down. Sometimes, giving means just giving it all up to God.

Looking back at the way I thought, things I said, or things I did, there are definitely some moments I am not proud of. But one of the hardest things we have to learn to give others, including ourselves, is forgiveness and grace. To give ourselves credit that we tried our absolute best at that time and grace that now we know better, we will do better and keep moving forward in the direction God guides us.

We will continue to make mistakes because we are human so extending forgiveness and grace to ourselves and others is ongoing. To forgive others that may have wronged us and to show grace again and again gives God the glory. After all, God freely and repeatedly forgives us and extends to us His undeserved favor.

"Bear with each other and forgive one another if any of you has a grievance against someone. Forgive as

the Lord forgave you." -Colossians 3:13

"For it is by grace you have been saved, through faith - and this is not from yourselves, it is the gift of God - not by works, so that no one can boast." - Ephesians 2:8-9

I encourage you to make "giving" a routine in your life. Whether it's giving of your personal possessions, finances, time, talents, tips, knowledge and suggestions, or giving your best effort, attention and quality time, or giving it up to God, or giving forgiveness and grace. Something happens in your heart when you give from a place of authenticity and love. It definitely helps keep you humble, grateful for what you have, and reminds us of Him to whom everything ultimately belongs to, and who gives it all to us to care for as He chooses and entrusts us.

"Give, and it will be given to you. A good measure, pressed down, shaken together and running over, will be poured into your lap. For with the measure you use, it will be measured to you." -Luke 6:38-40

Lesson Learned: We all have something to give and even the little things, like quality time and grace for others, holds immense rewards.

Opportunity Now: Give. Think about who you can give to from what you already have this Thanksgiving. Or begin to gather Christmas gifts that you can surprise and bless others with beyond your immediate circle. Think about who you can give attention and time to and block it off in your calendar. Or who you can mentor or share your knowledge and suggestions with. If you have a social media account, think about giving tips, inspiration, and sharing something of value with others on your feed. Reflect on whether there is anything you need to let go and give up to God? Or perhaps, is there forgiveness and grace you need to extend to someone with a simple apology, a humble acknowledgement, or a simple sweet gesture? Do you need to forgive yourself? Say a prayer...confess and ask for forgiveness from your Heavenly Father who loves you and wants you to return to Him.

"Get rid of all bitterness, rage and anger, brawling and slander, along with every form of malice. Be kind and compassionate to one another, forgiving each other, just as in Christ God forgave you."
-Ephesians 4:31-32

Hope For Our Future: When we are able to give forgiveness to others and ourselves and extend grace in the day-to-day frustrations, we are freed from the bitterness that would otherwise be held in our hearts and hold us captive from freely enjoying this life. There is so much power in forgiveness. And as you continue to go about your life, as you allow God to use you as a conduit and as the blessings He gives you flow through you to others, you will experience the true joy in giving!

My prayer for you my chocolate friend, is that you can fully experience the joy of giving. That it will give you a thrill as it does for me and my husband, Chris. And if there is forgiveness to give, I pray that you can find it in your heart to do so.

Giving is not just for this holiday season, but can become a regular routine in your life throughout the year. A little can go a long way when we do what we can and give the rest to God, to ultimately give Him the glory.

With love always,
Your chocolate friend, Erin

"Whoever can be trusted with very little can also be trusted with much..." -Luke 16:10

— NOVEMBER 16—

Week No. 36
Routine 16: Be Authentic

This is one of the most important routines I will write. Because in ALL the routines you do, I hope you will…

Be authentic.

Be real.

Be honest.

Be you.

Just "Be."

That is the ONE thing I can say I have consistently been in every single journal entry. I have been authentic in sharing with you who I really am, transparent in relaying my thoughts from my journal, and brutally honest when opening up my life to you. In fact, I wrote this week's contribution three different ways until I finally got a real flow that felt authentic.

This place of vulnerability is where connection happens, and that's really my intention for what I want to accomplish. I want to live out what we at Choco le`a always say to do: "Make connections and build sweet relationships through chocolates." This year, we have shifted our focus to be a "people" business, "Bringing peace to our world, one chocolate story at a time." God prompted me to carry this out by being completely myself and putting everything out there.

The words and sentiments poured out over these many weeks are everything I would tell a real friend. I hope my transparency and the risk of exposing my flaws has built something real, so that you feel a genuine connection to me, and to us.

This week was all about being authentic. From getting caught in unexpected pouring rain to taking three showers in one day, I was tired of reapplying my makeup and doing my hair and decided to just go out and be plain me.

"This is me," I thought to myself as I went to the market with a little nervousness about running into someone without "my face on." Honestly, I prefer to at least have my eyebrows drawn in and my hair straightened. But even more important than that, I wanted to go out and live life and go about my routines as me...not as an impossibly- difficult-to-accomplish version of myself.

However, this week, I did create a different sort of "version" of myself. I finally learned what a "memoji" was. I mean, I had seen it a long time ago and my mother in law Carolyn, my Uncle Colins, my Aunty Joan, and so many others in the generation before me had already made their own memojis before 2020. I am so late to the party sometimes and joke that I am "old school" since I still use a checkbook more than Venmo. But that's me!

I tried to make our company Christmas card and take a group photo as my team ran away from the camera (again) because that's who they are (camera shy). I realized that in this tech day and age, I could perhaps create a photo memoji-style since most of them already show up as their digital counterparts in their "Animal

Crossing" game.

As they whipped up their memojis, I Zoomed with our reliable (and younger) extended chocolate family member, Elise, and asked her how to do this and she sent me directions and screen shots to follow along. Then I started to create my own.

The funny thing is, at first, I started to make one that I thought was cute or how I wanted me to look with a nice tan, big eyes and super long lashes. I then realized this was not looking anything like how I really looked. I had to start again and sit in front of a mirror to get real and try to make it as close to me as possible.

Soon after I finished my five-year-old, who had been watching, wanted to try and whipped one up of herself right away wearing a chef hat since she wants to be a Chef, a Chocolate Maker, AND a Paleontologist! This way of technology, virtual connections, etc. is definitely going to be the future for these kids, if it's not already. We better make sure they have a positive outlook of who they really are, too.

The funny thing is even with the same set of memoji feature selections to choose from, everyone's memoji on our team came out different, but pretty similar, to what we really look like in real life. We all have very different strengths, quirks, body language, and character traits. It's what makes us have dynamic discussions in our meetings. It also brings out the best for the overall mission and work of the company, since we can do it from a place of humility, respect, and gratitude for our differences. We are real with each other about what's frustrating, what we need help with, what the challenges are we face within the company and need to solve together. Work is a place to just be real and honest and you can probably see a little of our real personas represented in these memojis!

Though I wanted to send my new memoji out into the world to get things done, I still had to show up as me and do the work this week. But there is something so freeing when you can move about and work and just be yourself. There's no major prep or planning involved.

This week I had an interview with Nolan Hong for his Elevate808 series on small businesses in Hawai`i. I only talked to him for a brief 5 minutes before we went to recording, but the funny thing is I was so comfortable because I felt like I already knew him. I've watched his posts and listened to his podcasts and seen him and his wife at our curbside pick-ups. He's so relaxed and real, it was like an unspoken invitation for me to be the same.

So I was. We talked story and I spoke freely about life in the pandemic, the inspiration behind business decisions, natto truffles, the reason for this season's Christmas specials, and some of the real, not yet announced plans for 2021!!! It was honestly a super authentic session, just talking story about all things with a friend.

Later in the week, Christine and I took a field trip to Ten Tomorrow to visit another entrepreneur we love, Summer Shiigi, and her team. We experienced their private in-shop appointment (something we are looking forward to doing in 2021) and shopped their new and innovative customized "designer experience." Summer and I probably talked for fifty of the sixty reserved minutes of our shopping appointment about all the real things we share in common as small business, local entrepreneurs learning as we go. I then spent 10 minutes actually shopping. It was my first time there and it was long overdue since being on my "to-visit list" for over a year.

Honestly, I truly fell in love with everything! The clothes were cute, comfy, great fit, made in Hawai`i and I love when I feel authentically great in the clothes I wear that represent people and brands I love! We laughed and stomped our feet so hard when we swapped similar business "mistake and failure" stories, screaming, "OH, I KNOW!" We had an instant, authentic connection that will lead to a collaboration I'm sure!

At the end of the week, my daughter asked if we had any new chocolates. When I told her we had six new truffle flavors for Christmas, she asked, "Oh can you please, please, bring them home and let us try them before you let anyone else try it? Can we be the first, and can we do a video?" These videos are all done on my phone with no rehearsal, no script, and no editing, either.

Although our Stories on Instagram are not professional and sometimes embarrassing, you all say they are your favorite because they are so real! I am video-bombed by little kids who are very authentic all of the time. I pronounce words incorrectly, I often say the same thing over and over, and apparently I smack my lips when I eat! Wait what? (Okay, Ally just made me aware of that one. Really?)

We tried the Christmas truffle specials, recorded the experience in one-take at home, and you can view it on our YouTube channel. I truly love our lineup for this holiday season! Even if every part of our house out of frame is really a mess, even if we're still working at home and trying to figure this out, at least we can have some fun together and share authentic sweet moments like this. Even if they say, "This chocolate is not so good," on camera and, "Oh my gosh, it's so good I want more," off camera!

On Saturday, curbside was fun as usual running out to the cars with a big smile - and that's REAL! My team knows how much I love seeing all of you and am always wanting to run out and see everyone and so do they!

I had no idea these curbside pick-ups were going to be our saving grace for the past eight months. You have all kept us alive to celebrate the holidays and look forward to planning 2021! That's the real deal. Even though everything is hard to predict, it was especially hard to really know what would happen with the business. We always just had to do our best in thinking ahead to what you might want and enjoy as we got to know the real you better.

Finally, the week ended with our chocolate family meeting to kick off The Angel Tree Christmas shopping. Together, we have raised over $1,500 for Kupuna and Keiki in need! Thank you Chocolate Angels!

The best thing about this experience was seeing how authentically awesome my chocolate family is outside of work too! I could see their real hearts for others in the way they shopped for the gifts! They were truly focused on a mission together of "Bringing peace to our world, one gift at a time."

But they all did it their own way. One made the spreadsheet, organized, grouped similar things together, and moved about efficiently and safely with gloves. Another was like a ninja moving quickly and silently and packed items in the cart so perfectly that it would all fit just right. A few checked prices and did quick cost benefit analysis of items, took notes and compared options. A few split up into groups, watched the time, worked down the list, and made a back-up plan. I did my usual: took photos and videos to include all of you in the experience and ran around checking up on all groups to make sure everyone was okay (which they totally were)! It was hilarious! I saw all of their personalities and strengths shine through. The roles they excel in reflected even in their shopping!

Though they are all different, they all share similar values and worked towards the same goal which was truly something special to witness in action outside of our chocolate kitchen and shop. They gave of their own talents, time, and finances and worked in teams to split up and find things, took their time to really think beyond what they would like to what the recipients would like. They checked for quality and went back when there was a little tear in the box or perhaps a better option and worked thoroughly at this like they do with the chocolates. They were committed to quality and worked at it until they knew they gave their best and were happy with what they were going to give away.

"We have different gifts, according to the grace given to each of us. If your gift is prophesying, then

prophesy in accordance with your faith; if it is serving, then serve; if it is teaching, then teach; if it is to encourage, then give encouragement; if it is giving, then give generously; if it is to lead, do it diligently; if it to show mercy, do it cheerfully. Love must be sincere. Hate what is evil; cling to what is good. Be devoted to one another in love. Honor one another above yourselves." -Romans 12: 6-10

Being surrounded with my chocolate family and throughout the week with family, friends, business friends, and real, genuine people, allows me to be my authentic self. These people don't try to change who you are. They see who you really are, bring out the best in you, and appreciate you for you.

Being authentic, to me, is one of the most important routines in life. With everything and everyone that can sway and influence us, we need to self-reflect and be in touch with ourselves and with God to make sure we are growing, doing, and being who He created us to be.

When you take the time to intentionally be authentic in your routines, it means that you **pray** the way that feels right. Find your **morning** routine that works and get

443

focused on what you **value**. **Prepare** for what kind of life you want to live and **celebrate** how you can along the way. Find how you best de-stress and what you consider as fun ways to **move**. **Connect** with people in your own special way. And when you need to **change** things up, do it. **Plan** again what works for you and the goals you have for your life. **Learn**, **try**, and **choose** what works and remember to take the **breaks** that you need. **Work** at it with all you've got and remember to **give** to others too. Do this all by being **authentic**! We still have four more routines to come to bring out the best version of the real YOU!

"I praise you because I am fearfully and wonderfully made; your works are wonderful, I know that full well." -Psalm 139:14

Lesson Learned: Being authentic, and being yourself is the best option. It's so much more joyful, rewarding, and easier to just be yourself rather than trying to pretend to be someone else. We were each given different skills, personalities, and dreams so there's more than one way to go about a routine or live the life that's in front of you. When we each can focus on being the best version of ourselves, surrounded by other people who make us better too, we can accomplish a lot more!

Opportunity Now: Be authentic and be yourself in everything that you do. Don't worry about who someone else says you should be. You can always listen and learn from others, but you ultimately need to figure out who YOU are, who God created you to be, and live that out authentically. It may be hard or scary at first but start showing little by little the real you. It will reveal who really loves you, for you.

Hope For Our Future: You will feel free! If we can stop comparing and trying to constantly follow someone else's example or expectations in everything and live the life you were created for, you will feel free … and that's just the person this world needs you to be.

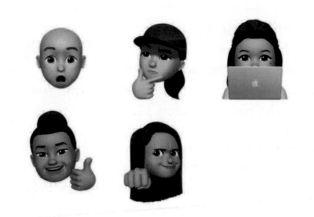

My prayer for you my chocolate friend, is that you find freedom, strength, and comfort in being yourself. That you find your own rhythm with these routines and make them your own. Be authentic. Be real. Be honest. Be you. That's the person I'd really like to meet and get to know.

With love always,
Your chocolate friend, Erin

"But those who hope in the Lord will renew their strength. They will soar on wings like eagles; they will run and not grow weary, they will walk and not be faint." -Isaiah 40:31

— NOVEMBER 23 —

Week No. 37
Routine 17: Thrive

Who's hungry for more energy? Especially after stuffing yourself with turkey on Thanksgiving and a busy Black Friday, Small Business Saturday and kick off to the holiday weekend?

I don't know about you, but this is USUALLY an insanely busy weekend for me filled with lots going on at the shop, lots of shopping, lots of cooking and prepping, large get-togethers with multiple sides of the family, picking out the Christmas tree, etc. and ends with me being completely exhausted by Monday. But this year, it was not like that all. It was quiet, sweet, and simple.

Every morning when I go through my routine and gratitude journal, I find myself thanking God for the most basic things that we often take for granted, like food on the table and good health. In this pandemic, I've become ultra-aware of my health and what could positively or negatively affect it. I wake up and thank God every day I have a breath, I ask for his protection, and pray for those who are going through COVID-19 and those with underlying health conditions or who are in unhealthy situations who are at greater risk.

Ironically, exactly one year ago on Thanksgiving week I was struck down with influenza A. I quarantined in isolation in my bedroom for six days. No hugs or kisses with my kids. I could hear the family laughing in the next room through the closed bedroom door. I had also just started a personal blog and wrote about what I was grateful for; however, also how it was not a surprise for me to be sick. I was always working and going at everything full speed, then getting really sick on my "fun, free days." It was a pattern in my life. Here's an excerpt from 2019:

This Thanksgiving is no different. Same pleads. Same alone time with God. Only this time, I will make that promise because I am sick and tired of being sick and tired. I will change my lifestyle and change my calendar to allow for what I know deep in my heart needs to be done. But my pride about accomplishing things one after another, my stubbornness than I CAN do it all, and my worries about putting myself first, keep getting in the way.

Well this is going to change. I am grateful I have another chance. I am grateful for another day to make a decision to live a better version of my life. God simply reminds me that I already know what I need to do, but I am just not being obedient.

So the life lesson learned: Don't let the same bad things keep happening to you over and over again. If you're missing out, it's because you're missing something in your life. It may be time to breathe, play, take care of yourself, get outside, walk, run or share a joke. Whatever it is, continue to have a heart of gratitude, but also adjust your life and live the changes you need so that you don't end up in isolation on Thanksgiving.

Who knew that four months after writing this in November 2019, I'd really have the opportunity to work on this and live this out? Who knew that this miserable one week in quarantine would become a "quarantine" lifestyle of now thirty seven weeks living in COVID-19?!

I don't want to just survive this pandemic. I also want to thrive in it! A vaccine is hopefully on the way, but while we wait for that, we can go ahead and make the changes in the areas we are in control of right now.

Washing our hands, wearing a mask, sanitizing, staying six feet apart, daily temperature checks, multiple baths, and other cleansing routines have become part of our daily lives. What was once perhaps new to some of us, hard to remember, and inconvenient, has become a healthy routine. It took conscious effort, reminders, and sacrifices of comfort and laziness to make this adjustment, but it is well worth it.

As I reflected on that, I realized it would seem incomplete if I didn't have a routine about health listed in my twenty routines. Although I already covered a lot of very important aspects of our health:

- **spiritual health** with prayer and devotions as part of the morning routine;
- **mental health** and stress management with preparation and planning routines; and
- **physical health** with rest and sleep via breaks

452

and exercise via my move routine,

I haven't yet talked about a very big component of health: **what we eat and drink**!

We need to eat and drink to survive and what we eat and drink can help us to also thrive!

Honestly, I guess I could say I was avoiding discussing healthy eating because I am far from being a master at this and definitely am not a nutritionist. I struggle with this routine a lot. I mean, I do have a major sweet tooth! Seriously, I am a chocolate shop owner! So, this doesn't make any business marketing or financial sense to keep writing this. But your opportunity to thrive towards better health IS important to me.

I truly want to thrive and want the same for you! One thing I have always been on these email blogs is honest. And honestly, eating has a lot to do with our ability to thrive or not.

Thrive is defined as: To grow, develop well, and flourish.

What we put in our bodies, as well as our minds and hearts, affects us. As the expression goes, "Garbage in, garbage out." To grow, develop well, and flourish, we need to really think about what we are doing to nurture that. The routines that came out of these COVID-19 reflections were a result of me being sick and tired of reflecting and wanting to start really LIVING in this pandemic. I am trying to live my best life, as the best version of myself, and am encouraging you to do the same too. COVID-19 forced me to reflect and then implement routines to help me achieve the goals and life I wanted, and good health helps us to do that.

I always find myself getting sluggish, my brain foggy, and my energy dying in the late afternoon to early evening. I need energy all day to lead my team and keep up with my very energetic kids and husband. So I started to think about how I could optimize the full use of the day and started to slowly change things to live a healthier life and see what would result.

I began noticing how much what I eat affects how I feel. I noticed that some foods affect the way I feel more than others. Fortunately for me, a little chocolate doesn't negatively affect me (phew!) What does negatively affect me is soda, too much fried or greasy food, fast food, and definitely when I have way too much of anything. My stomach can handle a little, but not a lot. On the flip side, my body needs A LOT of water, not a little. Staying hydrated is important and on the days I forget my massive water bottle, I notice I get headaches and don't feel as full.

It's weird, but once I started tracking it, I started noticing it. Consistent journaling helped me to discover what food and drinks were doing to my body and how it was making me feel. Some foods were slowing down my energy and I didn't want to just make up for it with another cup of coffee. I wanted to eliminate whatever was making me feel junk!

This routine is still a work in progress, but I have definitely come to understand two fundamental things that have changed the game:

1. I am certain that what I eat directly affects how I feel.

2. I know that I am the one that can choose how I want to feel and am in control of deciding what I will and will not eat.

This is mind blowing you guys!

How Am I Doing This?

With this information, I know how I thrive! For sure it is not easy, but when I know what's best for me then it's up to me to make the choice to make some small changes to get started. I never used to eat many vegetables, but I have come to really appreciate salads, cooked veggies, and fresh produce, especially from our garden. Other foods that feel clean and fuel me are fish and meats, food that's cooked simply with very little sauce or fanfare.

I have an accountability friend and coach who calls me from time to time to check in and see how I am doing. I'm reading a book about the habits of health and following a new cookbook of clean meals with simple ingredients I can follow. I order food from chefs who use fresh ingredients and have a nice assortment of protein and veggies. Again, I am far, far, far from being an exemplary healthy eater, but I'm enjoying the benefits of the small healthy changes I have started to make.

I sometimes totally go off course and eat aimlessly way too much, but I simply give myself some grace, and get back on it. It's like everything else in life: a lifelong balance and work to establish routines until we get in the rhythm! I'm also journaling how I feel to keep me aware. I eat frequently, usually something small every 2-3 hours, little fuelings, but it keeps me energized as opposed to big meals that make me want to unbutton my top button of my jeans and lie on the sofa!

I am not aiming for perfection or some ideal image. I am simply trying to stay away from feeling "blah" and feeling strong instead so that I can thrive in all areas of my life and the many things I want to accomplish. Lying on the couch and feeling guilty does nothing for me so I am taking care of what I can and enjoying what I want. I am just making sure it's a controlled proportion of quality indulgences that's worth it to me. No more emotional, unconscious, stuffing of my face with junk stuff that only makes me feel horrible after, but rather, the slow and savoring enjoyment of only the really, really good stuff.

I know what you're thinking, do I still eat our chocolates? Absolutely! Honestly, I eat a little daily, but I try to take my time and enjoy it as a reward rather than a given supply that I can just get more of, because truthfully, I can't anyway.

I could eat all of "The More The Merrier" nut mix we put up online weekly but because we are trying to make as much as we can for YOU, I cannot have all of those bags that I could easily indulge in. Instead, I grab one cluster in the morning with my coffee during my morning routine, one cluster at lunch after I get through my inbox and to do list, and one after dinner before bed. #thisisreallife

I have found that by making small and simple changes, while still enjoying the sweet things I love, I have the energy to do the things I really love and keep up with the people I love. Fortunately, this Thanksgiving I was not in isolation or in quarantine. My husband and I did our annual tradition of providing meals to those less fortunate. This always serves as a reminder to me that some people can't thrive simply because they don't have enough in their bellies to function. Sharing food and spiritual nourishment with others is another way we can all thrive. As you use the energy and strength God gave you to serve others, together, we can strengthen the communities around us.

"Then Jesus declared, 'I am the bread of life. Whoever comes to me will never go hungry, and whoever believes in me will never be thirsty."
-John 6:35

This is how we thrive! When I kept reflecting on how I can get more energy to thrive more, I realized I needed to make my own energy. A quote I love reads, "A power plant doesn't have energy, it makes energy." To receive that energy for me is a combination of some basic health fundamentals that I have been reading about now for the past several months:

-Sleep

-Hydration

-Exercise

-Meditation and prayer

-Social interaction and community

-What we eat

What That Looks Like

To give you an example: In my typical week, I sleep seven hours, but am striving for seven and a half now and trying to shut off devices earlier to better thrive. I drink at least ninety-six ounces of water daily and take my Yeti water bottle with me everywhere. I get outside daily even if for just a fifteen-minute walk and hike once a week.

Honestly, I will need to work on building muscle and strength training next. I wake up every morning with my routine of prayer, journaling, and gratitude. For social interaction, I keep in conversation with family and friends, cuddle and play with my kids, and see all of your bright shining faces on Saturday at curbside. I am eating more veggies, fish, and meat, and enjoying the quality stuff I really love in moderation. For me, yes, that does include at least one chocolate a day.

"Blessed is the one who does not walk in step with the wicked or stand in the way that sinners take or sit in the company of mockers, but whose delight is in the law of the Lord, and who meditates on his law day and night. That person is like a tree planted by streams of water, which yields its fruit in season and whose leaf does not wither -whatever they do prospers." -Psalm 1:1-4

It's kind of cool to look back now and see that most of these things were encouraged in my past routines. As we get into the rhythm of each of them one by one, some easier than others, we can move onto the next routine and for me, that's eating well and in moderation to give me the energy I need to thrive.

"So whether you eat or drink or whatever you do, do it all for the glory of God." -1 Corinthians 10:31

Lesson Learned: I want to thrive, not just survive, and with that takes some sacrifices, tough decisions, and controlled moderation of enjoying the things I absolutely LOVE. It takes work, but it is so worth the effort if the trade-off is worth something greater that you can do with your life.

Opportunity Now: Start making small changes you can stick to. As you get into the routine of making a few slight changes, you will be able to tackle them one at a time and add on a little more. The first thing you can do is to keep a journal of how you are feeling. What you ate, how you feel. What you did, how you feel. Just start with that and look at patterns in how you feel and at what time of the day and what you did and accomplished or didn't. You'll start to learn more about your body and energy levels and how different things affect you.

461

Hope For Our Future: We can give ourselves, and those we influence around us, the opportunity to live a longer, stronger, and fuller life of energy for the things that matter. We can set an example for others and be an inspiration. We can help our kids develop these healthy habits and even our kupuna to turn things around and live the second half of their lives even fuller than the first! Together, we can thrive!

My prayer for you, my chocolate friend, is that you find the little things you can change to help you thrive. I want you to be healthy and live a well-balanced life. We've got a lot yet to experience together!

With love always,
Your chocolate friend, Erin

"Dear friend, I pray that you may enjoy good health and that all may go well with you, even as your soul

is getting along well." -3 John 1:2

— NOVEMBER 30 —
Week No. 38
Routine 18: Dream

It's December, everyone! The Christmas lights are going up everywhere and for many, like me, this is our favorite time of the year. Something about those twinkling little lights brings me a little peace and joy. I suppose that simple little thing reminds me of God's light and how He sent His son, Jesus, to save the world.

"I am the light of the world. Whoever follows me will not walk in darkness, but will have the light of life."
-John 8:12

When I was a kid, I would sit on our driveway and stare at a single strand of twinkling lights lining the roof of my parents' house and dream. It was like the twinkling stars from far out in the sky were brought closer to me and within reach. Today, I have a strand of white twinkling lights up year-round in my living room that I turn on every single morning during my morning routine and another strand that I turn on every day at the chocolate shop.

This is the time of year when the air starts to cool, the Christmas music plays, the smell of pine trees and wreaths linger, and sparkly, smiling, Santa decorations and Christmas lights can be seen all over. It encourages me to dream like a little girl again. My heart always opens up to start thinking about the future and what I'd like to do in the next year. It also reminds me that the calendar year is almost over and I look back at what was accomplished this past year.

For many in 2020, so many dreams were crushed. Lives lost, businesses closed, dream jobs disappeared, travel plans canceled, celebrations diminished, leaving for college postponed, meeting new classmates and teachers in person delayed, friends missed, and division everywhere.

This year was definitely a tough one for us all, and truthfully, every year has its downs. There is always something that hurts us, challenges us, makes us cry, and makes us question our purpose or worth. The year

2020 brought a shutdown of our state, lock down time at home with my family, the rebuilding of my business, and the worry that life was so fragile and could end on any day. But for me, the best thing that came out of it was the opportunity to really dream again and make changes to live life with even more gusto, meaning, and purpose.

It was almost like a re-set button had been pushed. This year, my 20-20 vision of what I wanted for my life and what I thought was "best" was interrupted, re-set, and taught me to seek God's perfect vision again and not my own.

It is by far the year I have read the most, journaled the most, and prayed the most. I started to dream of a life outside this "bubble" and also what could still be done while living in a pandemic. To **dream** is a routine.

I believe that dreaming of endless possibilities and what could be is ongoing. I hope you will give yourself the chance to dream again. Envisioning great things, thinking of the big picture, and looking far ahead is something I have always enjoyed and comes natural to me. Dreaming of what could be is always on my radar.

What 2020 taught me was to dream from a place of who God created me to be and to do what He wanted me to do right now in THIS season. It also taught me to take small consistent steps focusing on the present, as well as how I could be used to ultimately bring the peace and joy I felt beyond the Christmas lights to others, so that they may find His peace.

"I have told you these things, so that in me you may have peace. In this world you will have trouble. But take heart! I have overcome the world." -John 16:33

This week I dreamed of what the tourism industry could like in the near future with a potential hotel partner. I dreamed of what the food industry could look like for us with a neighboring chef. I dreamed of what the retail industry could look like with a successful local boutique business owner and friend. I dreamed of what doors could be opened by being an author with a friend I had made at the chocolate shop, literally outside our doors. I dreamed together with a loyal, repeat customer-turned-friend about what we could do with our passion of writing and storytelling. As I got super excited about my dreams, I also got a little scared as doubt and fear crept in.

Thankfully, my small group of church friends reminded me:

"...being confident of this, that he who began a good work in you will carry it on to completion until the day of Christ Jesus." -Philippians 1:6.

I dreamed with my best friend, Traci, what living and working together in Hawai`i could be like, since she's been away from me on the mainland for over 15 years. I dreamed with my husband about future travels and what we hope we can show our kids one day.

I dreamed with my team about what our business could look like in 2021, in five years, and in ten years. I've only just begun to share with them the dreams of my heart and invited them to share their dreams with me. What really made me happy this week was hearing, "I HAVE my dream job, Erin! I'm living the dream!"

We dreamed about bringing back old favorite products, but also started dreaming up new creations, flavor profiles, products, and collaborations through 2021. With our Christmas specials selling out in minutes week after week, while at our max capacity, we began dreaming about how we could do more next

Christmas, how we could grow our chocolate family, and how we could make more and more of your chocolate dreams come true! This pandemic forced us to really think outside of the box and dream of the possibilities -any of the possibilities - that could work, and to just try and go for it. We just have to push past what we knew once worked!

For YOU, our chocolate friends, I dream that we will grow even closer as a community and you can fully experience what goes on behind the business ... the love and dedication that goes into the artisan craftsmanship of everything we make, fresh and on-site. I dream you can learn from our mistakes, laugh along, build a personal connection to our team. In the process, start sweet conversations and sweeten relationships through chocolates, to truly be a part of our ongoing BIG mission of "Bringing peace to our world, one chocolate at a time."

I shared the idea with my family that I was going to take some time this week, the start of December, to really tackle the manuscript that is now seventy-six thousand words long with a God-given deadline of December 31st. I told my kids I was going to take a little time every week to focus on getting this done I am not going to wait any longer to make this long-time dream come true. It would include the lessons I learned this year that I would want them to learn and one day read in a book when they were older and able to understand it all.

To this, my daughter replied, *"Oh can the book be about us?"* I replied, *"Of course! It totally has you in it!"* She was beyond thrilled and proceeded to ask, *"Can I help you with the book?"* To which I again said, *"Of course!"*

After all, Aubrey and Conner, whom I spent the most time with in 2020, provided most of the ideas and content and they are part of the reason why I continue to dream of a better world and future for all of our kids.

So that's what this week was about. Dreaming about our future together, and a BIG, BIG dream that has been placed in my heart from long before Choco le`a days : to write and publish a book. For years, I had NO IDEA what I would write about and started so many "books" without finishing them; I would make goal list after goal list that "one day I'd write a book."

Well, this is the year. No more dreaming about it. I am

writing it. I have a God-given deadline and in these last couple weeks with the holidays, it's absolutely crazy to me! As I've taken steps of faith week after week to write with the gnawing at my heart that this would become a book, I asked God, "When?" What He revealed to me was that this would be the year I finished it.

With my last chapter, week #40, routine #20, planned to come out days before Christmas on December 22nd, I'd have just one more week in the year to write a closing to wrap up 2020 and this book. Oddly enough, I found that I would need to get this to my editor by December 31st so that she, the publisher, and printer would have JUST enough time to get this to me by March 2021, exactly one year after all of these COVID-19 email reflections began.

With this deadline, we can re-visit the lessons learned, opportunity now, and hope for our future, week by week, with a book in hand. This is how I know it's God's dream, not mine. It's His timing, and definitely not mine. I'd like more time! The only way I will be able to do this and get the timing of every person and thing involved in this process to work is with God's power, strength, and blessing. More about that in our next chapter.

I believe He wants me to be able to carefully craft something from the heart that has no expiration date or shelf life, unlike chocolates. One that can easily be printed thousands of times to share with all of you. It should not sell out in minutes and if it does, more copies can be mass printed so that everyone will have an opportunity to enjoy sweet chocolate stories. This will be especially satisfying for those chocolate friends who have had a technically challenging year with everyone moving to online shopping, curbside pick-ups, social media information, Facebook Live sales, Zoom meetings, online learning, etc. while they are stuck inside. A book will be an old-school, familiar, physical, and tangible way to get in their hands and homes and connect with them again.

Please hang on and stay with me friends. In just a few months, we will hopefully be safely out and about, and re-reading together the week by week 20 reflections and 20 routines of 2020 that hopefully have changed us all to live life more fully, with love, with God, and with purpose, so we can begin to dream again.

Lesson Learned: The dreams in your heart that God has put there cannot be shaken. We must be obedient and follow through or we could lose the opportunity. Those dreams can be the plans He has for each of us and how He will use us, to bring His light, His peace, and His joy to the world.

Opportunity Now: Dream again. Dream BIG. Don't be afraid to say your dreams out loud and when they come true, God will receive the glory.

Hope For Our Future: Dreamers are all around us. Dreamers are people who believe that things can change for the better. They are visionaries who see the hope and gather those to rally behind a unified dream to start making BIG dreams come true. You may be one of them! We need the vision of leaders like you to lead us into a brighter future. Who knows what God will and CAN do with those dreams!

My prayer for you, my chocolate friend, is that when you see the Christmas decorations and lights, hear the music, smell the pine trees, feel the cool weather, and taste the fresh chocolates, you open your heart to dream of what God can do through YOU!

With love always,
Your chocolate friend, Erin

"You are the light of the world. A town built on a hill cannot be hidden. Neither do people light a lamp and put it under a bowl. Instead they put it on its stand, and it gives light to everyone in the house. In the same way, let your light shine before others, that they may see your good deeds and glorify your Father in heaven. -Matthew 5:14-16

— DECEMBER 7 —

Week No. 39
Routine 19: Lead

I almost titled this "Angels" since this past week, I felt like I was being being watched over by a guardian angel, worked and served with real angels on Earth, was an "angel" delivering Angel Tree gifts for others, watched the little angels in my life take off, and even made sand angels. But realizing "angels" is not a routine, I changed it to "**lead**." This week, I was led by angels.

Let's be real. Writing and reading about routines that are good for us is so much easier than doing them. And sticking consistently with them, especially when you don't experience immediate results, is even harder. But we must choose to lead ourselves through life and commit to what we know is good for us: to do what we know we should do despite what the rest of the world around us may be doing.

With just this and one more routine to go, I must include a topic I am very passionate about. A kick-in-the-butt-real-hard look at how to get things done. To get through these routines, we have to have the routine to **lead** ourselves.

One of my favorite mentors and leaders I follow who teaches on the topic of leadership is Dr. John C. Maxwell. He often says, "The hardest person to lead is yourself." #sotrue To turn all of these routines into a rhythm, or a habit, we must consistently get ourselves to do it.

Sure, having leaders to follow and leading a group yourself provides accountability. It definitely helps. But sometimes, it's just you and you. With no one watching. No one cheering you on. And for some of us who have had to be in quarantine isolation during this COVID-19 season, we understand what it's like to have no one else with us. We have to be the leader in our own life wherever we are and with whatever we've got. Sometimes all we've got is our choice; our perspective; our life and our time here on Earth.

I knew "leading" or "leadership" was a routine I was eventually going to cover, and this week, I really experienced leadership all around me. If you're thinking, "I am not a leader of a business or team," stop right there. That's not it. I've learned that leadership is *influence*. If you have influence over anyone, and you do, YOU are a leader! By definition, to lead is to *be a means of access in a particular direction, or an example for others to follow, or to cause a person to go with one by holding them by the hand while moving forward.*

I hope that's the leadership style you feel with me. I'm simply a friend, holding your hand, trying to move us both forward through reflections and routines.

The week began with me feeling pumped to lead my team through a discussion after last week's "dream" routine. We got to talking about 2021 and brainstorming how we can make more chocolates and bring more joy to all of you. We talked about how we would transition into opening the shop eventually again and improve the online experience. We talked about all of the exciting specials and collaborations we wanted to do in 2021. And we talked about so many other things with the vaccine on the way and a hopeful end of COVID-19 on the horizon.

We also delivered the Angel Tree gifts we purchased thanks to your generous contributions! Together we raised $1,865 to help kupuna and keiki in need in our local community. Thank you, Chocolate Angels! By a simple click of a button leading to a donation of any amount, you have led our team to be filled with excitement, hope, and joy through this particular project with more to come as we continuously work alongside The Salvation Army.

At this week's Angel Tree drop off, we experienced other angels on Earth working to do the most good for others. The hard-working staff members and volunteers of this non-profit organization reminded me of the leaders serving everywhere outside of our little chocolate home. They do this day in and day out all year long because the need is always there. We don't always witness the good work others are doing.

"Do nothing out of selfish ambition or vain conceit. Rather, in humility value others above yourselves, not looking to your own interests but each of you to the interests of others." -Philippians 2:3-4

I met virtually with one of my long-time business mentors, Keith, who led me through our finances as we looked at how Choco le`a did in 2020 and projected out how much harder we need to work in 2021 and the years to come to build again. The goal this year was just to make it and stay in business. Looking ahead, the next goal is to build Choco le`a again. Having leaders around me like Keith pushes me to prepare and think for "what could happen" or the possible challenging scenarios ahead so I don't stay in my "new normal comfort zone."

Leaders see first and farther ahead. Keith calls it the "chutes and ladders" game. He's seen me fall through so many chutes I didn't see as a new business owner and so leads me by trying to warn me where they may be. He directs me toward where the ladders are instead. With a leader like him, and many other mentors in my life, I have been able to grow. They've helped me avoid the chutes I could not see, but which they could, because of their years and wealth of experiences and their willingness to lead beside me.

"And he shepherded them with integrity of heart; with skillful hands he led them." -Psalm 78:72

I also met with other local business leaders online this week. At the end of 2019, we shared what our goals were for 2020. Here we were again, catching up at the end of a very unexpected 2020 and sharing our goals for 2021 as we lead our teams and ourselves through whatever comes next. I am so thankful for this group of business friends, led by my friend, Tanna. This is a group where we can honestly share the chutes we fell through and the ladders we found to climb back up on.

As Tanna always says, "Leaders need leaders." We learn so much from each other and we find connection when we can share the hardships and joys of leadership with others who are going through similar challenges.

"As iron sharpens iron, so one person sharpens another." -Proverbs 27:17

Part of this week also got a little rough and I needed to step to the side and not do the weekly work that I enjoy, like reviewing each order and running out to curbside. As a result, the dream team stepped up with no problem, no hesitation, and had the chance to lead through something I knew they were capable of but didn't have the opportunity to do because I always did it.

They are true leaders in their area of expertise, but Ally, Tori, Casey, Christine, Rena, and Carol together led the way to continue this week's work without missing a beat. In fact, they pushed themselves even harder to produce more chocolates for this past week's online pre-order sale. A huge reason why this business works is because I have a group of leaders, aka CEO's (Chocolate Everything Officer) unified and serving on one team. We are all on board for the same mission and work with the same set of values.

While the team was hard at work, I was led to a health care worker with so much heart for what she does. For those of you in this line of work, I think you've been and continue to be the angels serving on the front lines. Even though I didn't get to be with my team, I got to be with her team and believe I was led there to pray with them. Though we didn't know each other at all and met for only a few minutes, we shared common ground through COVID-19 and a shared a belief in the same leader that we could call out to for strength and resilience to lead us - God. He did.

"Being confident of this very thing, that He who has begun a good work in you will complete it until the day of Jesus Christ." -Philippians 1:6

Thanks to my team of leaders, leaders serving in our community, the first leaders in my life (my mom and dad), and my husband (whose leadership style is *suck it up, tough up, and move forward*), I was able to take care of what I needed to most at the moment, that being my kids and myself.

My husband and I are the greatest influencers, and therefore leaders, to our kids and with everything we say and do, they are growing to become the leader of their own life. I've always hoped for a daughter and wanted to name her "Aubrey." When she was born, I introduced her to my grandpa, who has since passed, but who led a lot of our family to the Lord. He asked me, *"What does 'Aubrey' mean?"* I laughed and said, *"I have no idea, grandpa!"*

We looked up the definition of "Aubrey" and found her name means: "Leader of the little people." I laughed! How perfect. I already knew this feisty, strong willed, yet super compassionate little girl would become a leader to others, starting with her little brother. We are all leaders. We all desire to have leaders we can respect and follow, and for others who may follow our lead. Even those that have already left us can continue to lead us through life as guardian angels who have passed on their wisdom and love that remains within us.

We all want to feel loved and that we belong. So how can we start to feel loved and as if we belong? We go first. "Leaders go first," is a quote that reminds me that I must be obedient and step out in faith first. I need to be willing to go someplace uncertain and out of my comfort zone first before anyone else will come along.

Leading can be a routine if we choose to make it a part of our daily life. I may not view it as leadership in the way the business world paints it, but to me, leadership is about going first and about influencing others. It is holding someone's hand to move them forward. It is a choice that needs to be made.

To illustrate that simply, it's being the first to go into the unknown tide pool to make sure it's safe. It's waving the kids in to encourage them to jump in. It's pointing out to them where the different ocean creatures could be and letting them explore. It's holding their hand on a muddy trail to guide them where to step. It's sometimes going ahead to set the pace and push them to keep up. And then it's letting them take off in front of you when they realize they're almost at the top and they want to be the first to see the view and yell back down to you that they did it!

Funny how the littlest angels in our lives can be the bravest and biggest leaders in our lives. Everyone can lead someone. We need to lead one another.

Who to follow or what to follow when you are trying to lead can be very confusing, so we must decide who and what that will be. The good news is the creator of the universe also serves as a loving Father in Heaven who leads us daily through His word in the Bible. As I always said, the guy at the top of our organizational chart for Choco le`a, is God. The ultimate leader of our family and my life is God. He leads with a servant's heart. He does everything He says and keeps His promises. He doesn't discriminate and does everything in love. Unlike me, or any of us, He is perfect. He is the ultimate example to me of what a leader should be and so I choose to follow Him.

"Do to others as you would have them do to you."
-Luke 6:31

That is why so often in my writing I provide an opportunity to lead you to Him, too. It's ultimately your choice and one that I whole-heartedly respect. Whether you believe in Him or not, I am a friend, willing to hold your hand and move forward with you. This was honestly hard for me to write for fear of you not liking me and what I have to say, but I write this because I am following what He is leading me to share.

"Therefore encourage one another and build each other up, just as in fact you are doing."
-1 Thessalonians 5:11

Lesson Learned: You are a leader. Everyone is. It's a responsibility we should not take lightly and a routine we need to continue to develop. Leading ourselves is definitely not easy and leading others is a great privilege, one that comes with great responsibility.

Opportunity Now: Find the leaders in your life. Who are you going to seek for advice and mentorship? Who are you going to surround yourself with so you can help lead one another on? Who will you influence and raise to leadership? Who and what will you ultimately follow as you learn to be a leader for yourself and for others? You must choose and move forward.

Hope For Our Future: God will never leave us or

forsake us. He is always with us. We will always have a leader to follow even when we feel completely alone. He sometimes sends his angels to us and He himself is within us every day.

My prayer for you, my chocolate friend, is that you lead the life you are meant to live. I hope that by leading you through the routines that I have found are working for me week by week, you find what works for you. From there, you follow God's **lead**.

With love always,
Your chocolate friend, Erin

"For he will command his angels concerning you to guard you in all your ways." -Psalm 91:11

— DECEMBER 14 —

Week No. 40
Routine 20: Love

It's week #40 and the final chapter. Only one way to wrap this up, guys - with **love**.

To love is the routine I knew I had to end our 20 reflections and 20 routines from 2020. It was an unbelievable year holding onto faith, believing in hope, and now choosing to end with love. If there's only one routine we can remember or implement, let's start with the last.

Let's choose to **love**.

"And now these three remain: faith, hope and love. But the greatest of these is love." 1 Corinthians 13:13

Love was, and still is, a choice wherever we are. I don't

know where week #40 finds you. I don't know what experiences of "loss" or even gain you've had since week #1. I don't know if you've been following this journey since the start in March or if you've just joined us in this final chapter. But I do know that this message is for you.

March 2020 marked the beginning of our COVID-19 reflections and it all began in week #1 with "loss." Loss of people we loved. Loss of routines and a normal way of life we knew and loved. Loss of jobs and businesses loved. Loss of freedom, hobbies, and physical connection with others, among other things we loved. In essence, we felt like we lost love itself. But did we?

Or did we, instead, perhaps get stripped of everything that we defined as "love" to be forced to look deep within ourselves and search for more? Through 20 weeks of reflections, we found ourselves missing something. Then in the next 20 weeks, we began the journey of developing routines to make ourselves feel whole again.

As I write this from the same red desk at home that I started these reflections and routines, my three-year-old son came walking over and asked me to sit with him on the couch. When I told him I needed to write, he asked if I can come over when I am done with my work to be with him. He is used to this now after nine months of mommy working from home. Since I'm writing about love, I asked him, *"Conner, what is love?"* He innocently responded, *"A hug,"* to which he came up to me and shoved his face into my lap, wrapped his arms around my legs, and gave me a hug right there in the chair. This is his expression and understanding of love.

Intrigued by his answer, I then asked my five-year-old daughter, *"Aubrey, what is love?"* She thought really hard then shrugged her shoulders at me, a little confused by this tricky question and seemed unsure of an answer.

When I rephrased it as, *"When do you feel loved?"* she responded, *"When you say, 'I love you.'"* To which she immediately jumped off the couch and into my arms and said, *"I love you, mommy."*

That's all our kids want. That's all any of us really want isn't it, to be seen, heard, and loved? But we look for love in all sorts of things as love is defined differently by us all. Sometimes we look for it in all the wrong places. We find a temporal love that's not lasting or eternal.

In this year of isolation, shut downs, social distancing, with a world of technology replacing face to face, we find the things that we may have identified as "love," like hugs and "I love you's" in person are no longer allowed. With that, it means we don't feel loved in the same way we used to, which has led to more problems, more division, and more loss in this life beyond the coronavirus, all simply because of feeling a lack of love.

May I reassure you, and myself, that this world is not lacking love. We're just lacking an understanding of the true meaning of love. The real source of love.

How timely that week #40 leads up to Christmas. With just a couple of days left in the year, and Hawai`i in what we call "tier two" of restrictions, a lot of things have been canceled. Large family get-togethers, company holiday parties, parades, and so many other holiday traditions cannot take place. But as my church pastor reminds us, "Christmas is not canceled." It can't be.

Christmas is the celebration of Jesus Christ's birthday,

and He is the source of love. The good news of God sending His son down to Earth to be with us is maybe the reminder we all need this year. That though we may still be able to drive around in our cars to look at lights on houses, eat gingerbread, chocolates, and candy canes, see Santa waving from behind a glass barrier, watch Christmas movies, and give and open presents, that's not what Christmas is really about. It's only what the world defines Christmas to be.

When this world experienced a global pandemic that no one saw coming, something that no one expected would last this long and have such a significant impact, we cried, we hid, we ran, we pivoted, we tried, we changed, we fought, we reflected, and we started new routines. We really didn't know what to do and when it would end, but it seemed that however we responded, when we chose to respond in love, it was the right thing to do.

Love was always the right answer. Love was the common denominator week after week. Love was the reason we chose to implement new **routines** into our lives. The love for our family forces us to **plan**, **prepare**, **work** hard and reminds us of our **values** and what we **choose** in this life. The love for friends is why we will stop and **celebrate** and **give** generously. The love for our team and our business is why we're willing to **change**, **try** new things, and stepped out to **lead**.

It's the love for our kids and a hope for a better future in our world that encourages us to **dream**. It's the love we learn for ourselves that allows us to take the time to start each day with a **morning** routine, take **breaks**, and courageously choose to **be authentic**. It's the love of community that makes us yearn to **connect** with others. It's the love to live this life to the fullest that we **move** our bodies and do what it takes to **thrive**. It's a love within that we can't quite grasp that brings us to our knees to **pray**.

So what is love? We know it's a part of life, but it's so complex and at the same time so simple. It's easy, but so hard to do. It's what God wants for us and what we want for ourselves, but sometimes don't know how to get it. As a friend, I'd like to reassure you that when you experience God's love, it fills your whole heart up to the brim and overflows so much that you must, must share it.

"Love is patient, love is kind. It does not envy, it does not boast, it is not proud. It does not dishonor others,

it is not self-seeking, it is not easily angered, it keeps no record of wrongs. Love does not delight in evil but rejoices with the truth. It always protects, always trusts, always hopes, always perseveres. Love never fails." -1 Corinthians 13:4-8

So how do you feel God's love? I believe it's different for everyone since we all respond to love differently. Our Heavenly Father knows that about us since He created each of us. For me, it's the gentlest whisper I hear in my heart even in the darkest moments. It's the warm touch of strong yet gentle hands on my shoulders that fills my body with light. It's a rush and flow of peace over me and reassurance that I am loved. It's something like nothing in this world can offer. Not even from my husband, kids, or parents. It's a love that I was always missing in my life until I opened my heart to Him and chose to let Him fill it.

God's love is also sometimes tangible and visible in my day-to-day life. Among the many moments I experienced loved this week, from seeing chocolate friends at curbside to delivering Angel Tree gifts with our extended chocolate family, there were two simple ones in which I felt God's love pouring and rushing over me.

One moment was when my chocolate family and I stood around "Diva" for the first time. This newest "mechanical" team member that we saved tens of thousands of dollars for, the team's dream addition for years just before the shut-down, finally had her chance to shine. Over one year later after sitting untouched because we were too busy, then being shoved in a corner with very little space as we downsized and said goodbye to so many of our things that once surrounded her, we held onto Diva in hopes she could help us create more new products at a future time.

Well, seeing her pour out her chocolate over everything that went under her, reminded me of God's love continuously pouring out on us from above. This simple moment meant so much to me as I knew how much work it took to get her and how long we had been waiting to use her, and to finally be here at this point in time. We made it through a crazy 2020, hung onto our faith and here we were working on things for a new year. Hope flowed again.

During this simple time of research and development in creating dark chocolate covered gummy bears, I was reminded how I still miss being with people and hugging, which is one way I personally like to express love. That inspired these "Chocolate Bear Hugs" to be created. As I watched the bears get covered with our signature dark chocolate, then cool and harden to a smooth tempered shell that hugged, and embraced them, it simply reminded me how alone and naked we can feel until we are covered and held by God's sweet love.

The second moment in the week when I felt God's love, was while hiking with my family up in the mountains on what we call our #familyfundaySunday. The rush of wind blowing over the mountaintops sending a cool breeze over our skin, the sound of the trees rustling against each other, the sight of orange butterflies coming out of the brush, and our kids joyously chasing after them felt like God's presence was all around us. It was so simple, but I loved the moment so much.

Hiking has become our hobby during lock down and even with everything there was still left to do this busy holiday season, we chose to take this time to spend with each other. We learned in this pandemic more than ever how hard marriage and parenting can be and that loving one another is a continuous choice. This year was especially hard on our marriage. In fact, my husband told me to include this and be totally transparent with the fact that we had to choose to love one another day after day. We openly share this with you as an honest reminder that we are all human and that love doesn't always come easy. It is a continuous choice to love one another.

But thank God that the source of love doesn't come from material things or even from another person in our life. It was created by and comes from God. In all the holiday movies we watch from the couch, love conquers all. Are you ready for the best news? Love really does conquer in real life. Because God is real. The battle has already been won. The King of Kings and Lord of Lords came to Earth and was born a baby in a manger on Christmas Day. Then that baby Jesus, gave His life for us because He loves us and so now His love is freely available to all of us.

"But the angel said to them, 'Do not be afraid. I bring you good news that will cause great joy for all the people." -Luke 2:10

Pandemic or no pandemic, it's what the answer has

been all along. Love is the answer. Love is the routine to sum up all routines. Love is such a powerful word. It is usually among the last words that are exchanged between people when there is no time left. It sums up everything left to be said in just three words: "I love you." At this time, I'd like to say to you all, *"God loves you."*

I already know this truth and when my time comes, I can go in peace. I know it sounds crazy, but a part of me wondered, at the beginning of all of these journal entries where I poured my heart out first on paper, then into these emails week after week, if the world was coming to an end. I wanted to be heard. I wanted you to feel loved. I wanted us both to find comfort and connection when we went through this as a community. Through it all we became chocolate friends. And over time, I even wondered if the first book I wrote would be my last. In case it is, it needs to be said, that I believe God is real, that He loves you, and that God is love.

"The first and second commandment says, "Jesus replied: 'Love the Lord your God with all your heart and with all your soul and with all your mind.' This

is the first and greatest commandment. And the second is like it: 'Love your neighbor as yourself.'"
-Matthew 22:37-39

If love is the greatest commandment, then to LOVE is the greatest routine.

Lesson Learned: Love comes from God. God IS love. Love is free, it never runs out, it is always available, and it is for everyone. Love is something all of us can give to one another.

Opportunity Now: Choose love. Go to the source of love to continuously fill every inch of your heart so that you can pour it out and love on others. If you are ready to receive His love, then I invite you to say this prayer out loud or in your heart:

"Dear Jesus. I believe that you are the son of God. I believe that you came to Earth and died on the cross for my sins and rose from the dead, and that whoever believes in you, will have eternal life. I repent of my sins and ask you to come into my life. Be my Lord and Savior. I want to start a relationship with you. I am ready to receive your love. I am ready to receive you into my heart. In Jesus's name I pray. Amen."

Hope For Our Future: If you said the prayer above, your new life with the Lord has begun. You are a new creation, born again and all of heaven rejoices! His love never fails. God is still with us. The Christmas story of Jesus being born in Bethlehem is still true. It's the tradition that continues to be celebrated and it can never be canceled.

Love. That is what it all comes down to. From week #1 loss to week #40 of reflections and routines together, love is the thread that holds it all together in both the good and the bad. Every single story shared was written from love. It is love that has gotten me through it all and it is love that will continue on.

503

My prayer for you, my chocolate friend, is that you accept the love God freely pours over you and you choose to love yourself and others. I pray that you experience a full life of love, knowing how much God loves you. Merry Christmas!

With LOVE always,
Your chocolate friend, Erin

"Greater love has no one than this: to lay down one's life for one's friends." -John15:13

— CONCLUSION —

Here we are at the very end of the most unprecedented year, 2020. Who else had a perfect 2020 vision of what this year would look like, with big goals and big dreams that not only didn't happen, but were also crushed?

Just like that, it's over. Well, the year is over. The vaccine is being distributed, but the pandemic is still very much here. With holiday travel and gatherings we anticipate a rise in cases again. It's unlikely that as soon as the clock strikes midnight and 2021 begins, all will be like it was before and everything will return to normal.

What we once knew as normal, has changed. Businesses have changed, hobbies have changed, people have changed, habits have changed, traditions have changed, and even cultures have changed. But isn't that what life is? Always changing. Never static.

As I reflect back on the past forty weeks, I remember beginning the year in the hustle and bustle of a busy hotel lobby in Waikiki where tourism was booming. I sat excitedly with a cup of coffee, our chocolates, my Bible, a journal, pen, computer, and my thoughts. I mapped out what I had hoped for 2020.

Now, I find myself at the end of the year in my new normal. Sitting at home, but still with a cup of coffee, our chocolates, my Bible, a journal, pen, computer, and my thoughts. I guess some things don't change. Our thoughts, what we reflect on and some of our routines may have changed. But the rhythms in our life, the routines we have consistently stuck to no matter what, the things that make us who we are, those remain steadfast.

Every year, I pray and ask God for a "word." Something to provide focus that will sum up EVERY single thing for the year. All throughout December 2019, I prayed about it and just didn't hear a thing. Then, no joke, right on January 1st, I heard it, "peace." It was NOT the word I was thinking of. I was hoping

He would reveal something like "growth" or "joy" or something more exciting but instead He simply whispered, "peace."

I knew instantly, somehow, that was it. In fact, I had a peace about it! I thought hard about what that meant. Did it mean I would have peace and quiet this year? Less craziness with the kids and my husband, and a more peaceful and a clean house? More peace in the business to run on its own so I could begin new adventures?

This is what I wrote at the beginning of 2020, straight from my journal:

"The start of a new decade. Will this be the year that I finally listen and slow down? I must. To live with peace in my heart that I did it and followed God's calling this season. I must step out in faith and make the changes I know I need to make, that He has been telling me again and again. This is going to be hard...I need to pursue the desires He put in my heart. Trust Him for success and focus on bringing peace into our home. To find peace with Him and not the world."

"Pursue righteousness, faith, love, and peace." -2 Timothy 2:22

"A heart at peace gives life to the body." -Proverbs 14:30

January and February 2020 took off with major investments in the business, additional new hires and managers to run everything in what was sure to be our biggest and fastest year ever. All the while, there was some kind of virus happening "far away" in China that we just heard about in the news and didn't really experience it in OUR world. In my journal on March 8, I wrote "Too much to do and not enough time. Still looking for the peace…" Then, less than two weeks later, COVID-19 came to Hawai`i and that's when this whole journey began. That's when the story of finding peace in this life and with who God created us to be, began.

"In me you may have peace. In this world you will have trouble. But take heart! I have overcome the world." -John 16:33

It's almost as if God called it in scripture, before this global pandemic hit us all. I wrap this up by saying that "peace" really was the word of the year. In the year of the greatest turmoil of my lifetime, I found peace.

I found peace in our business. I found peace in being small, simple, and still sweet. We strengthened our foundation based on our unwavering values but thought innovatively and pivoted in ways we never imagined we would so we could adapt and build again. All this while relentlessly fighting for our mission, "Bringing peace to our world, one chocolate at a time." We focused on trying to figure out how to do that, and how to stay connected with others, without chocolates. Thus my journaling and the start of this book was born.

A singular focus to keep this mission alive brought about a peace in knowing that we could survive if we stuck to why we started this all in the first place. I realized that we could each bring God's peace, one person, one relationship at a time, to the world within our reach. In time, and with the consistency to choose this mission founded in love again and again, our community of chocolate friends could help us spread peace to our entire world.

It's just like our reflections and routines. We're learning

a little every week. We're making little changes one by one in our daily routines. Over time, while intentionally choosing what we do and how we think, the decisions we make will ultimately change our life. As each of us work on changing our own individual "worlds" and where God has placed us, together, we can change our world as a whole. This gave me the hope I needed to persevere.

I found peace with my children, my husband, my family, and friends. We learned to find peace in it all, whether we were stuck with each other day after day while figuring out how to do distance learning at home while working from home, or being separated from the family and friends we were used to seeing and hugging regularly in each other's homes. We found ways to make peace with our situations of quarantine, stay-at-home, do-not-gather, but still share the love we knew was there for one another. We had to make peace in knowing that the relationships would survive even if we felt absolutely crazy after being with each other daily; or felt absolutely heartbroken that we hadn't been with each other at all, all year. We found different, creative, ways to express this love and realized more than ever just what, or who, really mattered.

510

I found peace with a new way of life. My usual activities of dancing, shopping, lunches and coffee, professional development training, meetings, travel, go-go-go, and so much more changed to hiking, swimming, cooking, reading, simplifying the house, and teaching. I found peace with new routines that had to be created. As I consistently stuck to these routines, I started to find the peace in this "new normal" as the routines became rhythms in my life that I have come to appreciate and enjoy.

Most importantly, I found peace with myself : a peace about who I am and who God created me to be; how I could still fulfill my dreams, if I changed my perspective to search for HIS peace.

There were **lessons learned** about strengths and perseverance, learning that I needed to learn to rely on God even more; that I have the power to choose what I focus on, that sometimes less becomes more; that routines really do help; that I can never get this time back; that relationships matter most and that there is still a lot to be grateful for.

I've sought out **opportunities now** like taking the time to rest and make changes. To connect and reach out to others, thank them, show kindness, and celebrate. I'm also taking this time to reflect, simplify, and find new ways to have fun. I am stepping out of my comfort zone, asking for help more often, and continuing to learn as I move onward.

I still have great **hope for our future** that this is only a season and we must hold onto our faith. I see the hopefulness that even our crazy kids have for life as an attitude we should follow because it can help us reshape our own perspective. The "aloha spirit" is still alive here in Hawai`i and we will still live with that culture when our economy opens back up. We found that our world is more connected than ever before, and that perseverance prevails, and love wins. We can learn a lot from each other as we grow and can count on God who still answers prayers.

The really cool thing about it all, is that the peace of God was always there, from the beginning of the year to the end. Through it all, He has remained the same God, the Prince of Peace. He gave me the peace and confidence in myself that I could accomplish one of my greatest goals and dreams, to write a book. It has been on my heart for so many years, but I had no "time" to do it or content worthy to share. He reminded me that although with God, all things are possible, that I still had to make up my mind to have a Godly perspective and do my part, with no excuses. No pandemic can stop the desires God has put in our hearts.

"But the Helper will teach you everything and will cause you to remember all that I told you. This Helper is the Holy Spirit whom the Father will send in my name. I leave you peace; my peace I give you. I do not give it to you as the world does. So don't let your hearts be troubled or afraid." -John 14:26-27

As I write this closing, at this, the closing of the year, it is now that the title of my book has been made so obvious. What this year was about, was peace. It all points back to the word for this year. It comes back to the mission of our business, Choco le`a, since its beginning, but with a new twist:

"Bringing Peace To Our World, One Chocolate Story At A Time."

Bringing the peace to our world starts with your world and my world, one story, one reflection, one routine, one week at a time. The search for peace, which can

513

only be found in God, has always been available to us, just revealed in the most unexpected way.

Thank YOU for reading these stories and for being on this journey with me to search for peace in the most turbulent year.

My prayer for you, my chocolate friend, is that you take the stories, the reflections, routines, lessons learned, opportunities now, and hope for our future, and you find the peace in your world at this time, a peace that comes from a new perspective, from God's point of view…a.k.a. "2020" vision.

With love always,
Your chocolate friend, Erin

"And the peace of God, which transcends all understanding, will guard your hearts and minds in Christ Jesus." -Philippians 4:7

"A child has been born to us; God has given a son to us. He will be responsible for leading the people. His name will be Wonderful Counselor, Powerful God, Father Who Lives Forever, Prince of Peace." -Isaiah 9:6

"May the Lord of peace Himself give you peace at all times and in every way." -2 Thessalonians 3:16

ABOUT THE AUTHOR

Erin Kanno Uehara's personal mission is to "Live a life of faith, learning and leading through God's love." She is doing this through her chocolate and people business, Choco le`a, volunteer work with her church and community, and in her daily routines with her family and friends. She is a woman of faith, a wife, mom, friend, entrepreneur, leader, speaker, brand and community ambassador, and now author. She enjoys hiking, dancing, acting, modeling, creating, collaborating, reading, writing, learning, connecting with others, and cuddling with her kids. Erin was born and raised in Hawai`i where she resides with her husband Chris, daughter Aubrey, and son Conner.

You can find Erin on
Instagram @yourchocolatefriend &
online at www.erinkannouehara.com

You can find her business, Choco le`a, on
Instagram @chocolcahawaii &
online at www.chocolea.com